SHIELD OF DREAMS

STEPHEN J. CIMBALA

SHIELD OF DREAMS

Missile Defense and U.S.-Russian Nuclear Strategy

NAVAL INSTITUTE PRESS
Annapolis, Maryland

Naval Institute Press
291 Wood Road
Annapolis, MD 21402

Library of Congress Cataloging-in-Publication Data

Cimbala, Stephen J.
  Shield of dreams : missile defense and U.S.-Russian nuclear strategy / Stephen J. Cimbala.
     p. cm.
  Includes bibliographical references and index.
  ISBN 978-1-59114-116-7 (hardcover : alk. paper) — ISBN 978-1-59114-117-4 (pbk. : alk. paper)
  1. Ballistic missile defenses—United States. 2. Ballistic missile defenses—Russia (Federation)
  3. Nuclear warfare—Prevention—International cooperation. 4. Nuclear arms control—
  International cooperation. 5. Nuclear nonproliferation. 6. Deterrence (Strategy) I. Title.
  UG740.C55 2008
  358.1'740973—dc22
                              2008023342

Printed in the United States of America on acid-free paper

14 13 12 11 10 09 08   9 8 7 6 5 4 3 2
First printing

Book design: David Alcorn, Alcorn Publication Design

Contents

Illustrations

Preface and Acknowledgments

THIS BOOK BEGAN AS A DRAFT MANUSCRIPT and has evolved through various stages, always somewhere between completion and "still another" revision. Thankfully the end game has arrived. I owe considerable thanks to the persons named below and to others without whose encouragement I would have given up. Special thanks are due Richard Russell, director of the Naval Institute Press, for his encouragement and support in getting me across the finish line; to Elizabeth Bauman, assistant editor, for leadership and management of the project toward a finished product; and to Karin Kaufman for diligent and thoughtful copyediting of the manuscript.

There are numerous publications on missile defense technology. This is not one of them. This book is a policy study that provides a focused discussion of missile defenses and their relationship to Russian-U.S. nuclear arms control and nuclear deterrence relationships and nuclear proliferation, especially the spread of nuclear weapons and missile or airborne delivery systems in Asia. The analysis makes some necessary assumptions about the expected performances of nuclear weapons and nuclear strikes as well as missile defense systems. These scenarios are hypothetical but realistic and are tested under variable assumptions with regard to force size and operational guidance. In other words, I make technical assumptions as necessary to support or refute policy arguments.

This is an academic policy study with no political agenda. Although I hope it proves useful to policy makers and other nonacademic readers, it is not intended to sway political debates in a particular direction. Nationwide missile defenses, a "what if" item during the Cold War, are now being deployed by the United States, and other powers may follow with ballistic missile defenses—or offensive countermeasures—of their own. The future of intercontinental (and shorter-range) nuclear weapons is therefore headed away from the simplicity of offensive-only nuclear forces and toward the complexity of offensive-defensive interaction between opposed forces. The world has now entered a deterrence regime in which deterrence by denial of the attacker's objectives will coexist with deterrence by credible threat of unacceptable nuclear retaliation.

Gratitude for insights pertinent to this topic is extended to Stephen Blank, Ivo Daalder, Martin Edmonds, David Glantz, Colin Gray, Aaron Karp, Jacob Kipp, Lawrence Korb, Julian Palmore, Keith Payne, Peter Rainow, and C. Dale Walton. Special thanks are due James Scouras for use of his AWSM@ model for analyzing nuclear force exchanges, and to James J. Tritten for use of an analytical model first designed by him for the same purpose. Neither Scouras nor Tritten is responsible for any of the analysis or argument here.

The long march from concept to fruition for this study included some detours to publish articles in various journals from the ever-growing database on nuclear arms control, proliferation, and missile defenses. I am grateful in particular to the editors and publishers of these scholarly journals for their interest and support. Some of this work also contributed to my book *Nuclear Weapons and Strategy* (Routledge, 2005), and I am grateful to editor Andrew Humphrys for his interest and support.

None of the above-named people bears any responsibility for the contents of this work.

I am grateful to Pennsylvania State University–Brandywine for administrative support for this and other research studies.

I thank my wife Betsy for her love and steadfastness through all things, and my sons Christopher and David for dragging me into the modern world.

Abbreviations

ALCM	Air-launched cruise missiles
APC	Armored personnel carriers
ASAT	Antisatellite weapon
BMD	Ballistic missile defense
C4ISR	Command, control, communications, computers, intelligence, surveillance, and reconnaissance
CFE	Conventional Forces in Europe
DAY	Day-to-day alert
DOD	Department of Defense
DPRK	Democratic People's Republic of Korea (North Korea)
EMT	Equivalent megatonnage
EU	European Union
FSB	Federal Security Service (Russia)
G8	Group of Eight
GEN	Generated alert
GLCM	Ground-launched cruise missile
IAEA	International Atomic Energy Agency
ICBM	Intercontinental ballistic missile
INF	Intermediate Nuclear Forces
JCS	Joint Chiefs of Staff
LOW	Launched on warning
MARV	Maneuvering reentry vehicle
MDA	U.S. Missile Defense Agency
MIRV	Multiple, independently targetable reentry vehicle
MRV	Multiple reentry vehicle
MT	Megaton
NMD	National missile defenses
NPT	Non-Proliferation Treaty
PRC	People's Republic of China
RKSD	Medium-range missile complexes
ROA	Ride out attack
ROK	Republic of Korea (South Korea)
RV	Reentry vehicle
SDI	Strategic Defense Initiative
SDIO	Strategic Defense Initiative Office

SLBM	Submarine-launched ballistic missile
SLCM	Sea-launched cruise missile
SNDV	Strategic nuclear delivery vehicle
SNUAV	Strategic, nonnuclear UAV
SORT	Strategic Offensive Reductions Treaty
SRAM	Short-range attack missile
SSBN	Ballistic missile submarine
SSPK	Single shot kill probability
START	Strategic Arms Reductions Treaty
TMD	Theater missile defenses
UAV	Unoccupied aerial vehicle
WMD	Weapons of mass destruction

Introduction

Missile Defenses in a New Nuclear Century

T he U.S government found itself confronted with an unexpected threat from a source of its own construction in January 2008. An American spy satellite carrying toxic fuel had become damaged and was headed for a crash landing somewhere on Earth in February. In response U.S. officials set up a high-powered team that included U.S. Navy missile defense experts and defense contractors and scientists from the Johns Hopkins University Applied Physics Laboratory. The result of these consultations was a decision by the Department of Defense (DOD), approved by the president, to shoot down the wayward satellite by launching antimissile defense weapons. Navy ships equipped with the Aegis missile defense system would attempt to intercept the spacecraft about 130 miles over the Pacific. The SM-3 missile would destroy the satellite by direct hit (or kinetic kill), colliding with the spacecraft at high speed after zeroing in on it via a heat-seeking sensor.[1]

The Aegis missile defense system had evolved from a state-of-the-art air defense system for the U.S. Navy into a component of the evolving U.S. global missile defense system proposed by the Department of Defense and its Missile Defense Agency. The use of this system to knock down the satellite would be an opportunistic test for the system, although not necessarily the scenario for which it was intended. The satellite provided a smaller target signature than a ballistic missile would, and there was no guarantee that the sea-based ballistic missile defense (BMD) system would destroy the satellite completely. The satellite carried some one thousand pounds of hydrazine fuel in a fuel tank lined with beryllium, both highly toxic substances.

The U.S. government deployed six rescue teams around the country, prepared to act in case of an intercept failure and a crash landing in or near populated areas.[2] Much to the relief of U.S. officials and others, the intercept was an apparent success. The Aegis-class cruiser *Lake Erie* fired a single SM-3 missile on the evening of February 20, 2008, and the interceptor's kill vehicle collided with the dying satellite, which was traveling more than seventeen thousand miles per hour. According to the Pentagon, a network of land-based, sea-based, airborne, and space-based sensors confirmed that "the U.S. military intercepted a nonfunctioning National Reconnaissance Office satellite which was in its final orbits before entering the Earth's atmosphere."[3] Regardless of the outcome, technology and the "fog of war" (or disaster) had conspired to raise the visibility of missile defenses in technical discussion and policy debates.

The end of the Cold War was not the end of the nuclear age. Failure to recognize the continuing risks of nuclear war, or of nuclear arms races that can lead to war, by politicians and warlords in the twenty-first century is almost a certainty. The 1990s were a decade, at least in the United States and other developed democracies, of unprecedented rapid economic expansion and political euphoria. The terrorist attacks of September 11, 2001, and the possibility of further strikes by state or nonstate actors against the U.S. homeland or against U.S. forces and allies with weapons of mass destruction (WMD), reminded heads of state and military planners that governments lived in a dangerous world. Experts feared that terrorists or rogue states might, among other possibilities, acquire and use nuclear weapons for missions of coercion or destruction against the United States or other nations. For these and other reasons missile defenses returned to the top of the U.S. national security agenda, as seemingly inevitable as they were eternally controversial.

In matters of strategy and national security policy, as Colin S. Gray reminds us, context is all.[4] This introduction establishes the context for further, more specific discussion to follow.

The First Nuclear Age

Japan's defeat in 1945 was expedited by the first nontest use of an atomic bomb. The first nuclear age begins with the U.S. bombing of Hiroshima in 1945 and ends with the end of the Cold War and the collapse of the Soviet Union. The post–Cold War era, or second nuclear age, begins in the 1990s and carries forward into the twenty-first century.[5] The period from 1945 to 1991 was one in which a bipolar distribution of international military power, combined with a two-sided ideological competition between capitalism and communism, overshadowed all other military activity. During this time U.S. influence was thought to rest on military persuasion through the selective application of threat of force mixed with reassurances that the threatened party could escape punishment by acquiescing to the demands made on it. The use of the most powerful weapons in actual war fighting would be self-destructive. So instead, for the duration of the Cold War, the Americans and Soviets used nuclear weapons as instruments of political influence short of war.

Two means of influence were predominant among those chosen by policy makers and their advisors in bringing military instruments to bear on problems short of war: deterrence and coercive diplomacy. The first means, deterrence, is the more passive of the two; it aims to prevent an action that a hostile state has not yet taken but appears to be seriously considering. Deterrence is before the fact. The second means, coercive diplomacy, is the more active form of influence by means of threat of force and, possibly, selective reassurances. Coercive diplomacy, as Alexander L. George has explained, is intended to stop an action already in progress or to undo and reverse an action already completed.[6] It therefore requires more exertion and commitment on the part of the threatener, and it usually requires of the threatened party, in order to comply with the threatener's demands, to make a greater adjustment in its current behavior. President John F. Kennedy's demand that Soviet premier Nikita Khrushchev remove his missiles from Cuba in October 1962 is an example of the application of coercive diplomacy in order to stop, and then undo, an action regarded as contrary to U.S. national interest. Kennedy first imposed a naval blockade around Cuba to prevent the shipment of additional Soviet missiles there (the "stop" aspect of coercive diplomacy). Then he demanded that the Soviet Union remove the missiles previously deployed in Cuba as soon as possible (the "undo" aspect).

The Cuban Missile Crisis displayed the two-sided character of nuclear weapons when employed as instruments of military persuasion. Enormous coercive power could be derived from the threat of nuclear first use or escalation even if the threat was not explicitly stated in the course of an international negotiation. On the other hand, the devilish paradox of nuclear deterrence was that for deterrence to be credible, both the willingness and the capability to use nuclear weapons had to be apparent to the other side. Capabilities could be measured and, after the deployment of reconnaissance satellites, counted with reasonable fidelity. But intentions were another matter. Intentions were contingent on the exigent circumstances of the moment as much as they were derived from any generalized mind-set of a state's leadership. Thus U.S. leaders might assume that Soviet Cold War aims included political expansion backed up by selective military pressure. But this assumption about Soviet mind-sets in general did not tell U.S. intelligence whether Khrushchev would deploy missiles to Cuba, nor whether he would pull them out attendant to a U.S. crisis time demand to do so.

This duality of nuclear weapons, enticing for their coercive potential and dangerous on account of their capacity to destroy modern civilizations in several hours, made it of first importance for policy makers and commanders to grapple with the concept of escalation. If a conventional war in Europe began, could it be stopped short of nuclear first use? If not, could some stopping point between nuclear first use and Armageddon be agreed to as NATO and Warsaw Pact armies clashed on the central front? Did the Soviets even recognize any concepts such as "escalation control" and "war termination" as discussed in the U.S. deterrence and arms control literature?[7] The matter of escalation, like the coercive power potential of nuclear weapons, was Janus-like. If escalation from conventional to nuclear war, or from smaller to larger nuclear wars, were *certain to occur*, then no rational head of state would start either a conventional or nuclear war, at least not in Europe. On the other hand, if escalation were *guaranteed not to happen* and states were confident that "firebreaks" could be preserved between conventional and nuclear war, or between limited and total nuclear war, then states would be free to play with fire either at the level of conventional war or within a spectrum of nuclear wars.

But to the confounding of nuclear theory, neither condition was certain: Neither the absence of escalation nor its presence could be foreseen. The uncertainty of escalation in any particular case was the effective deterrent as much as the firepower behind it. While this might provide interesting speculative material for applied psychologists, it drove military planners to distraction and drove scholars and policy advocates in either of two directions: toward more insistent demands for nuclear arms control and/or disarmament or toward more insistent demands for increased nuclear war preparedness. During the early years of the Kennedy administration these two theoretically opposed sets of demands actually coincided in time and space, with large clusters of expert and lay opinion weighing in on both sides.

When all of the dust had cleared after four decades or so of actually operating nuclear forces, of conducting arms control negotiations, and of reaching various agreements to prevent accidental nuclear war or escalation growing out of incidents between American and Soviet forces, it fell to President Ronald Reagan and the Soviet Union's President Mikhail Gorbachev to bell the cat. Nearing the end of the Cold War, both acknowledged from different perspectives that the basic issues of the first nuclear age had been thought through and fought out. Those shared understandings from the archdeacon of capitalism and the last dying emperor of Soviet socialism, held with more or less reluctant acquiescence by their respective militaries, were as follows:

1. Nuclear war could neither be fought nor won in the traditional (prenuclear) sense. Victory was not attainable at an acceptable cost in any nuclear war involving more than a few demonstration shots at noncritical targets.
2. No technology then in existence or immediately foreseeable could provide an effective defense of the U.S. or Soviet national territories against

large-scale attack. (Reagan's Strategic Defense Initiative, or SDI, called for a research and development program for a *future* [read: futuristic] nationwide defense system, not for imminent deployment of one as some misperceived.)

3. It was in the interest of both the United States and the Soviet Union, as well as of the civilized world, that nuclear weapons' spread be confined to the smallest number of state actors (and, preferably, to no nonstate actors, such as terrorists).

4. The safe and secure operation of nuclear weapons' and forces, including the alerting and crisis management of nuclear-capable forces, was a requirement for maintaining peace and security in the Cold War and for stabilizing the nuclear relationship between Washington and Moscow (accordingly, both sides worked out "rules of the road" to reduce the possibility of misunderstanding, such as prenotification of test missile launches within certain geographical areas).

5. Although NATO was a voluntary alliance of democratic states and the Warsaw Treaty Organization was not, both the U.S. and Soviet leadership agreed that neither wished to be dragged by allies into a catalytic nuclear war. Accordingly, the nuclear potential of allies or erstwhile allies was limited by multilateral agreement and diplomatic persuasion (as in NATO), by imposition of Soviet military domination (as in the Warsaw Pact), or by a combination of sticks and carrots (as between the Soviet Union and China).

These were important areas of agreement during the first nuclear age. Not a single one of them can be taken for granted as a policy consensus shared by nuclear or nuclear-aspiring powers as the second nuclear age passes through the twenty-first century. Why not?

The Second Nuclear Age

The second nuclear age replaces the erstwhile determinant bipolar competition between two nuclear-armed superpowers with a more fluid and unpredictable international order. The two "policemen," or principal constables, of the Cold War antiproliferation system, the United States and the Soviet Union, have been reduced to one. This subtracts from the strength of regulatory forces. In addition, Russia, the nuclear successor state to one of the two Cold War constables, has financial and other incentives to join the ranks of nuclear and missile technology suppliers. There is considerable evidence that it already has done so. For example, Russia has aided in the development of the nuclear industry and missile technology infrastructure in North Korea. U.S. intelligence cannot say for certain how much weapons-grade material (plutonium or enriched uranium) has leaked from holdings in Russia into the hands of other states or terrorists.

On account of the condition of its conventional military forces in the 1990s, Russia became more reliant on its nuclear weapons to cover a variety of contingent threats to its security. These threats were not limited to nuclear attack on Russia or on a Russian ally. Overlapping with growing nuclear dependency in Russia was NATO's decision to enlarge its membership in several stages beginning in 1999. Although NATO declared that it had no "intention, plan or reason" to station nuclear weapons in any of these newly admitted members, NATO enlargement brought the alliance's nuclear guaranty up to doorstep of Ukraine and Belarus. And Russian president Vladimir Putin's efforts to realign military doctrine in Russia fell short of convincing leading elements within the Russian General Staff and Defense Ministry that NATO was still Russia's principal adversary.

The President George W. Bush administration proceeded to abrogate the Anti-Ballistic Missile Treaty of 1972 and began to deploy national missile defenses (NMD) for U.S. territory in 2004. Russia had no comparable technology on offer. In addition, some Russian (and U.S.) arms control experts expressed fears that any U.S. nationwide defense would overturn stable deterrence based on offensive retaliation, which had served the Soviet Union well during the Cold War. There was some irony and a taste of "retro" in Russia clinging to a doctrine that the Cold War Soviets had first opposed vehemently and then reluctantly embraced as a way to slow down the Americans in the arms race. Now Russia supposedly feared that the United States might invent its way into a defense technology that would be good enough to negate Russia's nuclear retaliatory strike, even if it could not defeat a surprise first strike. If Russia's retaliatory strike were up for grabs, then Russia in a political crisis might be forced to operate its nuclear retaliatory forces on a hair trigger.

Given the preceding discussion, it was not only "assured destruction" based solely on offensive retaliation that was in danger of falling out of favor in the twenty-first century. Equally unclear was the fate of deterrence itself as a central concept for understanding the arms debate and as policy-prescriptive tool for organizing alternatives. Deterrence had grown up with the Cold War and nuclear weapons. It provided a common nomenclature within which academics, policy makers, military planners, and others could debate military and political options. Deterrence, to paraphrase Clausewitz, became not only a common grammar of reference for inter-elite nuclear debates but also a logic unto its own for answering virtually any question about strategy and military policy. Eventually deterrence was even extended downward on the ladder of escalation into the bowels of so-called low-intensity conflict of unconventional warfare.

As deterrence became an all-purpose talisman by which virtually any policy or strategy could be analyzed, its ubiquitous application came at the expense of explanatory or predictive power. All deterrence analyses or forecasts were made equal. By the time two decades of the nuclear age were history, it had been forgotten that the theory of deterrence (unlike the practice of it, which had existed since the beginning of human interpersonal conflict) had grown up under very special conditions in the early years of the nuclear age, when policy makers needed advice about how to deal with these new weapons of unprecedented destructiveness. Thus sharp debates were held in academic journals and at conferences in the 1980s, for example, as to whether "conventional deterrence" on the central front in Europe would suffice to preclude an outbreak of war, ignoring the inescapable commingling of nuclear and conventional forces in both Soviet and NATO forward deployments and war plans.

But the major weakness of deterrence was not conceptual overstretch, important as that was. A more important limitation of the theory of deterrence, relative to the probable practices of states in the twenty-first century, was inherent in its assumptions about rational decision making. When deterrence theory worked as an explanation or prediction for real political phenomena, it "worked" because heads of state or other political leaders behaved according to a simplified rational policy model. The model assumed that individuals in a competitive bargaining game behave according to a certain game-imposed logic that requires them to engage in value-maximizing behavior within a set of carefully drawn rules. Change the rules or the assumption of value maximizing behavior, as defined by the observer, and all bets are off. In other words, deterrence is a quasi-experimental open system subject to fluctuation in behavior to the extent that the mice choose to cooperate, or not, with the designers of the maze.

The assumption of rationality on which deterrence theory was based was itself criticized for being politically naïve, but this criticism was sometimes overstated.[8] One had to make some assumptions, and rationality was not the worst place to start. A more important limitation in deterrence models was the assumption of a U.S. or Western kind of rationality in decision making—the assumption that "they" think like "we." So it was assumed by some policy makers and analysts, for example, that the Soviets would look on nuclear weapons and nuclear arms control from the same frame of reference as did their U.S. and allied Western counterparts. When in the event this expectation of strategically identical "apes on a treadmill" was proved wide of the mark, Soviet leaders were disparaged for their inability to comprehend the realities of the nuclear age.

Even more challenging to deterrence theory were the so-called low-intensity conflicts, mostly unconventional wars, raging in a variety of states in the so-called Third World outside of U.S. and Soviet direct political control and military influence. A common misunderstanding is to see this mostly Asian, African, and Middle Eastern landscape as relatively pacified by the Cold War superpowers until the breakup of the Soviet Union and the end of the Cold War. Here there is a collective memory loss. In fact, neither the Americans nor the Soviets, nor the former colonial powers numbered among U.S. allies, succeeded very well in applying deterrence theory to the practice of preventing or "deterring" revolutionary-guerrilla warfare. The U.S. policy and strategy of extending containment to Southeast Asia crashed and burned in Vietnam. The Soviets invaded Afghanistan in 1979 with the expectation of quickly imposing their will on a scattered rabble of Afghan mujahideen opposition; they withdrew in embarrassment and defeat a decade later. The French were driven first from Indochina and then from Algeria, although the latter was legally defined as part of metropolitan France and French withdrawal provoked part of the army to mutiny.

One could argue that revolutionary-guerrilla and other unconventional warfare is embedded in local causes too numerous to generalize about, and that it therefore lies outside the ambit of deterrence theory. This may be so, but it was not only deterrence that failed in the cases listed above but also the inability of policy and strategy to resolve the matter once a state of war had supplanted a state of peace. U.S. officials who were responsible for committing American forces to the war in Vietnam between 1965 and 1973 now acknowledge, for example, that they misunderstood in fundamental ways the politics, society, and culture of Vietnam. This phenomenon was not isolated during the Cold War—or since.

Not understanding the "otherness" of states in the new world order includes not understanding how new nuclear powers might view their arsenals, compared to the five original and officially sanctioned members of the nuclear "club" (also permanent members of the UN Security Council). In the United States and in NATO nuclear weapons are now treated as weapons of last resort and something of a post–Cold War embarrassment. Since the Persian Gulf War of 1991 the weapons of first choice for the United States and others who want to play in the league of major powers have been the high-technology, information-based conventional weapons for long-range, precision strikes; stealth technology; and advanced systems for C4ISR (command, control, communications, computers, intelligence, surveillance, and reconnaissance). This "revolution in military affairs" is thought by some to have established a dividing line between those states that can afford to play in this high-tech military world of "smart" or future "brilliant" weapons and those who cannot afford the price of entry.

On the other hand, it is entirely possible that those who cannot afford the price of entry into information-based warfare, of which "information warfare" or cyberwar is a subspecies, will play other strategies consistent with their history, strategic culture, and available options. Iraqi leader Saddam Hussein, for example, was widely discussed in the West in 1991 as someone who had "lost" the Persian Gulf War because his forces had been expelled from Kuwait and decimated by U.S. smart firepower. This is the outcome of the war as seen from a U.S. perspective. But it is not the only possible vantage point. From Saddam Hussein's perspective and that of some others in the Middle East, Iraq had successfully stood off a coalition of thirty states headed by the world's sole superpower and survived with its regime and much of its modern army intact. Nevertheless, a peace was imposed on Iraq that required it to dismantle many (although not all) of its weapons of mass destruction in the 1990s and UN-imposed sanctions (most notably, restraints on its ability to export oil) cut drastically into its economy.

Moreover, Saddam Hussein remained in power in 2001, long after George Herbert Walker Bush had departed the presidency and in time to watch George W. Bush, son of the former president, assume the highest U.S. executive office. Repeated air attacks by the Clinton administration and a widely known if officially unacknowledged CIA effort to dislodge Hussein from power by fomenting a rebellion among dissident Kurds in northern Iraq failed to change the regime in Baghdad. So who "won" in Iraq in the 1990s? The answer depends on the perspective by which one defines winning and losing. And those states or revolutionary movements fighting against the top dogs in any international system, including the international system of the next two decades, may calculate winning or losing with a calculator powered by the batteries of faith, nationalism, or simple warrior mentalities that are unfamiliar to laws regarding and casualty averse Western audiences.

In this regard the availability of ballistic missiles and nuclear weapons to new powers from the Middle East to the Pacific Rim should cause U.S. policy makers and strategic planners to rethink their military-strategic geography. One reason for this is inherent in the technical properties of missiles apart from culture. Medium- and long-range ballistic missiles shrink the geography over which conflicts can be fought quickly and, if those missiles are carrying weapons of mass destruction, with much greater devastation than hitherto. But more important than the technical properties of ballistic missiles are the variations in the way missiles can be used, depending on the imagination of the user.

Western military experts tended during the Cold War to disparage the utility of early generation ballistic missiles sold to countries outside of NATO or the Warsaw Pact due to those missiles' low accuracy. The measure of a missile's value was, in addition to its range, its ability to strike with high accuracy against military forces, that is, counterforce targets. But non-Western leaders had other ideas. During the Iran-Iraq War of the 1980s both sides fired conventionally armed ballistic missiles at each other's cities as terror weapons, like the German V-2 rockets fired at London during World War II. And during the Persian Gulf War, Iraq used its Scud missiles to launch terror attacks against Israeli cities; although the missiles carried no chemical or biological weapons, U.S. and Israeli intelligence knew that Saddam Hussein had deployed some Scuds that were capable of launching chemical or biological weaponized warheads. Hussein undoubtedly knew that the United States and Israel knew and exploited this knowledge in his effort (unsuccessful but nonetheless energetic) to try to divide the coalition.

Hussein's Scuds were also a weapon of terroristic counterdeterrence. Because they might be mated to some chemical or biological warheads, especially the latter, they could be used to checkmate any opportunistic expansion of war aims on the part of the United States and its victorious allies. Subsequent to the expulsion of Iraq's invading armies from Kuwait, some contended that the United States had ended the war too soon. It was felt by critics of the U.S. decision to terminate the ground war after one hundred hours that additional pursuit of Iraq's fleeing forces might have destroyed additional components of the crack Republican Guard armored forces that were vital to Saddam Hussein's postwar survival. Other critics of the prompt war termination were unhappy that the United States and its allies did not persevere until the entire power structure of Hussein's regime was forced out of office or destroyed. But the United States suspected that Saddam Hussein would pull out all stops to stay in power, including an apparent willingness to have prepared Scuds with biological weapons pretargeted at cities in Israel and in Kuwait. In the event of an enemy storming of Baghdad to dislodge the regime, the deadly missiles armed with germ weapons would fly automatically.[9]

The willingness to employ biological and other weapons of mass destruction stamps Asian and Middle Eastern leaders as backward in the eyes of Western advocates of precision, information-based warfare. But this sort of thinking misses the leverage WMD may confer on aspiring hegemons who seek to dominate their regions and to keep outside powers like the United States from interfering. For actors of this type the lack of accuracy of Scud missiles, for example, may not be dissuasive. These Soviet-designed ballistic missiles may not provide the pinpoint accuracy of smart weapons, but they are adequate to target the rear echelon forces and supporting bases of U.S. expeditionary forces. Knowing this, the United States may be deterred from forcible entry into hostile zones. As Paul Bracken has explained:

The great administrative and technical intricacies of the Western military effort are not seen at the tip of the military spear, but at its shaft. The tip—the front-line units—needs ammunition, fuel, and spare parts for its complex vehicles, radars, and radios. Biological weapons attack the shaft, the long, vulnerable part of the Western spear, comprising trucks, parts inventories, repair shops, and air and sea transportation. The shaft of the spear is not nearly as well protected as the tip is.[10]

If cultural dissimilarity will impede Western understanding of the strategies that adversaries in Asia and the Middle East armed with ballistic missiles will pursue, another potential vulnerability lies in asymmetrical information strategies available to opponents both above and below the threshold of mass destruction. One potential U.S. vulnerability is the casualty aversion in the minds of U.S. politicians (but not necessarily among the public or the armed forces) that has grown up with the advent of the all-volunteer force and the spectacular success of U.S. and allied armies in Desert Storm. This casualty allergy can be manifest in two ways: It can enhance the counterdeterrent effect of the enemy's threat to employ nuclear or biological weapons against intervening U.S. forces or their bases of support or it can be used to intimidate the American public by running up casualties in protracted conventional, or unconventional, conflicts. Iraq's strategy for deterring U.S. military attack in 1990 and 1991 was to threaten a ground war of attrition that would cause tens of thousands of U.S. casualties, as predicted even by some Americans. This strategy failed because superior U.S. air power and knowledge-intensive warfare blinded and deafened Iraq's war machine, allowing its head to be disconnected from its body so that it flailed helplessly to self-destruction. However, the strategy of exhaustion of the U.S. body politic by means of casualty attrition worked for North Vietnam and the Vietcong from the Tet Offensive until the withdrawal of American combat forces in 1973.

More recently the Clinton administration was moved to withdraw combat forces from Somalia in the wake of a shootout with the unconventional warriors of warlord Mohammed Farah Aideed in October 1993 that resulted in eighteen U.S. and hundreds of Somali deaths in Mogadishu. But the most recent showcase for policy planners motivated by casualty aversion was NATO's war against Yugoslavia (Operation Allied Force) in the spring of 1999. Political leaders, including President Bill Clinton, ruled out a ground offensive at the outset of the air campaign. Knowing this, Yugoslav president Slobodan Milošević was unimpaired in accelerating his ethnic cleansing of Albanians resident in the Serbian province of Kosovo. In addition, the NATO air sorties against

targets in Serbia were mostly held above fifteen thousand feet in order to mini-
mize the loss of pilots (in the event, no pilots were killed by hostile fire). But one
result of this limitation on air tasking was that ground targets, including tanks
and armored personnel carriers, were difficult to identify clearly and to hit precisely. After-action reports compiled by the NATO staffs were unable to verify
more than about twenty destroyed tanks, despite claims by the U.S. Joint Chiefs
of Staff and high NATO officials that the air campaign had actually knocked out
hundreds of tanks and armored personnel carriers (APCs).

Admittedly these examples are not examples of deterrence or counterdeterrence by means of WMD, but that is precisely the point. In the case of NATO
we have a nuclear armed alliance centered on the sole global superpower at the
end of the twentieth century, and collectively disposing of about two-thirds
of the world's gross national product. In the other corner we have the state of
Yugoslavia, whose government is under siege from within and is unprotected by
its former superpower patron, the now defunct Soviet Union. From the standpoint of military-strategic capability, it was a most unequal match. However,
strategy can confer additional points of advantage, or disadvantage, on military
combatants and the policy makers for whom they work. NATO's no-casualty
strategy left the Milošević regime on the ground to accomplish its war aims of
expelling Albanians from Kosovo, after which Milošević agreed to say uncle
and negotiate an end to the fighting. Thereafter NATO found itself embroiled in
a peace operation that required the restraint of Albanians who, having returned
to Kosovo, sought to get even with their erstwhile Serbian oppressors.

The nuclear past, incorrectly interpreted, offers a misleading guide to the
nuclear future. Nuclear proliferation outside of Europe will create a new map
of geostrategy, especially in the Middle East and Asia. And deterrence as prac-
ticed in the Cold War was insufficiently cognizant of the importance of cultural
and social variables in comprehending the mind-set of other state and nonstate
actors. In the next section, we consider a third aspect of the attempt to project
the twenty-first-century role of nuclear weapons: technology.

Bringing Back Classical Strategy?

In the first nuclear age, military traditionalists were frustrated by the dominance of offensive over defensive technology. Antibomber defenses were developed and deployed by the United States in the 1940s and 1950s with mixed
success. Once ballistic missiles became the dominant arm of the Soviet strategic nuclear forces, air defenses seemed superfluous and the United States ener-
getically pursued a variety of research programs on missile defense. The ABM
Treaty of 1972 between the United States and the Soviet Union permitted each

side to deploy ABM systems at two sites: one to protect the national command authority and one other. The United States chose to deploy its Safeguard system at Grand Forks, North Dakota, in the early 1970s to defend an intercontinental ballistic missile (ICBM) field, but Congress chose to dismantle the system in 1975.

From the mid-1970s the issue of missile defenses remained off the radar of the U.S. policy debate until the Reagan administration. President Ronald Reagan in 1983 called for a research and development program to create national missile defenses for the U.S. territory, and Congress authorized the creation of the Strategic Defense Initiative Office (SDIO) in the Pentagon to review a number of technology and policy issues related to the president's directive. The SDIO spent a considerable amount of money and time on the problem, but the technology was not available, nor imminently foreseeable, to fulfill the president's ambitious objective. But the Reagan proposal and SDIO did keep the issue alive into the next administration.

Recognizing that neither the money nor the political support for Reagan's original and ambitious Strategic Defense Initiative would be available to his successors, President George H. W. Bush and Secretary of Defense Dick Cheney downsized and reoriented the missile defense research and development program toward the goal of limited rather than comprehensive national missile defense. The first Bush missile defense program was intended to defeat small attacks of nuclear missiles caused either by accidental launches or by deliberate strikes from "rogue" states such as North Korea, Iraq, Iran, or Libya. The Clinton administration later adapted the downsized Bush program as its own, with less apparent enthusiasm but in recognition of the sunken costs already invested, of the congressional support from members of the Republican majority in 1994, and as a hedge against an uncertain threat environment created by the proliferation of weapons of mass destruction and ballistic missiles.

The George W. Bush administration took office in 2001 and indicated its resolve to deploy national missile defenses and to withdraw from the ABM Treaty of 1972, described by Bush officials as a Cold War "relic." (The United States officially withdrew from the treaty in 2002.) The Putin administration spoke with two messages on NMD. In principle, Russia preferred that the United States adhere to the ABM Treaty and not deploy missile defenses, judged to be destabilizing by Moscow. In practice, Putin recognized that the Bush administration was determined to deploy missile defenses as soon as it became technologically feasible to do so. Pragmatism in Moscow dictated that Russia settle for a seat at the table.

Russian and U.S. defense experts have exchanged views on missile defense technology and on the possibility of research and development cooperation related to BMD. Although Russia reacted with diplomatic correctness to initial American BMD deployments in 2004 on U.S. national territory, the Kremlin was far more sensitive about possible U.S. deployments in Europe. This sensitivity was acute with respect to U.S. plans announced in 2007 to deploy missile defense interceptors in Poland and BMD radars in the Czech Republic. The United States insisted that these deployments posed no threat to Russia and that limited BMD deployed in Europe was meant to counter possible threats from Iran. Russia, however, reacted sharply in the negative, despite these reassurances. Putin announced in April 2007 that Russia would suspend its compliance with the Conventional Forces in Europe (CFE) Treaty, signed by member states of NATO and the Warsaw Pact in 1990 and requiring the relocation or destruction of major battle equipment for conventional forces deployed by both alliances during the Cold War.[11]

Despite Putin's nationalistic and more assertive foreign policy in his second term, the possibility of cooperation between the United States and Russia on missile defenses was not precluded. At his meeting with President Bush at Kennebunkport, Maine, on July 2, 2007, Putin expanded on an earlier proposal for a shared U.S.-Russian missile defense system to be developed jointly under the aegis of the NATO-Russia Council. Putin's plan included use of a modernized radar site in Azerbaijan and another early detection system in southern Russia, in addition to information exchange sites in Moscow and Brussels.[12]

The difficulty in arbitrating debates about missile defense is that the applied scientific research is so embedded with political advocacy. This has been true since the earliest U.S. debates about missile defense in the Cold War. The 1980s were an especially active decade of aggressive confrontation between proponents and opponents of BMD. How to sort out the technology and policy issues attendant to BMD or NMD? Let us try some provisional constructs for categorizing two important aspects of the problem: the technology and strategy environments within which current and future policy makers will have to decide. First, let's compare possible present and/or future conditions with regard to the technology available for missile defense. Of course, we are not merely interested in the technology as a test bed, but in how well defense technology compares to the evolving threats it is expected to meet. The possibilities that present themselves are summarized in table I.1.

Numbering the cells from left to right and from top to bottom, we can see that cells 2 and 3 (simple technology/complex threats or complex technology/ simple threats) are *asymmetrical* conditions in which either the defense (cell 3) or the offense (cell 2) is favored. Cells 1 and 4, on the other hand, present *symmetrical* conditions in which offensive and defensive technologies are more or less in balance. A symmetrical condition is one in which neither the offense

TABLE I.1. POSSIBLE TECHNOLOGY AND THREAT ENVIRONMENTS FOR BMD

1 Simple defense technology / simple threat environment	2 Simple defense technology / complex threat environment
3 Complex defense technology / simple threat environment	4 Complex defense technology / complex threat environment

nor the defense can leap ahead by a generation and outperform its rival so much that the nuclear stalemate is broken and first-strike capability is within reach for one or more nuclear armed states. Symmetry is a frozen woolly mammoth in your cellar: interesting to look at and not disruptive of existing living arrangements. An asymmetrical situation, in contrast, is a condition such that one or more states have been able to leapfrog a generation ahead in offenses or in defenses, thus placing at risk the second-strike capability of one or more other actors. In an asymmetrical situation your woolly mammoth has thawed out, come back to life, and now remembers the hunger pangs that it had before being frozen. In other words, a symmetrical relationship between technology and threat environment is probably going to be stable, that is, less prone to war, whereas an asymmetrical relationship will be more war prone.

Notice, however, that symmetrical and asymmetrical conditions describe a *relational* attribute between technology and threat environment, not technology itself. We might, as some have done, compare the probable state of offensive and defensive technology five, ten, or fifteen years from now. But comparing technology with technology misses the point. We are less interested in offensive and defensive missile technology than we are in the *strategy* or military uses for these technologies. Offensive technology (long-range ballistic missiles) can be used to support a defensive strategy, as we saw during the Cold War; deterrence was based on *retaliation* (a defensive strategy) after having absorbed an offensive first strike. Conversely, it would be possible to use missile defense technology as part of an offensive strategy: launching a nuclear first strike, then using defenses to mop up the other side's ragged retaliation.

What makes a threat environment complex or simple? A simple threat environment is one that is more or less predictable based on available intelligence and one for which existing or near-term technology provides an appropriate and available response. A complex threat environment is a condition that is difficult to predict on the basis of existing intelligence and for which no available or near-term technology provides an appropriate response. What makes a threat environment complex as opposed to simple is not necessarily how complicated the technology is, but the *degree of ingenuity* of exploitation of the technology on the part of the users. Thus, for example, Germany leaped ahead of Britain and France between the world wars in its ability to wage tank warfare not on account of superior technology (British and French tanks were better in some respects) but due to Germany's superior concept of armored warfare, including uniquely constituted panzer divisions, specially tasked supporting tactical air power, and radio communications that allowed superior information flow up and down the chain of command.

By analogy, it is not necessarily the first power that parks weapons in space that will dominate the future of antimissile technology but the power that incorporates space-based weapons into an overall strategy for the denial of mission superiority and political coercion to its opponent. Some of the more important missions foreseen by the U.S. Department of Defense for space-based weaponry are summarized in table I.2.

Space-based weapons may be vulnerable to prompt kills from antisatellite weapons (ASATs) or to degradation or spoofing from information warfare. Or the leading-edge state in space-based weapons may nevertheless be intimidated from employing its weapons by the superior fanaticism or ruthlessness of its opponent. Say, for example, that the United States deploys some first-generation, space-based kinetic weapons and informs a potential aggressor that if it launches a ballistic missile in the direction of U.S. territory or that of our allies, we will blow it out of the sky with our space-based weapons and then consider strikes against its armies or cities. The response might be, Do that, and we will launch hundreds of mobile ballistic missiles and cruise missiles with biological warheads at your cities and the cities of your allies. In addition, we will set off twenty prelocated biological weapons already set on "command detonate" in twelve U.S. cities. Europe and North America will suffer plagues for which there are no existing cures.

The scenario is imaginary, but the illustration of a relationship between technology and strategy points to a more enduring reality. Nuclear weapons and antinuclear defenses will contribute either to the avoidance of twenty-first-century warfare or to its greater likelihood, on the basis of the policies laid down by governments and the strategies preferred by their national security managers. The relationship between war and peace, or in nuclear deterrence theory between offense and defense, is both relational and paradoxical. In order to understand why a war broke out, you have to explain why peace broke down. And vice versa: an explanation for why peace happened is tantamount to at least part of the explanation for why war did not. Explaining a failure of deterrence presumes that you have already defined some standard for the successful practice of deterrence: Explaining why deterrence worked in a particular case implies that you have some concept of a deterrence failure. In each case,

TABLE I.2. POSSIBLE MISSIONS FOR U.S. SPACE-BASED WEAPONRY

SURVEILLANCE	PROTECTION	PREVENTION	NEGATION
Precise detection, tracking, and identification of space objects	Detection and reporting of space system malfunctions	Prevent adversarial use of U.S., allied, or third-party capabilities	Precision negation of adversarial use of space
Ability to characterize objects as threats or nonthreats	Characterization of an attack and location of its source		Strike assessment or BDA against target sets
Detection or assessment when a threat payload performs a maneuver or separates	Withstanding and defense against threats or attacks		
	Restoration of mission capability		

Source: Office of the Secretary of Defense, *Space Technology Guide*, 10-2.

in order to have a viable research hypothesis one must have an equally robust "null" hypothesis with which to juxtapose and contradict it.

It follows that missile defenses may make nuclear deterrence more stable or less stable, depending on how the investigator defines pre–missile defense experience. If the history of the first nuclear age, covering approximately the same years as the Cold War, is regarded as mostly stable and peaceful, then that appraisal will be used as a marker to cast doubt on the contribution of missile defense to stability, or, to say it another way, to predict that missile defenses will make the international system less stable. Conversely, if the assessment of the observer is that nuclear deterrence in the Cold War was more precarious than many judge it to have been, the observer is likely to be more willing to entertain the possibility that missile defenses could improve, instead of detract from, stability.

Of course "stability" is a loaded term with a number of possible predicates; stability can be political, technological, social, cultural, military-doctrinal, and so forth. When a number of these dimensions undergo simultaneous upheavals, they constitute a "military revolution" or, in cases of lesser turbulence for the status quo, a "revolution in military affairs."[13] The twenty-first century is guaranteed to surprise us in ways that will confound existing policy and strategy paradigms. Even as we speak some of the most notable "big ideas" of the 1990s and early twenty-first century have been sorely tested against U.S. experience in Iraq since the ouster of Saddam Hussein in 2003 and the insurgency that followed.

These big ideas now being chased into rewrites or at least partial nullification include the inevitable march of history toward a determinate outcome favorable to market economies and political democracies, the necessity for a U.S. "empire" supported by a willingness to fight imperial wars across the breadth of the greater Middle East (from the sands of Morocco to the heights of the Hindu Kush), and the declaratory strategy of a "global war on terror" that lends itself to acronym abuse and indeterminate definition of enemies.

Conclusions

Traditional diplomatic strategies to prevent the further spread of nuclear weapons, including arms control agreements like the Non-Proliferation Treaty (NPT), are important statements of international consensus and policy preference. They cannot, however, guarantee a stable world. The expectation of stability with regard to war, including its causes and outcomes, is guaranteed to mislead. In the worst case it can lead to military misjudgment and defeat. Therefore, the United States' and other states' future consideration of nuclear proliferation will take place not in the (comparatively) stable world of the first nuclear age but within the unfolding dynamic of the second (or later).

The modern international system is driven by many forces, including ideological, technical, and economic, over which politicians may have little control and that cross state borders with impunity. In addition to wars between states, future wars may occur within states (failed, failing, or otherwise), around states (near and across borders), and above and below states. Prudent planners will therefore investigate off-the-shelf and other candidate technologies for military effect, including antimissile defenses not previously conceived or deployed. Hedging against uncertainty is neither elegant nor intellectually satisfying, compared to assumptions of stability-based generic prescriptions for military planning and arms control.

On the other hand adaptive hedging against uncertainty draws on U.S. strengths in culture ("Yankee ingenuity"), bottom-up innovation (Bill Gates, Steve Jobs), and disciplined but nontraditional military thinking (Andrew Marshall in the Pentagon's Office of Net Assessment). Historian Max Boot emphasizes the importance of innovative thinkers within the military establishment as well as the ideas of talented outsiders in bringing about military revolutions. In addition, technology innovation must be matched by adaptive organization, doctrine, and training, among other military attributes. Whether states are democracies or dictatorships is less significant than many suppose. According to Boot, the "key to successful innovation, whether for a dictatorship or a democracy, is having an effective bureaucracy."[14]

Chapter 1

Russian and American Nuclear Force Reductions

A more assertive Russia poses challenges for U.S. security and arms control policies. George W. Bush administration plans to deploy some parts of global missile defenses in Eastern Europe, as well as existing and proposed agreements on nuclear arms reductions and nonproliferation, are intersecting with an improved Russian economy for defense, the results of a new presidential election in Russia, and the uncertainty attendant to Vladimir Putin's transition from the office of president to that of prime minister, along with his replacement in the former office by his protégé, Dmitri Medvedev. As well, Russia must anticipate the arrival of a new U.S. administration in January 2009.

On the other hand, some arms control experts and former officials contend that, even in this expressive diplomatic climate, the United States and Russia could reduce significantly the numbers of their deployed strategic nuclear weapons without compromising the viability of their deterrents or diminishing deterrence or arms race stability. In addition, reductions in Russian and U.S. strategic nuclear forces could help to discourage nonnuclear states from acquiring nuclear weapons and encourage current nuclear powers to cap or reduce their existing arsenals.

Are U.S. and Russian Interests Convergent or Divergent?

Despite recent disagreements over the planned deployment of U.S. missile defenses in Eastern Europe, the United States and Russia have more common than opposed interests. One of these interests is prevention of the spread of nuclear weapons among additional states, especially those with grievances against regional neighbors or the existing international order. Another common interest is keeping nuclear weapons out of the hands of nonstate actors, including terrorists, who may be beyond the reach of nuclear deterrence. A third shared interest between the United States and Russia is prevention of the outbreak of accidental or inadvertent nuclear war or the onset of a crisis with a significant probability of leading to war.

In order to accomplish these objectives, the United States and Russia must fulfill their obligations under the Non-Proliferation Treaty and reduce their own arsenals of deployed nuclear weapons on intercontinental launchers: land-based ballistic missiles, submarine-launched ballistic missiles, and long-range bombers. So long as the Americans and Russians maintain larger than necessary (for deterrence) nuclear arsenals, the incentives for other nuclear powers to increase, or at least not to reduce, their own nuclear weapons inventories are powerful. Russia and the United States are the "gold standards" against which other nuclear states measure their relative power positions.

However, getting the United States or Russia to reduce its reliance on long-range nuclear weapons is easier said than done. Both states have maintained large inventories of nuclear weapons, including deployed weapons on intercontinental launchers, long after the end of the Cold War and the demise of the Soviet Union. In part this attachment to nukes is cultural. As nuclear arms control expert Joseph Cirincione has noted, "In the United States, perhaps more than in any other country, the atom is tied directly to the national ego. For many political leaders, it is inconceivable that the United States would give up the weapon we invented."[1]

U.S. interest in maintaining a strategic nuclear arsenal second to none is driven by factors other than nostalgia. First, since the end of the Cold War the United States has assumed an ambitious geopolitical profile in world politics. Under both the Clinton and second Bush administrations the United States assumed a responsibility for world order that would have been unthinkable during the Cold War years or earlier. From its traditional role as an offshore balancer in Europe and Asia, the United States has evolved into something its critics refer to as a global hegemon and its defenders call an international sheriff.

Whether one approves of or disparages this higher profile of U.S. global reach and responsibility compared to the Cold War, the relationship between a higher demand for U.S.-provided security and nuclear weapons is at best indirect. This is so for two reasons. First, U.S. military primacy since the Cold War is primarily due to its lead in advanced technology, conventional weapons, and delivery systems: especially those for C4ISR (command, control, communications, computers, intelligence, surveillance, and reconnaissance). As U.S. military prowess at the high end of conventional warfare improves, its need for nuclear weapons as anything other than a residual deterrent against enemy nuclear weapons is diminished.

A second reason the connection between U.S. nuclear weapons and the political influence supported by military power is indirect is the character of nuclear weapons themselves. They are, in their military, political, and social effects, the opposite of long-range, precision-guided weapons that have been the trumps of warfare since Desert Storm. Nuclear weapons have not been used in anger since 1945 because even their possessors recognize that they exist for the purpose of war avoidance, not for the actual fighting of war. The notion of military victory as most Americans and other civilized peoples understand it is missing in the collateral damage attendant to even small numbers of nuclear weapons.

There remain three reasons for U.S. interest in maintaining a large number of deployed long-range nuclear weapons: the three Ps of protection, prestige, and politics.[2] Protection refers to the inclusion of U.S. allies under the umbrella of American nuclear deterrence. Protection of allies in Western Europe against the threat of a Soviet conventional invasion was one of the reasons for deploying U.S. nuclear weapons in Europe during the Cold War. Prestige attaches to nuclear weapons for some states because they are symbols of great-power status and give a "seat at the table" or access to important international forums. Other states have not failed to notice that the five permanent members of the United Nations Security Council are also the first five states to have built and deployed nuclear forces.

The third P supporting U.S. interest in a second-to-none nuclear arsenal is politics—domestic politics, in this instance. Powerful interest groups combine with government bureaucrats and members of Congress to form "iron triangles" on behalf of particular defense programs. Members of Congress need to "bring home the bacon" of military deployments in their districts, including bases and other installations. Although nuclear weapons are not big spenders in domestic politics compared to conventional armies, navies, and air force elements, nuclear weapons programs have their own momentum in the service of DOD bureaucracies or on Capitol Hill. In addition, the nuclear motivations of prestige and protection also have their own foreign pressure groups and U.S. domestic constituencies.

Russia's Concerns

Russia has motives of its own for its continuing interest in nuclear weapons, apart from the motives it might share with the United States of nuclear deterrence and its own version of the three Ps. Russia's conventional armed forces crashed and burned, in quantity as well as in quality, during the first decade after the end of the Cold War. During the 1990s its nuclear weapons were its only justification for claiming major power status. Beginning in 2000 President Vladimir Putin began to rebuild Russia's military, aided by expanding worldwide demand for energy. His defense plans included improvements in conventional forces and the modernization of strategic and other nuclear forces.

Russia military doctrine under Putin made clear the perceived necessity of its military leadership to plan for the use of nuclear weapons, apart from situations of possible nuclear attack against Russia. In addition, Russia will consider the first use of nuclear weapons in case of invasion of Russian state territory or attacks on or near the periphery of Russia with the potential for causing significant damage to Russia.

Russia's willingness to entertain the possibility of nuclear first use in case of conventional attack is a departure from the Cold War Soviet precedent of no first use. Of course, declaratory policies may not always be honored in the event of actual crisis or war. But the disposition of Russia's political leaders and military planners since 1991 to rely on prompt use of nuclear weapons reflects the parlous state of Russia's conventional forces—for deterrence and for prevailing in war if deterrence fails.

One reason for Russia's concern about the balance of power in Europe is NATO expansion since 1991. NATO, an alliance of some sixteen western states during the Cold War, has now extended its membership in several stages to include twenty-six countries. A number of these states were formerly members of the Soviet-dominated Warsaw Treaty Organization (Warsaw Pact) military alliance during the Cold War. NATO's pub crawl to the doorstep of Russia's borders since the end of the Cold War is taken by many Russians as a breach of a tacit promise by former U.S. Secretary of State James Baker, during the first Bush administration, that the unification of East and West Germany would mark the end of NATO expansion.

Related to this is Russia's frustration over the Conventional Forces in Europe Treaty negotiated during the Cold War and adapted in 1999. The adapted treaty has yet to come into force because NATO has linked its ratification to the implementation of the "Istanbul commitments" by Russia—that is, the withdrawal of Russian troops from Georgia and Moldova. For its part Russia wants major changes in the adapted CFE, including the removal of all "flank" restrictions on force deployments (increasing flexibility for Russia) and the addition of collective ceilings on heavy weapons (limiting NATO's tanks and infantry fighting vehicles deployed in its easternmost members).[3] From the perspective of "order of battle," NATO does not appear to be more threatening to Russia than hitherto. As of September 2007 NATO's twenty-six member states had 20 percent less manpower and equipment than its formerly sixteen members were permitted under the original 1990 treaty.[4] But Russia is concerned as much about U.S. and NATO political intentions as it is about current force capabilities.

Apart from the expansion of NATO and the imbalance of NATO and Russian military forces in Europe, Russia has two other concerns that lead to its decision to modernize its nuclear forces and to limit its strategic nuclear force reductions. The first concern is the preservation of Russia's deterrent in the face of U.S. existing and future deployments of ballistic missile defenses. The second is the uncertain balance of military power in Asia and the possibility of an increasing nuclear arms race in Asia among existing and/or additional nuclear powers there. Russia's more immediate concern is the question of missile defenses in Europe (more discussion follows), but Russia is also mindful of the uncertainties attendant to nuclear arms competition in Asia.

Already nuclear Asia includes Russia, China, India, and Pakistan. North Korea declared itself into the ranks of nuclear powers in 2005 and conducted its first nuclear test in 2006. The United States and four other states (Russia, China, Japan, and South Korea) reached an agreement with North Korea (DPRK) in February 2007 that would freeze and eventually dismantle its nuclear programs, and a timetable established in early September 2007 called for declaration of, and dismantling of, all of North Korea's nuclear weapons and production facilities. According to the chief U.S. envoy for the North Korean negotiations, Christopher R. Hill, "One thing that we agreed on is that the DPRK will provide a full declaration of all of its nuclear programs and will disable their nuclear programs by the end of this year, 2007."[5]

If North Korea is successfully disarmed of nuclear weapons capability, it would reverse the momentum of nonproliferation negativity in the region, beginning in 1998 with the nuclear "coming out" tests by India and Pakistan and followed by North Korea's walkout from the NPT several years later. The prospect of an irrevocable North Korean nuclear weapons arsenal was dangerous to regional rivals, such as Japan and South Korea, but also to major powers in Asia, including Russia, China, and the United States. A shift in Bush administration approach to North Korea during Bush's second term, encouraging multilateral talks with the DPRK as well as selected one-on-one conferences between diplomatic principals, paid dividends in a breakthrough in principle in 2005 and a more conclusive agreement among the six states in 2007.

Reversing North Korea's nuclear status and slowing down the risk of unconstrained proliferation in Asia creates more maneuver space for Russia and China with respect to their bilateral relations, and with respect to their relations with the United States. A regional nuclear arms race might have created, in addition to new nuclear states, additional uncertainties among the Moscow-Beijing-Washington triangle with respect to the control of nuclear weapons and the reliability of nuclear deterrence. A more stable nuclear Asia opens the door wider for arms reductions between the Americans and Russians.

It also encourages nuclear restraint on the part of China, which has already been moving toward greater political and military cooperation with Russia, including joint military exercises of unprecedented size.

If its back door in Asia is not bubbling over, Russia can be a more confident participant in Russian-U.S. discussions about nuclear arms reductions. On the other hand, the apparently stabilizing containment of North Korea's nuclear ambitions might be offset by Russia's objections to U.S. plans for the deployment of components of its global missile defenses system in Poland and the Czech Republic.

Russia's objections to U.S. missile defenses are not limited to those parts of any BMD system deployed in Eastern Europe. In fact, Russian skepticism about American missile defenses dates from the Cold War and continues into the post–Cold War world. But the current political climate of adversity that influences Russian views of U.S. and NATO security policies is the result of two cascading forces: a growing sense of self-confidence on Russia's part and an undisguised resentment of the 1990s during which many Russians felt weak and dominated by the West.[6] Added to this is the suspicion on the part of Russian leaders that the United States intends to operate globally as a hegemonic power. In an address to the Russian Federal Assembly in May 2006, Putin referred to the United States as "a wolf which knows who to eat and is not about to listen to anyone, it seems."[7] Putin created greater waves with his harsh rhetoric in February 2007 at the Munich Security Conference, where he criticized the "unipolar" (meaning U.S.-dominated) international system and added, "Today we are witnessing an almost uncontained hyper use of force—military force—in international relations, force that is plunging the world into an abyss of permanent conflicts."[8]

From this perspective of Russian reaction to perceived U.S. unilateralism and imperialism, Putin's objections to U.S. ballistic missile defenses, especially if deployed in Europe, become of more than passing significance. Russian foreign minister Sergei Lavrov emphasized this point in a speech on September 3, 2007, to students at the Moscow State Institute of International Relations. Lavrov referred to opposition to U.S. missile defenses in Eastern Europe (and Russia's policy on Kosovo) as "red lines" that were beyond negotiation.[9] In July 2007 Russia had already indicated its intent to suspend temporarily its cooperation with NATO under the CFE Treaty on account of the U.S. plan to deploy BMD interceptors in Poland and radars in the Czech Republic.[10]

At the Kennebunkport "lobster summit" with the two Presidents Bush in early July, Putin took the diplomatic advantage by offering a substitute plan for the U.S. plan to deploy BMD components in Eastern Europe. Putin's plan called for the use of radar installations in Azerbaijan and in southern Russia, which

Russian experts contended would be more appropriate if, as the United States claimed, the BMD system was really intended to detect missiles launched from Iran.[11] In connection with this plan, Putin also proposed that Russia and NATO fulfill earlier expressions of intent to establish shared missile warning centers in Moscow and in Brussels.[12]

In addition to the "carrot" of BMD cooperation, Putin and other Russian officials have not been slow to play the "stick" card of offensive force modernization to offset U.S. defenses. Russia has undertaken strategic nuclear force modernization plans that include deployment of newer land- and sea-based missiles (ICBMs and submarine-launched ballistic missiles, or SLBMs) as well as a new generation of ballistic missile submarines. Reportedly Russia has also experimented with maneuvering reentry vehicles or other technologies and techniques to defeat any defense that might otherwise weaken nuclear retaliatory strikes.[13] Further to the image of improved strategic force readiness and assertiveness, Russia has resumed its former Cold War practice of flying nuclear bomber sorties near U.S. military airspace or territory on a regular basis.[14]

Policy Issues

Does the preceding catalog of U.S. and Russian security concerns, and their possible reasons for continuing interest in larger than necessary nuclear arsenals, argue for a continuation of the status quo in their nuclear deterrence and arms control policies? Not necessarily. Pressures against the status quo are considerable, and from at least three directions. First, maturing missile defense technologies may improve the performance of candidate BMD systems significantly, especially against threats posed by small powers. Second, proliferation remains a threat to existing security communities in Europe and Asia. Even with the favorable assumption that North Korea is effectively disarmed of a nuclear weapons capability by the end of the calendar year 2008, other stresses loom for the nonproliferation regime. For example, Iran continues to work against the clock of UN sanctions in order to position itself for a nuclear weapons breakout, if the leadership in Tehran should so determine.

Third, the continuation of political distrust between the United States and Russia threatens to turn the issue of mutual deterrence, and the role of missile defense technology, from a matter of cooperative security into an issue of competitive rivalry. As in other matters, so too in nuclear arms control: Politics drives strategy. Deterioration of their political relationship makes it more difficult for the United States and Russia to engage in additional disarmament of their respective long-range nuclear arsenals. Stalemate (or worse) between the United States and Russia discourages other nuclear states from arms limitation or reductions, and it encourages other states to consider the possibility of going nuclear.

On the other hand, it is easier for theorists to advocate for or against security policies than it is to accomplish them in political action. The gravitational forces pulling in favor of the status quo in nuclear weapons deployments are formidable. Certainly in the case of the United States any movement of national policy from the status quo requires painstaking incremental adjustments and negotiated compromises among competing interests and power centers. Large changes occur only in the aftermath of crisis or war, but prudent nuclear policy is intended to avoid both.

Politicians in Russia and the United States will also depend on their professional armed forces and other experts for advice about nuclear arms control and deterrence. Although there are experts aplenty in nuclear physics and in the politics of nuclear arms control, there are (thankfully) no experts in nuclear wars. Conventional military conflicts over the centuries have provided a database that acts as a sifter of hypotheses and theories. Expectations about the outcomes of nuclear wars, and about the performances of nuclear forces fired in a war between two or more states, are at best logical deductions from hypothetical scenarios.

The preceding point about the character of nuclear war as an abstraction or deduction is important because it permits analysis to drift toward the extremes of policy debate. For example, during the 1980s proponents of Reagan's SDI and others contended that the Soviet Union was bent on acquiring a nuclear first-strike capability against the U.S. land-based missile force (the so-called window of vulnerability). Opponents of missile defenses contended that it would provoke a new arms race in offensive nuclear weapons and increase the risk of nuclear war. In fact, SDI in the 1980s was a vu-graph proposal for a series of technology demonstrations, not even close to a workable or deployable BMD system.

Future administrations, including the Clinton and the first and second Bush administrations, ran away from SDI and scaled back the military objectives and the technology ambitions for missile defenses. Instead of a system providing comprehensive societal protection against massive attacks, U.S. national missile defense research emphasized protection against accidental launches and limited strikes. As a result of this experience, the present debate about missile defenses is more realistic with respect to BMD capabilities against responsive threats. Current U.S. BMD research and development programs include a variety of technologies for land-based, sea-based and airborne intercept.[15]

Despite some progress in midcourse and terminal theater and nationwide missile defense technologies, there is no breakthrough over the horizon that will remove states and their societies from their nuclear hostage condition.

In fact, nuclear deterrence has outperformed the predictions of its worst critics throughout the Cold War and subsequently. One reason for the unexpected durability of nuclear deterrence is the slower-than-anticipated spread of nuclear weapons among states. Projections made in the 1960s suggested that there might be an avalanche of nuclear weapons states by the end of the twentieth century, instead of the actual seven declared (excluding North Korea, which declared only in the present century) and one de facto but undeclared nuclear power (Israel).

But another reason for the durability of nuclear deterrence and the widespread assumption of a nuclear "taboo" is the progression of time that has elapsed since the bombing of Nagasaki. States with nuclear arsenals have, at least since the Cuban Missile Crisis of 1962, for the most part refrained from nuclear brinkmanship and other adventurism supported by explicit or tacit nuclear threats. This caution on the part of nuclear states does not argue for complacency about the viability of deterrence in the new world order. But it does indicate that experienced nuclear powers such as the United States and Russia should no longer be fixated on maintaining arsenals of certain size and character for reasons of inertia or braggadocio. It requires very few nuclear weapons to create a good deal of menace.

Analysis

If the preceding arguments have merit, then the United States and Russia should be able to reduce the sizes of their nuclear arsenals even below those agreed under the Moscow Treaty of 2002, otherwise known as SORT (for Strategic Offensive Reductions Treaty).[16] SORT requires that Russia and the United States reduce their numbers of operationally deployed strategic nuclear weapons to 2,200–1,700 for each state by December 31, 2012. The treaty allows each state to determine its own force structure of weapons and launchers with freedom to mix among different types under the overall ceiling of "deployed warheads." The treaty does not mention verification protocols with respect to its provisions, although it does provide that the earlier START I (Strategic Arms Reductions Treaty) remains in force.

How far could Russian and U.S. reductions in strategic nuclear weapons go and still meet the requirements of stable deterrence? Some expert opinion is optimistic. Gen. Eugene Habiger, commander in chief of U.S. Strategic Command in the 1990s, told an international conference in 1995 that Russia and the United States could reduce their arsenals to 600 warheads each.[17] Physicist Wolfgang K. H. Panofsky, who served as science policy advisor to Presidents Eisenhower, Kennedy, and Carter and worked on the Manhattan Project from

1943 to 1945, argues that deterrence has not become obsolete in the post–Cold War world. However, the character and requirements of nuclear deterrence in the present international order differ from those of the past. According to Panofsky, "Deterring Russia, as well as China and other states that have acquired nuclear weapons, remains a justifiable function of U.S. nuclear weapons policy. But several thousand U.S. nuclear warheads are not needed to discharge that mission; a few hundred would suffice."[18]

Harvard University political scientist Stephen M. Walt advocates a "grand bargain" in which the United States exchanges for a more viable nonproliferation regime several concessions: (1) abandon Bush administration plans to build a new generation of nuclear weapons; (2) reduce significantly the U.S. nuclear arsenal, retaining "a few hundred" warheads as a deterrent against direct attacks on the United States; and (3) reduce the threat posed by the United States to so-called rogue states provided those states, such as Iran and North Korea, give up their nuclear ambitions.[19] Rejecting anticipated criticism that his recipe amounts to a form of appeasement, Walt adds, "Unless it makes a series of catastrophic blunders, the United States will be the strongest country on the planet for the next several decades, and its primacy will not be altered whether it has five thousand nuclear warheads or only fifty."[20]

Agreement that U.S. forces could be reduced well below Moscow Treaty levels crosses the political spectrum and includes prominent officials and advisors to Republican presidents. Frank Miller, a former official with the National Security Council and DOD, stated in November 2005, "It's my personal belief that the levels of U.S. strategic weapons can and should decline further from those allowed in the Treaty of Moscow. I would hope that the administration takes steps in the next year or so to produce that."[21] And according to former Reagan administration official and George W. Bush defense policy advisor Richard Perle, "I see no reason why we can't go well below 1,000. I want the lowest number possible, under the highest control possible. . . . The truth is we are never going to use them. The Russians aren't going to use theirs either."[22]

Are these optimistic expressions about the possible scope of Russian and U.S. strategic nuclear arms reductions within the range of political feasibility and operational plausibility?[23] Political feasibility is a larger subject than the present study, but operational feasibility is something that can be addressed here. One can ask in this context whether sub-SORT nuclear arms reductions can leave in place the expectation that both Russia and the United States can fulfill their requirements for deterrence and arms control stability. If they can do so at lower levels, the accomplishment should have blowback in favor of proliferation restraint by nonnuclear states and less ambitious growth in the arsenals of existing nuclear powers.

Applying the Model

The analysis here proceeds in several steps. First, hypothetical Russian and U.S. SORT-compliant strategic nuclear force structures are created, projecting for the 2012–15 period.[24] Second, these forces are compared for their ability to provide surviving and retaliating warheads after having absorbed a counterforce first strike. Third, in addition to testing variable force structures for each state, their performances are modeled under each of four operational conditions: (1) generated alert and launch on warning, (2) generated alert, riding out the attack, (3) day-to-day alert and launch on warning, and (4) day-to-day alert, riding out the attack. In general, the gradation from posture 1 to 4 should provide for progressively fewer surviving and retaliating warheads.[25]

The alternative force structures tested in this analysis are, for Russia, (1) a balanced triad of land- and sea-based missiles and bomber-delivered weapons, (2) a dyad of land- and sea-based missiles without bombers, (3) a dyad of bombers and ICBMs without SLBMs, and (4) a force composed entirely of ICBMs. For the United States the alternate force structures are (1) a balanced triad, (2) a dyad of SLBMs and bombers, (3) a dyad of ICBMs and SLBMs, and (4) a force composed entirely of SLBMs. These alternative force structures are not equally "realistic" by design. Current Russian and U.S. plans are to deploy a balanced triad of land- and sea-based missiles and bomber-delivered weapons. The alternative forces are heuristic devices that permit comparative perspective on the performances of retaliatory forces. These alternatives might become more important if future U.S. or Russian force modernization plans change. For example, even modest U.S. missile defense deployments might suggest to Russian planners that they place additional emphasis on bomber delivered weapons compared to land- and sea-based missiles.

With the preceding "inputs" to the analysis, we want to ascertain the performance of Russian and U.S. forces at different force sizes, using three benchmarks: (1) SORT-compliant forces within a ceiling of 2,200 operationally deployed strategic nuclear weapons, (2) a smaller "minimum deterrent" force with a maximum limit of 1,000 deployed warheads, and (3) an even smaller "micro deterrent" force with a ceiling of 500 deployed warheads. Comparison of force performances by type of force structure, by operational posture, and by force size is summarized in tables 1.1–6.

The results summarized in tables 1.1–6 show that Russia and the United States have, under most operational conditions, sufficient retaliatory striking power to perform their assured destruction or assured retaliation missions for all force sizes.[26] Only Russian forces at 1,000 or 500 levels, and in the most unfavorable operational circumstances (day-to-day alert, riding out the attack), would be unable to deliver more than 100 surviving and retaliating warheads

TABLE 1.1. TOTAL DEPLOYED STRATEGIC WEAPONS, 2,200 LIMIT

UNITED STATES				
	BALANCED TRIAD	NO ICBMS	NO BOMBERS	ALL SLBMs
ICBMs	300	0	300	0
SLBMs	1,344	1,680	1,848	2,184
Air	512	520	0	0
RUSSIA				
	BALANCED TRIAD	NO BOMBERS	NO SLBMs	ICBMS ONLY
ICBMs	800	1,300	1,300	2,020
SLBMs	528	660	0	0
Air	840	0	820	0

TABLE 1.2. SURVIVING AND RETALIATING WEAPONS, 2,200 LIMIT

UNITED STATES				
	BALANCED TRIAD	NO ICBMS	NO BOMBERS	ALL SLBMs
GEN-LOW	1,732	1,740	1,767	1,769
GEN-ROA	1,489	1,740	1,524	1,769
DAY-LOW	999	912	1,273	1,185
DAY-ROA	756	912	1,030	1,185
RUSSIA				
	BALANCED TRIAD	NO BOMBERS	NO SLBMs	ICBMS ONLY
GEN-LOW	1,760	1,705	1,476	1,818
GEN-ROA	1,169	911	682	684
DAY-LOW	806	1,277	1,170	1,818
DAY-ROA	115	170	117	182

TABLE 1.3. TOTAL DEPLOYED STRATEGIC WEAPONS, 1,000 LIMIT

UNITED STATES				
	BALANCED TRIAD	NO ICBMS	NO BOMBERS	ALL SLBMs
ICBMs	300	0	300	0
SLBMs	392	686	686	980
Air	308	314	0	0
RUSSIA				
	BALANCED TRIAD	NO BOMBERS	NO SLBMs	ICBMS ONLY
ICBMs	440	530	470	980
SLBMs	264	456	0	0
Air	288	0	530	0

TABLE 1.4. SURVIVING AND RETALIATING WEAPONS, 1,000 LIMIT

UNITED STATES				
	BALANCED TRIAD	NO ICBMS	NO BOMBERS	ALL SLBMS
GEN-LOW	812	785	826	794
GEN-ROA	569	785	583	794
DAY-LOW	483	372	642	532
DAY-ROA	240	372	399	532
RUSSIA				
	BALANCED TRIAD	NO BOMBERS	NO SLBMS	ICBMS ONLY
GEN-LOW	820	846	809	882
GEN-ROA	504	458	469	210
DAY-LOW	439	551	423	882
DAY-ROA	61	85	42	88

TABLE 1.5. TOTAL DEPLOYED STRATEGIC WEAPONS, 500 LIMIT

UNITED STATES				
	BALANCED TRIAD	NO ICBMS	NO BOMBERS	ALL SLBMS
ICBMs	120	0	108	0
SLBMs	196	294	392	490
Air	184	204	0	0
RUSSIA				
	BALANCED TRIAD	NO BOMBERS	NO SLBMS	ICBMS ONLY
ICBMs	190	307	250	500
SLBMs	120	192	0	0
Air	180	0	250	0

TABLE 1.6. SURVIVING AND RETALIATING WEAPONS, 500 LIMIT

UNITED STATES				
	BALANCED TRIAD	NO ICBMS	NO BOMBERS	ALL SLBMS
GEN-LOW	401	387	415	397
GEN-ROA	304	387	327	397
DAY-LOW	214	160	310	266
DAY-ROA	117	160	222	266

TABLE 1.6 *CONT.* SURVIVING AND RETALIATING WEAPONS, 500 LIMIT

	RUSSIA			
	BALANCED TRIAD	NO BOMBERS	NO SLBMs	ICBMs ONLY
GEN-LOW	399	432	407	450
GEN-ROA	286	224	294	86
DAY-LOW	190	307	225	450
DAY-ROA	27	43	23	45

on the opponent's territory. It is unlikely that Russian forces (or U.S. forces, for that matter) would be operating in this relatively laid-back posture during any political crisis involving the threat or possible use of nuclear weapons.

In order to test the retaliatory performances of these forces more severely, tables 1.7–9 add in the element of missile defenses for both states. Admittedly Russia currently denounces U.S. existing and planned BMD deployments, but Russia has also offered to share technology development on national missile defenses with the United States and has been working with NATO on theater missile defenses.[27] Therefore, for purposes of symmetry, Russia and the United States have each been assigned national missile defenses that are sufficiently competent to intercept 50 percent of the other side's retaliating warheads. This is admittedly, and deliberately, a higher performance standard for defenses than current or immediately foreseeable technology can meet. It provides a tough "road test" for the various retaliatory forces at deployment levels of 2,200, 1,000, and 500 warheads. In tables 1.7–9 the performances of the various Russian and U.S. nuclear retaliatory forces against opposed missile defenses are summarized.

It turns out that even against defenses that are very effective by present and near-term standards of technology, U.S. and Russian nuclear retaliatory forces at levels of 2,200, 1,000, and 500 warheads, under most operational conditions, can provide for sufficient numbers of surviving and retaliating warheads to accomplish the mission of assured retaliation based on unacceptable damage. As in the case of nuclear force exchanges without defenses (tables 1.1–6), the weak link in the chain is the case of Russia on day-to-day alert and riding out the attack. Opposed by U.S. defenses that allow for 50 percent leakage (i.e., successfully intercept half of the retaliating ballistic missile warheads), Russian retaliatory forces, on day-to-day alert and riding out the attack, can provide for fewer than 100 surviving and arriving warheads at deployment levels of 2,200, for fewer than 50 warheads at deployment levels of 1,000, and for fewer than 25 warheads at deployment levels of 500.

TABLE 1.7. SURVIVING AND RETALIATING WEAPONS VS. DEFENSES, 50 PERCENT EFFECTIVE, 2,200 LIMIT

UNITED STATES				
	BALANCED TRIAD	NO ICBMS	NO BOMBERS	ALL SLBMs
GEN-LOW	1,053	1,059	883	885
GEN-ROA	931	1,059	762	885
DAY-LOW	500	456	636	593
DAY-ROA	378	456	515	593
RUSSIA				
	BALANCED TRIAD	NO BOMBERS	NO SLBMs	ICBMs ONLY
GEN-LOW	1,186	852	891	909
GEN-ROA	891	455	494	342
DAY-LOW	403	638	585	909
DAY-ROA	57	85	59	91

TABLE 1.8. SURVIVING AND RETALIATING WEAPONS VS. DEFENSES, 50 PERCENT EFFECTIVE, 1,000 LIMIT

UNITED STATES				
	BALANCED TRIAD	NO ICBMS	NO BOMBERS	ALL SLBMs
GEN-LOW	518	507	413	397
GEN-ROA	397	507	291	397
DAY-LOW	241	186	321	266
DAY-ROA	120	186	200	266
RUSSIA				
	BALANCED TRIAD	NO BOMBERS	NO SLBMs	ICBMs ONLY
GEN-LOW	515	423	598	441
GEN-ROA	357	229	428	105
DAY-LOW	219	275	212	441
DAY-ROA	30	42	21	44

TABLE 1.9. SURVIVING AND RETALIATING WEAPONS VS. DEFENSES,
50 PERCENT EFFECTIVE, 500 LIMIT

UNITED STATES				
	BALANCED TRIAD	NO ICBMS	NO BOMBERS	ALL SLBMS
GEN-LOW	268	268	207	198
GEN-ROA	219	268	164	198
DAY-LOW	107	80	155	133
DAY-ROA	59	80	111	133
RUSSIA				
	BALANCED TRIAD	NO BOMBERS	NO SLBMS	ICBMS ONLY
GEN-LOW	265	216	295	225
GEN-ROA	209	112	238	43
DAY-LOW	95	154	113	225
DAY-ROA	13	22	11	23

However, to emphasize the singular case of Russia on day-to-day alert and riding out the attack is to miss the forest for the trees. Under operational conditions that are more plausible, even Russia's "micro deterrent" force of 500 deployed warheads provides ample retaliatory power. Under conditions of intermediate retaliation (generated alert, riding out the attack or day-to-day alert, launch on warning), most of Russia's 500 deployed warhead forces can provide for more than 100 surviving and retaliating warheads. The exceptions are the "ICBM only" force for Russia in the "generated alert, riding out the attack" posture and the "balanced triad" force in the "day-to-day alert, launch on warning" posture. In the latter case, however, the number of surviving and penetrating warheads is almost 100.

The more alarming finding from an arms control and crisis stability standpoint lies in the apparent difference, across various Russian force sizes and structures, between the numbers of surviving and retaliating warheads under conditions of launch on warning, compared to riding out the attack. Russia derives a statistical "premium" in opting for prompt, compared to delayed, launch of its nuclear retaliatory forces. This finding is driven by Russia's high dependency on land-based missiles, and especially ICBMs that are silo based, compared to mobile land-based missiles, submarine-launched missiles, and bomber-delivered weapons. Russia's force modernization plans, including a new generation of nuclear ballistic missile submarines and submarine-launched missiles, is therefore important in reducing Russia's perceived need to rely on prompt launch for force survivability.

Conclusions

Findings in this chapter lend themselves to several generalizations. First, mutual deterrence between Russia and the United States is possible at deployment levels of SORT or lower. The claim by some experts that the United States can reduce its numbers of operationally deployed strategic nuclear weapons to hundreds instead of thousands, without necessarily jeopardizing its deterrent, is conditionally true.

Second, the conditionality of this argument lies in the fact that the U.S. and Russian deterrents are interactive by virtue of latent possibility—even if no political hostility exists between them. Thus it does not automatically follow that if the United States can safely reduce its numbers of deployed warheads on intercontinental launchers to several hundred, Russia can do the same.[28] Russia is still catching up from the aftershocks of the 1990s that dragged down its economy, including that part of the economy supporting conventional and nuclear forces.

Third, as a result of the preceding two conditions, the United States has an interest not only in reducing the size of U.S. and Russian strategic nuclear deterrents but also in modernizing Russia's deterrent qualitatively. In particular, the United States should encourage improved Russian early warning and command-control systems, safe and secure weapons management policies, and reliable personnel recruitment and evaluation procedures, with respect to the peacetime and crisis operation of Russia's nuclear retaliatory forces.

Fourth, Russia needs to be encouraged toward a force mix less reliant on prompt launch and, to a lesser extent, on generated alert for survivability. Russia's strategic bombers and ballistic missile submarine fleets were allowed to atrophy in the 1990s, and their rebuilding is a priority for Putin. Mobile versions of the Topol-M land-based missile (the sea-based variant is Bulava, planned for the *Yuri Dolgoruky* class of ballistic missile submarines) are intended to improve force survivability and to provide for additional countermeasures against missile defenses, including warheads in conjunction with multiple, independently targetable reentry vehicles (MIRVs).

Fifth, the United States should rethink its plan to deploy missile defenses in Eastern Europe. Russians are more frightened of missile defenses than they need to be. Granted that some of Putin's rhetoric on this topic was part of the buildup for the 2008 presidential election to choose Putin's anointed successor—not excluding the possibility that "popular demand" may find a way around the constitution for a third Putin term. In addition to Russian domestic politics, however, there are genuine fears of U.S. technological breakthroughs in BMD going back to the Cold War. And pushing American missile defense systems so close to Russia's borders invites diplomatic and military countermeasures that, in themselves, could complicate future relations between Moscow and Washington on other issues, including nonproliferation.[29]

Chapter 2

Missile Defenses: The Priority of Politics

Missile defenses have reentered the arena of policy debates and U.S.-Russian political controversy. U.S. abrogation of the ABM Treaty and initial deployments of components for a national missile defense system beginning in 2004 raised flags among members of the strategically attentive and arms control communities in Russia. And recent U.S. plans to deploy missile defense interceptors and radars in Eastern Europe caused emphatically negative political repercussions in Moscow.[1]

Issues of Immediate Concern

The United States' plan to deploy elements of a missile defense system in Poland and the Czech Republic provoked assertive diplomatic responses from Russia's President Vladimir Putin and other officials. Putin put forward carrots and sticks in an effort to derail the U.S. ballistic missile defense initiative or to absorb it within a larger framework more subject to Russian influence.

With regard to carrots, Putin proposed on July 2, 2007, during the "lobster summit" at Kennebunkport, Maine, with President George W. Bush, that radars in Azerbaijan and southern Russia be used instead of installations in Eastern Europe.[2] The regional BMD system would be operated under the aegis of the NATO–Russia Council.[3] The Russian president's proposal also included revitalization of an existing agreement between the United States and Russia to create a Russian-U.S. center for sharing information about missile attack warning. The agreement is ten years old but has never been implemented. Putin's proposal called for an expansion of the concept to include missile attack warning centers in Brussels and in Moscow.[4]

In addition to his effort to offer inducements as alternatives to the U.S. proposal, Putin also issued warnings and threats of countermeasures both diplomatic and military. On July 14, 2007, Russia notified NATO governments that it would suspend its cooperation with the Conventional Forces in Europe Treaty, a Cold War arms control agreement signed in 1990. Russia's suspension was to take effect in 150 days, suggesting that the door was open to further negotiation of aspects of the treaty that post-Soviet Russia now regards as obsolete. However, Russia's pique was also related to the U.S. decision on missile defense deployments in Eastern Europe.[5]

With regard to military responses to the U.S. missile defense deployments, Putin and other Russian officials indicated confidence that new missiles under development or in deployment can penetrate any missile defense system. On May 29, 2007, Russia test launched an improved version of its Topol-M intercontinental ballistic missile, capable of carrying MIRV warheads and reportedly intended to penetrate any U.S. missile defense system.[6] A submarine-launched ballistic missile variant of the Topol-M land-based missile, designated "Bulava," is also in development and scheduled for deployment aboard a new *Borey*-class of ballistic missile submarines (SSBNs). The Bulava will carry 6 MIRV warheads and is a flagship project of Putin's, despite reports of test failures in 2006 and some doubters among Russian navy experts.[7] If the Topol-M and Bulava missiles are expected by Russian planners to circumvent U.S. missile defenses, the Russian ICBMs and SLBMs may be equipped with "maneuvering" reentry vehicles, or MARVs, in addition to decoys of various sorts.[8]

In addition to the deployment of more capable offensive ballistic missiles, Russia has announced or implemented plans to raise the profile of other arms of service in support of its diplomatic profile suggesting greater military strength. In early August 2007 Russian generals announced that Russian strategic (long-range) bombers had resumed the Soviet Cold War practice of flying extended sorties into areas patrolled by NATO and the United States. For example, a Russian bomber flew over a U.S. military base on Guam on August 8 and "exchanged smiles" with U.S. pilots who were scrambled to track its flight path.[9] The head of long-range aviation in the Russian air force told reporters, "It has always been the tradition of our long-range aviation to fly far into the ocean, to meet [U.S.] aircraft carriers and greet pilots visually."[10] Maj. Gen. Pavel Androsov indicated that the flights by two Russian Tu-95MS bombers (designated "Bear" by NATO) originated from a base in the Russian Far East and lasted thirteen hours. One expert commentator noted that the flights were not that extraordinary. They had been scaled back in times of financial stringency for the Russian armed forces and were now being resumed in an improved fiscal climate.[11]

U.S. officials, recognizing that the missile defense issue had raised the temperature of Russian public diplomacy, and perhaps depressed the willingness of Russia to go further into arms control agreements, put forward some "high-concept" proposals in October 2007 with respect to European missile defenses.

One proposal offered to keep some parts of the U.S. missile defense shield deployed in Europe on "standby" status, short of full readiness. Under this proposal, the U.S. missile defenses in Poland and the Czech Republic would be built so they were fully operational but kept in a standby mode until future threat assessments were clarified.[12] The plan assumed further discussions between Russia and the United States with respect to the estimated date by which Iran, or other aspiring nuclear states, could threaten parts of Europe or the United States with nuclear armed ballistic missiles.

Russia's responses to this idea, and to other proposals advanced by Secretary of State Condoleezza Rice and Secretary of Defense Robert Gates at the "2+2" ministerial talks with Russia earlier in October, would depend on their future security relationships and on the trends in domestic politics within each country.[13] Presidential elections in the United States in 2008 will produce a different political leadership in 2009, but Russian legislative and presidential elections in 2007 and 2008 left Vladimir Putin in the role of prime minister and leader of the largest parliamentary party—a power still to be reckoned with and, after 2012, available to return to the presidential post. Not excluded within the realm of Russian domestic politics was the possibility of a post-Putin power struggle among his circle of *siloviki*, or security chieftains, with the potential to disrupt the continuity of Russian policy.[14]

Political Background

Putin's fusillades against U.S. missile defenses had a political backdrop in addition to the military-technical issues involved. There are several aspects to the political background relevant to Russia's view of missile defenses. First, Putin reflects the sensitivity of Russia's ruling elites about the decade of the 1990s, in which Russia's status as a great power, compared to the former Soviet Union, fell dramatically. In the difficult transition of the first post-Soviet decade, Russia's economic performance oscillated wildly. The defense budget was a matter of uncertainty for military planners, and even the commitments embodied in officially approved budgets were not always fulfilled. As a result, conditions in the armed forces, including the quality of personnel, the quantity and quality of equipment, and the amount of realistic training, deteriorated.

In this climate of financial uncertainty and scarce resources, Russia's conventional forces were no longer even a shadow of the Red Army that barricaded the Soviet Union and Eastern Europe against NATO. Post-Soviet Russia found itself in the 1990s with conventional military forces that were inferior to those of NATO, not only in quantity but also in quality. From Operation Desert Storm in 1991 through the war against Serbia over Kosovo in 1999, the United States and NATO demonstrated their superiority in information-based warfare, especially in long-range precision strike, stealth, command-control, reconnaissance, and other applications of computers and electronics to modern warfare. Russian president Boris Yeltsin was furious and helpless to stop NATO's air campaign against Serbia, Russia's traditional ally, in 1999.

One reason for Yeltsin's inability to stop NATO was the low credibility of Russia's military forces due to their performance in the first post-Soviet military campaign against rebels in Chechnya. The 1994–96 campaign revealed that Russia was lacking not only in military assets but also in military competency. Poor political and military leadership at the very top of the chain of command was compounded by indifference or negligence in field command. In 1996 Yeltsin was forced to sign a truce with Chechen rebels that postponed the final decision about the political status of that rebellious territory.

During this period of low credibility and disappointing performance on the part of Russia's conventional military, only its nuclear weapons, and especially its strategic or intercontinental-range nuclear forces, gave Russia credible claim to major power status in the new world order. Although Russia's strategic nuclear forces suffered along with the rest of the military establishment during the 1990s, they benefited from an expectation of parity or approximate equality with U.S. forces that carried over from the Cold War. This expectation of nuclear-strategic parity between the United States and Russia with respect to long-range nuclear forces was more theory than reality during the 1990s. On the other hand, Russia's nuclear forces were still superior to those of any third party, and the United States and Russia were uniquely tied together in START and other arms control regimes within which they were treated as equals.

A second source of Putin's sensitivity about U.S. missile defenses is the expansion of NATO since the end of the Cold War. NATO's twenty-six member states now reach to the borders of Russia, Ukraine, and Belarus. Russia's security space, compared to that of the former Soviet Union, has been moved eastward by many miles. The stationing of NATO troops and installations in member states of the former Soviet-dominated Warsaw Treaty Organization is a reminder of Russia's potential military vulnerability. Of course, NATO has no political intention to attack Russia; with respect to large-scale, interstate warfare, Europe is a relatively pacified or debellicized security community. On the other hand, history shows that prudent states base their military plans on the capabilities, not the intentions, of potential adversaries.

In addition, Russia currently requires a quiet western front because its southern and eastern fronts are anything but tranquil. To the south Russia faces challenges posed by the new politics and economics of Central Asia, the unsettled economic competition related to oil pipelines and the Caspian basin, and various forms of ethnonationalist separatism and terrorism in the Caucasus and Transcaucasus. To the east Russia confronts a rising great power in China, seen by some as a potential military peer competitor for the United States by mid-century. A waxing Chinese military capability holds the potential to complicate Russian interests in the Far East and Central Asia even sooner than China might compete with the United States for Asian or global military eminence.

Russia therefore needs as little turbulence as possible on its western frontiers. And NATO's nonbelligerent security policy with regard to Russia is reassuring to Russians only in the context of further improvement in Russian-U.S. and NATO-Russian relations. There is some reason for optimism in this regard, taking the longer view of history. First, the United States remains committed to its status as leader of the NATO alliance, albeit with a stronger "European pillar" than existed during the Cold War. The military presence of the United States in NATO reassures Russia against revanchist aspirations by individual European states, including past enemies of Russia. Second, Russia and the United States have no existing territorial disputes with the potential to erupt into war. Third, since 9/11 the United States and Russia have found common ground on the "war on terror" and in dampening the influence of Islamic extremism in Europe and the Middle East. Fourth, Russia seeks larger economic and political integration with the European Union, and NATO provides a military glacis behind which EU members can feel a sense of security in reaching out to Russia.

Despite this background of positives, Russia remains concerned about possible future expansion of NATO, which might include Ukraine and former Soviet Georgia. The democratic revolutions in those countries have caused great anxiety in Moscow. Ukraine's "Orange Revolution" in December 2004 was partly inspired by the success of Georgia's "Rose Revolution" in 2003–4. Both largely peaceful and prodemocracy revolutions grew out of protests against allegedly fraudulent parliamentary elections, among other issues. Putin was clearly not pleased at the success of either prodemocracy forces in Georgia or Ukraine, and the Kremlin continues its efforts to influence the domestic and foreign policies of both states. Russia supports two breakaway regions in Georgia and has declared its right to pursue fleeing terrorists from Russian territory into Georgia. The United States supports the democratic forces in Ukraine and Georgia and opposes the Kremlin's efforts to reverse the outcomes of the Orange and Rose revolutions. Although some Russians might (reluctantly) accept Georgia's accession to NATO, Putin and his likely successors would almost certainly resist Ukrainian membership in that alliance.

If two reasons for Russian sensitivity about missile defenses are the centrality of Russia's strategic nuclear forces for its image as a great power and Russia's fear of further NATO expansion, a third reason lies in Russia's historic experience with invasion from the West. It is impossible for many in the West to appreciate how much this fear is embedded in the "genes" of Russians based on their history. Within the past two centuries alone, Russia has faced invasion by Napoleon in 1812, by Imperial Germany in World War I, and by Nazi Germany in World War II. Each of these was a near-death experience—in both political and military terms. Russia's "Barbarossa complex" is not a fiction but a reality. Americans who doubt this should ask themselves how they feel about Pearl Harbor and 9/11, and then compare the casualties attendant to those events with Russian and Soviet twentieth-century experience.

I conceded previously that NATO and the United States have no intention of attacking Russia. That having been said, Russians know that wars have a way of starting for reasons neither politically logical nor strategically necessary. Despite the best efforts of some revisionist historians to make it appear otherwise, World War I was begun by political leaders and military planners who envisioned neither its ultimate outcome nor its protracted nature. And despite the hopes of war-ravaged states in Europe that the experience of World War I would never be repeated, it was repeated on an even larger scale two decades later. European politicians insisted on shaking and baking the international order until, by the end of the World War II, they had finally destroyed it. The Cold War that followed was marked by the preeminence of two superpowers, the Americans and Soviets, who dominated the global security agenda.

Vladimir Putin is sometimes wrongly described as desirous of returning to the "good old days" of the Soviet Union. But that assessment mistakes Putin's motives. He is more of a restorationist tsar than a Soviet commissar. He wants a modern Russia with a strong economy, which in today's world can only be based on market principles. On the other hand, Putin wants a Russian market that is subject to strong state oversight and regulation in support of maximizing Russian international power and influence. Thus the state under Putin and his successors will have direct and indirect controls over the distribution of "private" power in certain sectors—energy, for example. Putin's economic views resemble those of the modernizing Russian cabinet minister of the latter nineteenth century, Sergei Witte.

For Putin a worst-case scenario for Russia is that Russia becomes an object of decisions made by other state actors instead of a subject guided by its own international and domestic priorities. As Alexei Arbatov has noted,

> Despite overwhelming anti-Western sentiments and pressure from certain political circles inside the country, Russia's leadership does not wish for confrontation with the United States or the European Union, nor an end to cooperation. Furthermore, Russia does not view itself as

some sort of second superpower after the U.S. Moscow formulates its interests, first of all, in a trans-regional format and declares its rights at the global level only selectively.[15]

Arbatov went on to explain that, given this perspective on the part of the Russian leadership, a U.S. missile defense system deployed in Central and Eastern Europe might cause Russia to withdraw from the Intermediate Nuclear Forces (INF) Treaty and resume producing intermediate-range missiles of the kind that were scrapped by the treaty in 1987. In addition NATO might respond by deploying ballistic or cruise missiles of similar range in Europe, increasing the vulnerability of Russian strategic nuclear forces and their command-control systems.[16]

Even if this particular scenario of backsliding in European nuclear arms control does not result from deteriorating U.S.-Russian political relations, other negative consequences for arms control and nonproliferation are possible. According to Arbatov a multipolar world that is not moving toward nuclear disarmament leaves an open door to an expanding nuclear club. Absent cooperation between Russia and the United States, more states capable of developing nuclear weapons will decide to jump through the window of opportunity, and the "probability of nuclear weapons being used in a regional conflict will increase significantly."[17] Nor is this the worst possible outcome from U.S.-Russian political antagonism spilling over into lack of cooperation in security and arms control. Existing treaties on nonproliferation and arms control (for example, the nuclear Non-Proliferation Treaty, the Conventional Armed Forces in Europe Treaty, and the Comprehensive Nuclear Test Ban Treaty) will be at risk of abrogation or irrelevance. In addition, Arbatov notes, in a "worst-case scenario, there is a chance that an adventuresome regime will initiate a missile launch against territories or space satellites of one of the several great powers with a view to triggering an exchange of nuclear strikes between them. Another high probability is the threat of a terrorist act with the use of a nuclear device in one or several major capitals of the world."[18]

Arbatov's uncommon insights link the emerging multipolar world order with trends in American and Russian security policy and their relationship to the success or failure of nuclear arms control, deterrence and nonproliferation. The freezing of the frame in favor of continued peace in Europe, or the containment of adventurism on the part of new or aspiring nuclear states outside of Europe, cannot be taken for granted. Within this context, further reductions in Russian and U.S. strategic nuclear forces to levels at or below the Moscow Treaty of 2002 (SORT) are not merely a luxury or a fillip but a necessary part of a viable post-Putin and post-Bush security regime.

Background

The Moscow Treaty of 2002 requires that Russia and the United States each reduce its numbers of operationally deployed strategic nuclear warheads to between 2,200 and 1,700 by the end of the calendar year 2012. SORT takes the form of an agreed framework instead of a detailed list of specifications as to how the agreement is to be implemented and verified. The two states are free to mix their land-based missiles, sea-based missiles, and bombers in any combination, provided they stay within the appropriate ceiling.[19] Nor is it precluded that either or both sides could deploy fewer than 1,700 warheads if it chose to do so. Article II of the Treaty states that the START I of 1991 remains in force in accordance with its terms.

The Joint Statement on security cooperation, issued by the United States and Russia, along with the publication of the text of the Moscow Treaty, places the treaty within a broader framework of arms control and cooperative security. The Joint Statement alludes to a "new strategic relationship" emerging between Russia and the United States and to their new status as "partners" in the advancement of stability, security and economic cooperation.[20] The same statement also makes several specific and favorable references to future Russian-U.S. cooperation on ballistic missile defense.

First, the statement indicates that the two states "have agreed to implement a number of steps aimed at strengthening confidence and increasing transparency in the area of missile defense," including "the exchange of information on missile defense programs and tests" and the necessary steps "to bring a joint center for the exchange of data from early warning centers into operation."[21] Second, the United States and Russia also agree to "study possible areas for missile defense cooperation," including "the expansion of joint exercises related to missile defense" and the "exploration of potential programs for the joint research and development of missile defense technologies."[22] Third, within the framework of the NATO–Russia Council, the Joint Statement calls for the two states to "explore opportunities for intensified practical cooperation on missile defense for Europe."[23]

The SORT and the Joint Statement invite the creation of a new behavior space for Russian-U.S. cooperation with respect to nuclear arms. The explicit references to cooperation on missile defense research and development between Russia and the United States (presumably emphasizing national missile defense technologies) and between Russia and NATO (emphasizing theater missile defenses) have not led to as much shared work on technology development, shared warning information, or joint exercises as some proponents of BMD cooperation might have hoped. Nevertheless, from a legal or treaty standpoint, the door is open for further progress.[24] What is needed is the political will and a

sense of urgency with respect to combining joint work on defenses with SORT
or SORT-plus offensive arms reductions—if, that is to say, the two sides are
really agreed in principle that defenses are worth developing and have a meaningful role to play in future arms control.

Figure 1 shows Russian missile defenses in terms of their locations relative
to proposed U.S. missile defenses in Europe and Russian land-based missile
bases. Figure 2 depicts U.S. missile defenses current and proposed.

Data Analysis

This chapter's data analysis has two purposes. The first objective is to contrast
the performance of hypothetical but realistic U.S. and Russian SORT-compliant
strategic nuclear forces under various operational conditions: (1) forces are on
generated alert and launched on warning (GEN-LOW), (2) forces are on generated alert and ride out the attack (GEN-ROA), (3) forces are on day-to-day alert
and launched on warning (DAY-LOW), and (4) forces are on day-to-day alert and
ride out the attack (DAY-ROA). For this purpose, Russian and American forces
are compared at three levels: (1) the higher SORT-compliant warhead deployment
ceiling of 2,200 operationally deployed weapons, (2) the lower SORT-compliant
ceiling of 1,700, and (3) a contrasting "minimum deterrent" force of 1,000 warheads for each side.[25] The assumption is that these SORT forces or lower deployment levels might obtain beyond 2012 through the end of the decade under favorable political conditions.

The second objective is to test the performance of the forces enumerated
above against defenses of one or more layers for each side. Accordingly, the
scenario for each force level without defenses has been assigned a "compan-
ion" scenario with defenses added. The results of these analyses are summarized in tables 2.1–6. Tables 2.1 and 2.2 summarize the results for Russian and
U.S. forces at 2,200 levels with and without defenses. Defenses are shown as
a range of capabilities relative to retaliating offenses following a first strike:
(1) defenses are single-layered and capable of intercepting 20 percent of retaliating warheads, (2) defenses are two-layered and can intercept 40 percent of
retaliating warheads, (3) defenses have three layers and can intercept 60 percent
of retaliating warheads, and (4) defenses have four layers and can intercept 80
percent of retaliating warheads.[26]

Of course in the "real world" of engagements between offensive and defensive weapons, layers of the defense might not perform with equal reliability
or effectiveness relative to their missions. Different technologies are involved
for boost phase intercept, for example, compared to midcourse or terminal
defenses. ("Boost phase" refers to the initial stage of missile-powered flight or

FIGURE 1. RUSSIAN MISSILE DEFENSES

Source: Russian Nuclear Forces Project 2007, http://www.globalsecurity.org, via BBC.

FIGURE 2. CURRENT AND PROPOSED U.S. MISSILE DEFENSES

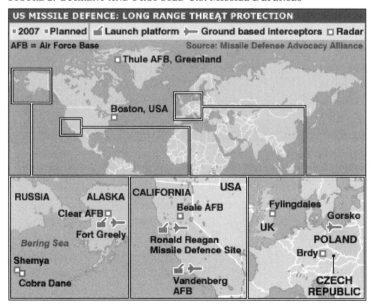

Source: Russian Nuclear Forces Project 2007, http://www.globalsecurity.org, via BBC.

the phase of a missile trajectory from launch to burnout of the final stage. For ICBMs this phase typically lasts from three to five minutes.) In addition, our numbers appear to be very generous to the probable competency of defenses— at least, to any defenses that can be built soon. For example, table 1 assumes the case of 5 warheads attacking a defense and compares the probability of 1 or more warheads penetrating the defense based on the total number of interceptors available to the defense and the single shot kill probability (SSPK) of each interceptor.

This example shows that based on random probabilities, and ignoring nuances such as the firing doctrines of the defender or the countermeasures available to the attacker, the defense faces an uphill battle even if its technology is very good. The reason for the higher bar for defenses compared to offenses is that the credible threat of even one or a few nuclear warheads arriving on target requires that defenses achieve perfect or near-perfect intercept. The relationship between nuclear offenses and antinuclear defenses is thus asymmetrical, in terms of the level of actual performance required against an opponent, relative to the highest possible performance.[27]

Having acknowledged that defenses face a higher "proof of life" against competitive offenses, tables 2.1–6 summarize the results of nuclear force exchanges at 2,200, 1,700, and 1,000 levels with and without defenses.

Findings and Implications

At SORT-compliant levels of operationally deployed strategic nuclear weapons, both the Russian and the U.S. deterrents will retain sufficient retaliatory capability to inflict unacceptable societal damage and to strike at a variety of other targets. This finding holds for forces at 2,200 and 1,700 prewar levels, and it applies for the most part even with very competent defenses. For example, Russian 2,200 forces provide a range of surviving and retaliating warheads from a high of 386 to a low of 193; Russian 1,700 forces provide a maximum of 339 and a minimum of 169 surviving and retaliating warheads (tables 2.1 and 2.3, respectively). Against U.S. layered defenses and retaliating on generated alert after riding out the attack, Russian 2,200 forces provide a high of 257 and a low of 64 surviving and penetrating warheads. Under similar conditions, Russian 1,700 levels provide a maximum of 226 and a minimum of 56 surviving and penetrating warheads (tables 2.2 and 2.4, respectively). Under similar operational conditions, U.S. forces provide for even greater numbers of surviving and penetrating warheads with or without Russian defenses.

The "minimum deterrent" forces of Russia and the United States (1,000 ceiling on operationally deployed warheads) are less capable than larger forces,

TABLE 2.1. PROBABILITIES OF WARHEAD INTERCEPTION AND PENETRATION

NUMBER OF ATTACKING WARHEADS	TOTAL NUMBER OF INTERCEPTORS	PROBABILITY THAT AN INTERCEPTOR WILL INTERCEPT ITS TARGET (SSPK)	PROBABILITY THAT ONE OR MORE WARHEADS PENETRATES DEFENSE
5	5 (1-on-1 targeting)	5%	99.999%
5	10 (2-on-1 targeting)	5%	99.999%
5	20 (4-on-1 targeting)	5%	99.98%
5	5 (1-on-1 targeting)	10%	99.99%
5	10 (2-on-1 targeting)	10%	99.98%
5	20 (4-on-1 targeting)	10%	99.5%
5	5 (1-on-1 targeting)	50%	97%
5	10 (2-on-1 targeting)	50%	76%
5	20 (4-on-1 targeting)	50%	28%
5	5 (1-on-1 targeting)	91%	38%
5	10 (2-on-1 targeting)	91%	4%
5	20 (4-on-1 targeting)	91%	.03%

Source: Gronlund et al., *Technical Realities*, 43.
Note: For an attack by five warheads, the probability that one or more warheads penetrates the defense is shown for five, ten, and twenty interceptors and for four different probabilities that an interceptor will destroy its target.

but they are more than adequate to provide for deterrence by credible threat of retaliation causing unacceptable damage. For example, Russian 1,000 forces provide for a high of 216 and a low of 108 surviving and retaliating warheads, without factoring in U.S. defenses (table 2.5). If U.S. defenses are added into the picture, Russian 1,000 forces provide for a maximum of 144 surviving and penetrating warheads and a minimum of 36 under operational conditions of generated alert and riding out the attack (table 2.6). U.S. 1,000 forces provide for a high of 367 and a low of 183 surviving and retaliating warheads without Russian defenses (table 2.5). Opposed by Russian layered defenses and retaliating on generated alert after riding out the attack, U.S. surviving and penetrating warheads range from a maximum of 245 to a minimum of 61 warheads.

The two preceding paragraphs summarize a large amount of data, but their purpose should not be misunderstood. The findings are not ends in themselves; they are benchmarks indicative of more general hypotheses and arguments, as discussed below.

Assuming appropriate force modernization on the Russians' part between now and 2015 or so, the strategic nuclear deterrents of Russia and the United States remain robust for their intended purpose. That purpose is reassurance as much as it is deterrence. A strategically reassured Russian and U.S. leadership is a necessary condition, albeit not a sufficient condition, for further progress between the two states on nuclear arms control and nonproliferation. Progress on both fronts is vital for world peace, and progress on neither front is possible without U.S. and Russian cooperation.

The implications of missile defenses for the viability of Russian and U.S. nuclear deterrents are marginal for *national* missile defenses until technology leaps another generation.[28] On the other hand, for theater or shorter-range missile defenses, it is possible that current or near-term technologies might improve the exchange ratios between offenses and defenses in favor of the defender.[29] This concern about theater missile defenses is probably what is motivating Vladimir Putin in his objections to U.S. missile defenses deployed in Europe. His own scientific and military advisors must know that viable national missile defenses are years away.

But theater missile defenses might complicate Russian plans to reboot the intermediate and shorter-range nuclear missile forces that were mothballed or destroyed under the INF Treaty. In addition, U.S. theater missile defenses for Japan might increase the difficulty for Russia in using coercive diplomacy against Japan to resolve outstanding diplomatic disputes. And although China and Russia in August 2007 conducted joint military exercises of unprecedented scope and now collaborate within the Shanghai Cooperation Organization on security and other issues affecting Central Asia, the possibility of future regional or border disputes between the two states cannot be discounted.[30] Even under present conditions China might take a dim view of Russian theater missile defenses and vice versa.

Chinese views of U.S. national missile defenses are related to its views of U.S. and Russian nuclear strategic modernization programs. Since 2002 China

TABLE 2.2. SURVIVING AND RETALIATING WEAPONS, 2,200 LIMIT

	GEN-LOW	GEN-ROA	DAY-LOW	DAY-ROA
Russia	386	322	257	192
United States	843	702	562	421

TABLE 2.3. SURVIVING AND RETALIATING WEAPONS VS. DEFENSES OF VARIABLE EFFECTIVENESS, 2,200 LIMIT

	PHASE IV DEFENSES	PHASE III DEFENSES	PHASE II DEFENSES	PHASE I DEFENSES
Russia	64	129	193	257
United States	140	281	421	562

TABLE 2.4. SURVIVING AND RETALIATING WEAPONS, 1,700 LIMIT

	GEN-LOW	GEN-ROA	DAY-LOW	DAY-ROA
Russia	339	282	226	169
United States	653	544	436	327

TABLE 2.5. SURVIVING AND RETALIATING WEAPONS VS. DEFENSES OF VARIABLE EFFECTIVENESS, 1,700 LIMIT

	PHASE IV DEFENSES	PHASE III DEFENSES	PHASE II DEFENSES	PHASE I DEFENSES
Russia	56	113	169	226
United States	109	218	327	436

TABLE 2.6. SURVIVING AND RETALIATING WEAPONS, 1,000 LIMIT

	GEN-LOW	GEN-ROA	DAY-LOW	DAY-ROA
Russia	216	180	144	107
United States	367	306	245	183

TABLE 2.7. SURVIVING AND RETALIATING WEAPONS VS. DEFENSES OF VARIABLE EFFECTIVENESS, 1,000 LIMIT

	PHASE IV DEFENSES	PHASE III DEFENSES	PHASE II DEFENSES	PHASE I DEFENSES
Russia	36	72	108	144
United States	61	122	183	245

has appeared to acquiesce to the inevitability of U.S. national missile defenses, but acquiescence is not tantamount to passivity.[31] China could react to U.S. or Russian missile defenses by modernizing and increasing the size of its offensive retaliatory forces. On the other hand, Chinese views of their military options with regard to America and Russia will also be politically nuanced. A dramatic increase in size or change in the character of Chinese strategic nuclear forces could complicate relations with Asian neighbors (including Russia) or with the United States. An immediate concern of China's would be whether their modernized ICBM forces (with additional mobility and MIRVed vehicles) would be sufficient to provide for minimum deterrence, in the form of survivable countercity retaliatory strikes, against U.S. or Russian state territory despite any missile defenses.[32]

Conclusions

The question of strategic nuclear deterrence between the Americans and Russians in the "new world order" has been ill served by the opposite errors of complacency and alarmism. Complacency regards nuclear deterrence as automatic and self-sustaining. Added to this is the assumption that a postnuclear world of advanced technology weapons has little use for nuclear weapons except for display in museums. On the other hand, alarmism regards the use of stray nuclear weapons by terrorists as imminent and inevitable or the proliferation of nuclear weapons among rogue state actors as equally inevitable and with necessarily devastating consequences.

Strategic nuclear deterrence and reassurance between the United States and Russia are necessary conditions for the preservation of peace and stability in Europe and Asia, and for the management of transition into a world of fewer and better managed nuclear weapons worldwide.[33] Missile defenses are not necessarily destabilizing of deterrence or reassurance with regard to U.S.-Russian relations or more broadly. Like other tools or instruments, the political and military impacts of BMD depend on the purposes for which they are used.

Russia and the United States could possibly reduce the sizes of their deployed offensive nuclear forces even below SORT levels and deploy limited national missile defenses without calling into question the viability of their nuclear deterrents. "Possibly" is the operative word, as the outcome depends on favorable political winds.[34] Although those winds were blowing in the wrong directions in 2007, political climates have a way of changing, and without regard for the state of military technology. Russian advanced air defenses, U.S. and NATO theater missile defenses, and other components of a European missile defense architecture could be built to help deter or defeat threats from the small arsenals of rogue states. First, however, political suspicions left over from the Cold War and Russian sensitivities about their "time of troubles" in the 1990s would have to be overcome in the interests of cooperative security.[35]

Chapter 3

Deterrence and Missile Defenses: Compatible or Antithetical?

B allistic missile defenses have become a matter of high policy attention and some dispute between Russia and the United States and, to a certain extent, Russia and NATO. There is uncertainty about how well missile defenses might perform even if they were eventually deployed in Europe, with or without Russia's cooperation. Some fear that missile defenses and other aggravations for the Kremlin could turn the political relationship between the United States and Russia into a new Cold War. Others fear that nuclear deterrence stability in and outside of Europe might be at risk.

This chapter sorts some of the wheat from the chaff with regard to some of the implications of U.S. and Russian BMD. Admittedly this is a large policy sweep, so a selective view of some aspects of the problem, supported by pertinent data analysis, is in order. The assessment here is aggressively antideterministic with respect to the options available to Russian and U.S. policy makers. They can use any military technologies, including missile defenses, in order to support arms control and cooperative security. Or they may fritter away the opportunity for European and transatlantic security on technological promissory notes and political unilateralism. A fork in the road appears ahead.

Background

Russia and the United States were on a collision course during the spring and summer of 2007 on a variety of fronts. Among the contentious issues between the two governments was the U.S. decision to deploy components of a ballistic missile defense system in Poland and the Czech Republic. Both before and after the Kennebunkport summit in early July between President Putin and President Bush, Putin criticized the U.S. plan to deploy antimissile systems in Eastern Europe.

For example, in a meeting with reporters before traveling to the Group of Eight (G8) summit in June, Putin dismissed the U.S. rationale for the system as necessary to deter or deflect future missile attacks from Iran. He described the long-range ballistic missile threat from Iran (and North Korea) to Europe as nonexistent and concluded, therefore, that the U.S. system was intended for use against Russia.[1] Putin warned that Russia would react to the U.S. deployments with countermeasures: "If a part of the strategic nuclear potential of the United States appears in Europe and, in the opinion of our military specialists will threaten us, then we will have to take appropriate steps in response. What kind of steps? We will have to have new targets in Europe."[2]

Russia had already issued warnings to Poland and the Czech Republic that they risked being targeted by Russian missiles if they agreed to accept parts of any U.S. missile defense system on their state territories. In February 2007 Gen. Nikolai Solovstov, head of Russia's strategic missile forces, argued that an Eastern European antimissile system would upset strategic stability and indicated that if Poland and the Czech Republic went ahead with U.S. plans, "the Strategic Missile Forces will be capable of targeting these facilities if a relevant decision is made."[3]

Of course the possibility that Russian weapons were *capable* of reaching targets throughout Eastern Europe and beyond was not news. But the latent possibility of Russian strikes was being used in this instance as a not very veiled threat against the specific plan to install BMD in Eastern Europe. At another news conference in March, General Solovstov emphasized Russia's current and future capabilities not only for targeting sites in Europe but also for overcoming any U.S. missile defenses deployed there.

With regard to targeting of Europe, Solovstov noted that Russia has on alert status missiles that can hit targets anywhere in the world. These missiles have a technical readiness coefficient, according to the general, of 0.97 to 0.98: "That is to say, out of every 100 missiles 97 to 98 are ready at any minute, at any second to perform their combat mission."[4] Presumably this reference was to Russia's land-based intercontinental ballistic missiles as opposed to its sea-based missiles or bomber-delivered weapons.

However, Solovstov also combined a political point about nuclear arms control with a military estimate and warning. Russia might, he noted, choose to augment its intercontinental nuclear-strike capabilities by revisiting the 1987 Intermediate Nuclear Forces Treaty. If Russia were to withdraw from that agreement, signed in 1987 by President Reagan and President Gorbachev, the strategic missile forces commander noted that the documentation still exists for reconstructing the banned intermediate and shorter-range missiles. Solovstov also said that Russia could move rapidly to build and deploy a new generation of nuclear-capable theater ballistic missiles in lieu of reviving the older models—different RKSD (medium-range missile complexes) with a new component base, control system, and new capabilities.[5]

Solovstov and other leading commanders have indicated that Russia might respond to regional BMD systems with new offensive weapons specifically tailored to circumvent missile defenses. In a February 2004 news conference, Yuri Baluyevsky, then first deputy chief of the General Staff, claimed that Russia had conducted an experimental flight by a device in a nonclassical orbital configuration using the atmosphere. In his March 2007 news conference Solovstov also alluded to research and development on missile weapons with vectored motion at hypersonic speeds.[6] Other experts, including officials at the Russian defense ministry, have told Russian reporters about research on warheads or missiles with hypersonic engines, making possible rapid changes of trajectory.[7]

Reentry vehicles capable of postlaunch maneuvered flight were the subject of some research and testing during the Cold War. This produced the acronym MARV, not to be confused with MIRV or MRV (multiple reentry vehicle, or a "bus" with several warheads but without the capability for assigning a unique trajectory to each warhead). The exact status of Russia's progress on this adaptive trajectory countermeasure is unknown, and particulars about the technology and its testing are unavailable.

Nevertheless, the policy message from Russia to the United States and NATO is unmistakable. Missile defenses deployed in Eastern Europe adjacent to Russian state territory, commanded and controlled by the United States and NATO and possibly aimed at Russia instead of Iran or other Middle Eastern threats, will cause both political and military-technical reactions from the Kremlin. To some this might mean that Putin was revisiting the Cold War reaction by the Soviet Union to the Reagan-proposed Strategic Defense Initiative of the 1980s.

Putin was more subtle and up-to-date than that. At the summit in early July the Russian president put forward the carrot as an alternative to the stick. If a unilateral U.S. missile defense system was unacceptable, Russia offered an alternative. The United States might join Russia in a shared missile defense system that made use of sites in Azerbaijan and in southern Russia, obviating the need for any U.S. deployments in the Czech Republic or in Poland.[8] In a related move at Kennebunkport, Putin also proposed that information exchange centers in Moscow and in Brussels be created to share missile launch warning data.

According to the Russian president, speaking the following day in Guatemala, his proposals for cooperative regimes in missile defense and in missile launch data exchange amounted to a new "global missile defense architecture."[9] Russia's first deputy prime minister, Sergei Ivanov, emphasized in Tashkent on July 4 that Putin's proposal for cooperation on missile defense "may be considered an innovation" that will have major results in Russia's relations with the United States and NATO: "A new space for trust will emerge. We may establish strategic partnership."[10] Ivanov further stated that if Russia's proposals were accepted, "this will inevitably lead to the exchange of technologies between Russia and NATO," including "the exchange of information from control systems."[11] Ivanov also emphasized that implementing the Russian missile defense and warning proposals would help "to create a 'pool' of states that will jointly fight the missile proliferation threat."[12]

Russia's sensitivity on the issue of missile defenses, and its alternating good news–bad news diplomacy related to nuclear arms control, have roots in a larger context of political and military issues. The next section considers this context.

Political and Military Context

Russia's reactions to U.S. missile defense systems deployed in Europe are based on growing self-confidence as a great power. Equally, and paradoxically, they are also based on Russia's sensitivities to its global position as less than equal to the United States, unlike the situation that prevailed during the Cold War. Both more assertive and more sensitive, Russia wants a voice in European security deliberations and a veto over developments that might impinge on Russian security interests.

At first glance it would seem that Russia's security interests in Europe are easily satisfied. Europe in the twenty-first century is a virtually debellicized continent. Although the 1990s were marked by the "wars of Yugoslav succession" and other outbreaks of ethnonationalist conflict related to the breakup of states, the prospect of major interstate wars among Europe's leading powers is substantively unthinkable. This is a remarkable shift in geopolitics. The first half of the twentieth century witnessed two world wars that began in, and were centered on, Europe. The Cold War was fought under the shadow of nuclear Armageddon over ideologies that had their roots in European political thought. The end of the Cold War and the demise of the Soviet Union should free a democratic Russia of fears of military attack.

Russia's perceptions of contemporary Europe are less benign than this. Russia's political and military leadership includes many persons who are either the products of the Soviet Cold War era or who, even if younger, use the Soviet Union as their referential gold standard for evaluation of international success or failure. Vladimir Putin has publicly stated that, in his opinion, the collapse of the Soviet Union was one of history's great tragedies. It was interesting that few commentators remarked on the oxymoronic aspects of that pronouncement. Most attributed his *nostalgie pour la boue* to his personal past in the KGB and to the fact that he has packed the presidential administration and the government with like-minded alumni of the Soviet and Russian foreign and domestic intelligence services.

But Putin's administrative and political decisions give no evidence that his style of ruling has been derived from classical Marxism. Nor have his pronouncements justifying policy decisions made much use of Marx or Lenin. Putin's style of leadership and management is best described as pragmatism.[13] He proceeds on a case by case basis and from issue to issue, balancing current problems against prospective opportunities. In that regard Putin behaves more as a portfolio manager of a competitive firm than as a Soviet apparatchik or commissar. One reason for this is personal temperament: Putin is ruthless but not given to rashness in judgment. He plays every issue close to the vest until a time for decision has arrived. He consults but does not commit. He is especially adept at sizing people up, particularly with regard to their character and hidden agendas. Above all, he respects strength.

Putin's handling of several issues since he became president validates the preceding assessment. First, he took personal control of Russia's disastrous policy in Chechnya, which had crashed and burned under his predecessor, Boris Yeltsin. Although terrorism and insurgency continue in that troubled region, Russia's military and political performance in Chechnya since 1999 has been a success story compared to its humiliation between 1994 and 1996.[14] Putin and his military leadership have tried a variety of approaches to counterterror and counterinsurgency in Chechnya, with mixed success. But Putin's resolve to keep this conflict simmering below the threshold of military contagion throughout the Caucasus, and to diminish its potential as a political issue that might erode his authority, has been unyielding.

Second, Putin moved in a step-by-step manner to improve Russia's economy as the basis for revamping its military. Russia emerged from the 1990s as a state with a military marked by qualitative and quantitative shortcomings. Budget cuts in the Yeltsin years and erratic presidential leadership of the armed forces left large deficiencies in military readiness, training, equipment, and personnel—especially in Russia's conventional forces. The former Red Army had been the pride of the Soviet Union and the exemplar of its claim to great-power status. At the turn of the twenty-first century post-Soviet Russia's military looked more like the army of Nicholas II than the army of Joseph Stalin. Desertions were rampant, draft dodging was epidemic, hazing in the barracks was out of control, and, most ominously, junior officers were leaving the army in droves—often because low salaries made it impossible for them to feed their families.

Putin began the process of stabilizing the decline in Russia's armed forces and even making some significant improvements. He sorted out the relationship between competing elements in the military chain of command—as, for example, between the defense ministry and the general staff. Putin also understood that the Russian military is an essentially conservative and bureaucratic institution in its mind-set. It expects and wants the president to provide leadership, that is, to provide overall guidance on national security policy that in turn creates a framework for military planning.[15]

Under Putin, Russia has begun to turn around the disastrous decline in its military power and potential that occurred during the first decade after Soviet collapse. Although its armed forces are still not capable of conducting large-scale, combined arms military offensives outside of Russia's borders, Russia's improved economy has permitted incremental gains in the purchase of new equipment, in training time, and in the recruitment and retention of enlisted personnel and officers. In particular Putin has emphasized the importance of converting parts of the Russian armed forces from conscription to contract service. In addition, Russia has reorganized the regional and functional alignment of its conventional forces in order to provide for more coherent command and control. Another improvement has been in the coordination of campaigns that include the military along with internal security forces, as in Chechnya, where the Federal Security Service (FSB) is now officially the lead agency with military support.

Another set of military improvements under Putin's leadership is related to nuclear forces and nuclear use policy. Putin's national security policy guidance has made clear the continuing importance of Russia's nuclear forces, especially its strategic missile forces. Putin recognizes that until Russia can rebuild its conventional forces to a higher standard of operational effectiveness, Russia's ability to deter large-scale aggression against its state territory or near its borders depends on its nuclear weapons.

Yeltsin's defense policy and the early years of the Putin administration were marred by disagreements between Anatoly Kvashnin, chief of the General Staff, and various ministers of defense with regard to the relative priority of conventional compared to nuclear forces (among other issues).[16] Putin settled the problem of rivalry within the chain of command by reorganizing the relationship between ministers of defense and the General Staff. In so doing he presided over a reformulation of military doctrine making it clear that both nuclear and conventional forces have their important roles in Russian military strategy and force planning.

However, during the 1990s Russia's nuclear forces deteriorated along with the rest of its military establishment. Under Putin a program to revise and reconstitute Russia's nuclear deterrent, based on a new generation of land- and sea-based ballistic missiles and a new class of ballistic missile submarines, was set in motion.[17] As in the case of its conventional forces, Russia's nuclear forces require modernization and improvement in training and personnel. As well, Russia's nuclear early warning and command-control systems were suspect throughout the 1990s and important deficiencies remain uncorrected.[18]

Despite these improvements in Russia's military performance and defense management since taking office, Putin remained dissatisfied with his military capabilities, relative to his ambitions and perceived threats to Russia. Among these, NATO's expansion to include twenty-six member states, including several that are contiguous to Russian territory, creates in the minds of some Russian leaders and planners a potential or actual danger. This pessimism on the part of some Russians is not altogether foreordained. As Dmitri Trenin has noted with respect to Russia's regular interaction with NATO via the NATO–Russia Council and in other forums, "The Russians certainly understand NATO much better today than they did in the 1990s. All this lends a degree of stability and predictability to the relationship, even though mutual expectations have been revised downward."[19]

Trenin notes that Russia's perceptions of NATO are ambivalent. NATO is considered as a geopolitical "factor" instead of a partner. Russia has a window on the NATO alliance but "still has no handle on it."[20] Among Russia's present concerns with respect to NATO are (1) possible enlargement of its membership to include Georgia and Ukraine, (2) the United States' temporary use of military facilities in Bulgaria and Romania, and especially (3) plans to deploy elements of an American BMD system in Poland and the Czech Republic.[21]

Russia's ambivalent relationship with NATO is part of the background for Putin's sensitivity with respect to U.S. missile defense deployments in Europe. Another part is the temporarily corrosive effect of the "Litvinenko affair" on relations between Britain and Russia. Prior to his death in London in November 2006 due to poisoning with polonium, Litvinenko accused Putin of having arranged the murder. A political and legal contretemps between London and Moscow followed during the winter and spring of 2006–7 and continued into the summer of 2007. British investigators identified Andrei Lugovoi, businessman and former FSB officer, as a suspect, and the British Foreign secretary requested that Russia extradite Lugovoi to the United Kingdom. Russia refused to do so, citing its constitution as not permitting extradition of Russian citizens.[22]

Under ordinary conditions, a matter of this nature would have been handled with minimum publicity between the respective intelligence services and without the involvement of high-level politicians. But the technology of the weapon chosen, and the sinister character of the apparent retaliation against Litvinenko, an outspoken Kremlin critic, touched a nerve in relations between Britain and Russia and across the Atlantic, as well as in other European capitals. It fed the flames of critics overseas and in Russia who regarded Putin as a backslider on democracy and a promoter of authoritarianism. As well, the Litvinenko affair was regarded as a signifier for a more assertive Russian foreign policy and forward leaning foreign intelligence profile.

Not only Kremlin critics but also President Putin made explicit the connection between more assertiveness in Russian foreign intelligence operations and disagreements with the U.S. and NATO over European missile defenses. Speaking in Moscow July 25, 2007, at a meeting with senior military and security officers, in remarks that were also posted on the Kremlin's web site, Putin promised to strengthen Russia's military capability and to increase spying abroad in response to U.S. plans to deploy missile defenses and troops in Eastern Europe. According to Putin, "The situation in the world and internal political interests require the Foreign Intelligence Service (SVR) to permanently increase its capabilities, primarily in the field of information and analytical support for the country's leadership."[23] Although Putin did not specify any nations as targets of increased attention by Russian foreign intelligence, U.S. and British officials had recently said that Russia had intensified its spying in those countries.[24]

Neither the Litvinenko affair nor the espionage wars that are normal among great powers even in time of peace were indicators of a New Cold War in progress. The ideological struggle between capitalism and communism is over with, and Russians, even troglodytes, recognize this. But Russia's desire for great-power status is a constant, and it remains as the basis for Russian foreign policy planning and national security decision making. The reasons for this priority have to do with the traditional rules of international politics since Thucydides (power commands respect), with the feelings of resentment over Russia's decline in the 1990s (much like Weimar Germany), and with the domestic political advantages of playing the "Russia deserves more respect" card.

No one can doubt that the Russian presidential elections of 2008 were related to the escalation of Putin's political rhetoric and his desire for improvement in Russia's armed forces. Playing the missile defense card and the "NATO is encircling Russia" card is smart politics for appealing to Russians who already feel besieged by terrorism, by the uncertainties of globalization and privatization, and by the absence of a clear state "enemy" against which to do military-strategic planning. On the other hand, these missile defense and NATO threat cards cannot be overplayed by Putin for several reasons: (1) impending changes in officeholders resulting from Russian and U.S. presidential elections in 2008; (2) Russia wants certain things from the West, including greater economic integration with the G8, and this requires a continuing security community in Europe devoid of major war; (3) Russia is already suffering from diplomatic scrutiny and public relations blowback over Putin's domestic policies, including alleged lapses in democratic practice related to the rule of law, press freedom, the right of dissent, and so on; and (4) peace and prosperity benefit Russia more than most in Europe because Russia's economy is now on a growth curve that energy, foreign investment, and other forces are driving in favorable directions.

The preceding discussion sketches only some of the political and military background pertinent to discussions among Russia, the United States, and NATO over missile defenses. One thing emerges above all: The present political condition of Europe is such that missile defenses are a political and military paradox. They are not immediate threats to deterrence stability as between Russia and the United States. Nor, on the other hand, are they escape hatches from mutual deterrence based on assured retaliation into a new world of defense dominance, as promoted by the Reagan administration. Whether missile defense technology over the next decade is even viable for the mission of deterrence and defense against rogue state attacks, a more attainable objective than comprehensive societal protection against circa 1980s Soviet nuclear strikes, is the subject of debate among military experts.

On the other hand, the politics of missile defense as between Russia and the United States, and Russia and NATO, do matter. If missile defenses become a divisive political issue instead of an enabler of U.S.-Russian or U.S.-NATO cooperation, then an important opportunity to strengthen security from the Atlantic to the Urals, regardless of regime changes in Washington or in Moscow, will have been lost. Therefore analysis should support sound policy making by separating myth from reality when it comes to the implications of missile defenses for deterrence and arms race stability. The analysis presented in the next section attempts a modest contribution toward that end.

Approach and Method

Signed by Russia and the United States in May 2002, SORT requires that both states reduce the numbers of their operationally deployed strategic nuclear warheads to a range of 2,200–1,700 by the end of the calendar year 2012. These overall reduction targets can be met by any mix of launchers and warheads—so long as the ceiling on warheads is not exceeded. Prior START I restrictions on multiple warhead missiles are superseded by SORT. However, START I inspection provisions theoretically remain in place until 2009 when that agreement officially expires.

SORT has opposite implications for missile defenses. On one hand, at least hypothetically, it makes the task of missile defenses easier: Fewer warheads require fewer and less capable interceptors, ceteris paribus. On the other hand, offensive force reductions cause some to argue that the case for missile defenses is thereby weaker. If offenses are in the business of self-destruct via the process of arms control, why deploy defenses? Defenses might even abort the cycle of offensive arms reductions and provide a rationale for a new arms race, according to pessimists.

TABLE 3.1. VIEWS OF DEFENSE OPTIMISTS AND PESSIMISTS ON NATIONWIDE BMD

	DEFENSE CAPABILITIES	DEFENSE POLITICAL IMPACTS
Defense optimists	Weak now relative to offenses but growing better with improved technology; since ballistic missiles are an old technology, it is only a matter of time and engineering before defenses catch up with offenses.	Should be reassuring because they provide insurance against rogue attacks or accidental launches and do not threaten deterrence in the present or the foreseeable future.
Defense pessimists	Nationwide BMD technologies have been ineffective relative to offenses since the Cold War, and there appears to be no breakthrough in the near future that would suggest otherwise.	Nationwide BMD systems would destabilize a secure U.S.-Russian deterrent relationship that was important during the Cold War and is important now for stability in Europe, control of nuclear proliferation, and other reasons.

Relative to the above issues the analysis in this section proceeds in several steps. First, both the United States and Russia are assigned four SORT-compliant strategic nuclear force structures.[25] Second, each force structure is played against the other's "balanced triad" in an exchange model. Third, the numbers of surviving and retaliating warheads are compared for the two states and their various forces under the following operational conditions: (1) forces are on generated alert and launched on warning (GEN-LOW), (2) forces are on generated alert and launched after riding out the attack (GEN-ROA), (3) forces are on day-to-day alert and launch on warning (DAY-LOW), and (4) forces are on day-to-day alert and riding out the attack (DAY-ROA). In general the numbers of surviving and retaliating warheads should diminish progressively as we move from operational condition 1 for the defender to operational condition 4, but that does not always happen—depending on actual force structures and other variables.[26]

In a fourth step defenses are added into the exchange models above, with a range of capabilities relative to the retaliatory strikes by offenses: (1) defenses capable of intercepting 25 percent of the other side's retaliating warheads (simulating single-layered defenses), (2) defenses able to intercept 50 percent of the retaliating warheads (defenses with two layers), and (3) defenses capable of intercepting 75 percent of the retaliating warheads (simulating a three-layered defense). These simulated defenses are constructed by reversing the analysis and "dumbing down" the penetrating capabilities of offensive ballistic missiles (but not bomber-delivered weapons).[27]

Data Analysis

The tables in this chapter summarize the findings from the preceding data analysis. Table 3.2 summarizes the SORT-compliant force structures for the United States and Russia within a warhead limit of 2,200. Tables 3.3–6 summarize the results of nuclear force exchanges with no defenses and with defenses at three different levels of effectiveness (as noted above). Table 3.7 summarizes the SORT-compliant force structures for Russia and the United States within a warhead limit of 1,700. Tables 3.8–11 summarize the results of nuclear force exchanges with no defenses and with defenses at three different levels of effectiveness (as noted above).

These tables condense a considerable amount of information, but certain indicators stand out. For example, in table 3.6 we see the "worst case" for Russia and the United States, with regard to their numbers of surviving and retaliating warheads, under an initial deployment ceiling of 2,200 weapons and against defenses with an overall effectiveness of 75 percent. Those defenses are heroically effective compared to anything now deployed or foreseeable in the next decade. Nevertheless, for Russia's balanced triad, the numbers of surviving and retaliating warheads ranges from 899 (GEN-LOW) to 29 (DAY-ROA). In the canonical case often used for analysis of generated alert and riding out the attack, Russia's balanced triad provides for 751 surviving and retaliating warheads against three-layered defenses as simulated here.[28] For the U.S. balanced triad retaliating against Russian defenses, the numbers of surviving and retaliating warheads in this "worst case" for the retaliator range from a high of 713 to a low of 189 warheads.

If we fast forward to table 3.11 for the numbers of surviving and retaliating warheads for Russian and U.S. forces, under a lower deployment ceiling of 1,700 weapons, and retaliating against defenses of maximum effectiveness (capable of intercepting 75 percent of retaliating warheads, or allowing only 25 percent "leakage" through the defenses), Russia's balanced triad provides a range of surviving and retaliating warheads from a high of 639 (GEN-LOW) to a low of 25 (DAY-ROA). A U.S. balanced triad under similar conditions provides for a high of 569 and a low of 140 surviving and arriving warheads.

Space prevents extended discussion of each table, but the results in tables 3.2–11 show that even very good defenses cannot create a paradigm shift from deterrence stability based mostly on assured retaliation. This is true for balanced triads and for other force configurations tested for both states. Neither deterrence nor arms race stability between the two largest strategic nuclear powers is therefore at imminent risk as a result of missile defense deployments—even if BMD much more competent than hitherto can be developed and deployed.

TABLE 3.2. TOTAL DEPLOYED STRATEGIC WEAPONS, 2,200 LIMIT

	UNITED STATES			
	BALANCED TRIAD	No ICBMS	No BOMBERS	ALL SLBMs
ICBMs	300	0	300	0
SLBMs	1,344	1,680	1,848	2,184
Air	512	520	0	0
	RUSSIA			
	BALANCED TRIAD	No BOMBERS	No SLBMs	ICBMS ONLY
ICBMs	800	1,300	1,300	2,020
SLBMs	528	660	0	0
Air	840	0	820	0

TABLE 3.3. SURVIVING AND RETALIATING WEAPONS VS. DEFENSES, 25 PERCENT EFFECTIVE, 2,200 LIMIT

	UNITED STATES			
	BALANCED TRIAD	No ICBMS	No BOMBERS	ALL SLBMs
GEN-LOW	1,732	1,740	1,767	1,769
GEN-ROA	1,489	1,740	1,524	1,769
DAY-LOW	999	912	1,273	1,185
DAY-ROA	756	912	1,030	1,185
	RUSSIA			
	BALANCED TRIAD	No BOMBERS	No SLBMs	ICBMS ONLY
GEN-LOW	1,760	1,705	1,476	1,818
GEN-ROA	1,169	911	682	684
DAY-LOW	806	1,277	1,170	1,818
DAY-ROA	115	170	117	182

TABLE 3.4. SURVIVING AND RETALIATING WEAPONS VS. DEFENSES, 25 PERCENT EFFECTIVE, 2,200 LIMIT

	UNITED STATES			
	BALANCED TRIAD	No ICBMS	No BOMBERS	ALL SLBMs
GEN-LOW	1,392	1,400	1,325	1,327
GEN-ROA	1,210	1,400	1,143	1,327
DAY-LOW	750	684	955	889
DAY-ROA	567	684	772	889

TABLE 3.4 *CONT*. SURVIVING AND RETALIATING WEAPONS VS. DEFENSES, 25 PERCENT EFFECTIVE, 2,200 LIMIT

	RUSSIA			
	BALANCED TRIAD	NO BOMBERS	NO SLBMs	ICBMs ONLY
GEN-LOW	1,473	1,278	1,184	1,364
GEN-ROA	1,030	683	588	513
DAY-LOW	604	958	878	1,364
DAY-ROA	86	128	88	136

TABLE 3.5. SURVIVING AND RETALIATING WEAPONS VS. DEFENSES, 50 PERCENT EFFECTIVE, 2,200 LIMIT

	UNITED STATES			
	BALANCED TRIAD	NO ICBMS	NO BOMBERS	ALL SLBMs
GEN-LOW	1,053	1,059	883	885
GEN-ROA	931	1,059	762	885
DAY-LOW	500	456	636	593
DAY-ROA	378	456	515	593
	RUSSIA			
	BALANCED TRIAD	NO BOMBERS	NO SLBMs	ICBMs ONLY
GEN-LOW	1,186	852	891	909
GEN-ROA	891	455	494	342
DAY-LOW	403	638	585	909
DAY-ROA	57	85	59	91

TABLE 3.6. SURVIVING AND RETALIATING WEAPONS VS. DEFENSES, 75 PERCENT EFFECTIVE, 2,200 LIMIT

	UNITED STATES			
	BALANCED TRIAD	NO ICBMS	NO BOMBERS	ALL SLBMs
GEN-LOW	713	719	442	442
GEN-ROA	652	719	381	442
DAY-LOW	250	228	318	296
DAY-ROA	189	228	257	296

TABLE 3.6 CONT. SURVIVING AND RETALIATING WEAPONS VS. DEFENSES, 75 PERCENT EFFECTIVE, 2,200 LIMIT

	RUSSIA			
	BALANCED TRIAD	NO BOMBERS	No SLBMs	ICBMs ONLY
GEN-LOW	899	426	599	455
GEN-ROA	751	228	400	171
DAY-LOW	201	319	293	455
DAY-ROA	29	43	29	45

TABLE 3.7. TOTAL DEPLOYED STRATEGIC WEAPONS, 1,700 LIMIT

	UNITED STATES			
	BALANCED TRIAD	No ICBMS	NO BOMBERS	ALL SLBMs
ICBMs	300	0	300	0
SLBMs	980	1,078	1,372	1,568
Air	416	616	0	0
	RUSSIA			
	BALANCED TRIAD	NO BOMBERS	No SLBMs	ICBMs ONLY
ICBMs	680	1,180	880	1,680
SLBMs	480	504	0	0
Air	534	0	820	0

TABLE 3.8. SURVIVING AND RETALIATING WEAPONS VS. NO DEFENSES, 1,700 LIMIT

	UNITED STATES			
	BALANCED TRIAD	No ICBMS	NO BOMBERS	ALL SLBMs
GEN-LOW	1,367	1,322	1,381	1,270
GEN-ROA	1,124	1,322	1,138	1,270
DAY-LOW	802	585	1,015	851
DAY-ROA	559	585	772	851
	RUSSIA			
	BALANCED TRIAD	NO BOMBERS	No SLBMs	ICBMs ONLY
GEN-LOW	1,390	1,470	1,390	1,512
GEN-ROA	880	757	758	556
DAY-LOW	690	1,144	792	1,512
DAY-ROA	100	147	79	151

TABLE 3.9. SURVIVING AND RETALIATING WEAPONS VS. DEFENSES, 25 PERCENT EFFECTIVE, 1,700 LIMIT

UNITED STATES				
	BALANCED TRIAD	NO ICBMS	NO BOMBERS	ALL SLBMS
GEN-LOW	1,101	1,104	1,036	953
GEN-ROA	919	1,104	854	953
DAY-LOW	601	439	761	638
DAY-ROA	419	439	579	638
RUSSIA				
	BALANCED TRIAD	NO BOMBERS	NO SLBMS	ICBMS ONLY
GEN-LOW	1,140	1,103	1,192	1134
GEN-ROA	757	568	718	417
DAY-LOW	517	858	594	1,134
DAY-ROA	75	110	59	113

TABLE 3.10. SURVIVING AND RETALIATING WEAPONS VS. DEFENSES, 50 PERCENT EFFECTIVE, 1,700 LIMIT

UNITED STATES				
	BALANCED TRIAD	NO ICBMS	NO BOMBERS	ALL SLBMS
GEN-LOW	835	886	691	635
GEN-ROA	714	886	569	635
DAY-LOW	401	293	507	425
DAY-ROA	279	293	386	425
RUSSIA				
	BALANCED TRIAD	NO BOMBERS	NO SLBMS	ICBMS ONLY
GEN-LOW	890	735	994	756
GEN-ROA	635	379	678	278
DAY-LOW	345	572	396	756
DAY-ROA	50	74	40	76

TABLE 3.11. SURVIVING AND RETALIATING WEAPONS VS. DEFENSES,
75 PERCENT EFFECTIVE, 1,700 LIMIT

UNITED STATES				
	BALANCED TRIAD	No ICBMS	No bombers	ALL SLBMs
GEN-LOW	569	667	345	318
GEN-ROA	508	667	285	318
DAY-LOW	200	146	284	213
DAY-ROA	140	146	193	213
RUSSIA				
	BALANCED TRIAD	No bombers	No SLBMs	ICBMs ONLY
GEN-LOW	639	368	796	378
GEN-ROA	512	189	638	139
DAY-LOW	172	286	198	378
DAY-ROA	25	37	20	38

With or without defenses, Russia faces a particular problem when its forces are postured on day-to-day alert and planning to ride out the attack. This contingency is very unlikely for either state. A nuclear war would not begin with a surprise attack "from the blue" but as the result of some political crisis. During the crisis management phase, decision makers would have the option of alerting some or all of their retaliatory forces. They would also have the option of tasking some or all of their forces for prompt as opposed to delayed launch—either preemption or launch under attack (see below).

Do the preceding points make an affirmative case for nationwide U.S. or Russian BMD systems? No, they fall short of that because other political judgments are entailed. First, missile defenses may be judged as irrelevant to the deterrent or arms control relationship between the United States and Russia but important for other reasons. One of the other reasons might be increased protection against rogue state attacks or accidental launches. Another reason might be that missile defenses would be seen as part of a package of technologies leading to future space dominance, including antisatellite weapons and next-generation command-control and reconnaissance systems.

A third reason for interest in defenses, apart from Russian-U.S. deterrence stability, might be to deter nuclear proliferation by increasing the likelihood that future proliferators would face improved "deterrence by denial" as well as deterrence by threat of assured retaliation. A fourth reason for interest on the part of either Washington or Moscow in missile defenses might be to help extend deterrence over parts of Europe or Asia to allies who would be provided with theater or other local missile defenses linked to a U.S. or Russian national missile defense warning and control system. Each of these four reasons for U.S. or Russian interest in nationwide BMD presents a set of important policy issues tangent to the present discussion, but they are beyond the scope of our current analysis.

If the calculations summarized above show that not even very competent defenses can threaten nuclear strategic stability, what might? Some clues are hidden in the data. To tease out their implications, four additional tables provide x-rays of the relative vulnerability of each state's balanced triads under 2,200 and 1,700 limits. How much real difference in performance is there between unalerted and alerted forces, or between forces that are launched on warning of attack as opposed to retaliating after riding out an attack? In tables 3.12–15 we provide snapshots of the answers to that question.

Table 3.12 summarizes the differences between the performances of Russian balanced triad forces on generated alert and day-to-day alert and between Russian forces launched on warning and those riding out the attack and then retaliating. The left side of the table shows the sensitivity to generation of Russian forces: first, when riding out the attack, and second, when launched on warning. The right side of the same table shows the sensitivity to prompt launch for the same Russian forces: first, on day alert, and second, on generated alert.

Thus, for example, on the left half of table 3.12 Russian forces riding out the attack on day alert provide for only 10 percent of the number of surviving and retaliating warheads as do Russian forces riding out the attack but on generated alert. But when they are launched on warning, the difference between day and generated forces' performances is reduced—the number of surviving and retaliating warheads on day alert is 46 percent of the number of surviving and retaliating warheads on generated alert if forces are launched on warning.

Table 3.13 summarizes information similar to table 3.12, for U.S. forces instead of Russian forces. Tables 3.14 and 3.15 provide information parallel to that appearing in tables 3.12 and 3.13, but in the latter case for U.S. and Russian balanced nuclear triads within a lower SORT ceiling of 1,700 deployed warheads instead of the higher ceiling of 2,200 warheads for forces depicted in tables 3.12 and 3.13.

The information provided by tables 3.12–15 sheds additional light on the analysis and identifies priority problems for policy makers. Both states' forces are significantly improved in performance by being placed on generated alert and by choosing prompt over delayed launch. The statistical sensitivities to generation and prompt launch are worse, that is, more pronounced, for the Russians than for U.S. forces. These findings to some extent reflect force structure. Russia is more reliant on land-based missiles compared to sea-based missiles for survivability;

TABLE 3.12. SENSITIVITY TO GEN AND LOW, RUSSIAN BALANCED TRIAD, 2,200 LIMIT

	Sensitivity to GEN (ROA vs. LOW)				
RF force 1	ICBM	72	129	720	720
RF	SLBM	43	428	86	428
Balanced triad	Air	0	612	0	612
	All	115	1169	806	1760
	Stability, ratio	10%	10.18	46%	2.18
	Sensitivity to LOW (DAY vs. GEN)				
RF force 1	ICBM	72	720	129	720
RF	SLBM	43	86	428	428
Balanced triad	Air	0	0	612	612
	All	115	806	1169	1760
	Stability, ratio	14%	7.02	66%	1.51

Note: Stability is the percentage obtained by dividing the number for All in each left column by the number for All in each right column. For example, in the lower half of the table, 115 is 14 per cent of 806. The corresponding ratio is 7.02, meaning that 806 is 7.2 times 115.

TABLE 3.13. SENSITIVITY TO GEN AND LOW, U.S. BALANCED TRIAD, 2,200 LIMIT

	Sensitivity to GEN (ROA vs. LOW)				
U.S. force 1	ICBM	27	27	270	270
U.S.	SLBM	729	1,089	729	1,089
Balanced triad	Air	0	373	0	373
	All	756	1489	999	1,732
	Stability, ratio	51%	1.97	58%	1.73
	Sensitivity to LOW (DAY vs. GEN)				
U.S. force 1	ICBM	27	270	27	270
U.S.	SLBM	729	729	1,089	1,089
Balanced triad	Air	0	0	373	373
	All	756	999	1,489	1,732
	Stability, ratio	76%	1.32	86%	1.16

TABLE 3.14. SENSITIVITY TO GEN AND LOW, RUSSIAN BALANCED TRIAD, 1,700 LIMIT

SENSITIVITY TO GEN (ROA vs. LOW)					
RF force 1	ICBM	61	102	612	612
RF	SLBM	39	389	78	389
Balanced triad	Air	0	389	0	389
	All	100	880	690	1,390
	Stability, ratio	11%	8.79	50%	2.02
SENSITIVITY TO LOW (DAY vs. GEN)					
RF force 1	ICBM	61	612	102	612
RF	SLBM	39	78	389	389
Balanced triad	Air	0	0	389	389
	All	100	690	880	1,390
	Stability, ratio	15%	6.89	63%	1.58

TABLE 3.15. SENSITIVITY TO GEN AND LOW, U.S. BALANCED TRIAD, 1,700 LIMIT

SENSITIVITY TO GEN (ROA vs. LOW)					
U.S. force 1	ICBM	27	27	270	270
U.S.	SLBM	532	794	532	794
Balanced triad	Air	0	303	0	303
	All	559	1,124	802	1,367
	Stability, ratio	50%	2.01	59%	1.70
SENSITIVITY TO LOW (DAY vs. GEN)					
U.S. force 1	ICBM	27	270	27	270
U.S.	SLBM	532	532	794	794
Balanced triad	Air	0	0	303	303
	All	559	802	1,124	1,367
	Stability, ratio	70%	1.43	82%	1.22

the United States, on the other hand, emphasizes sea-based ballistic missiles over land-based missiles. I previously noted Russia's precipitous decline in the numbers of surviving and retaliating warheads in the "fourth" option among operational postures: day-to-day alert and riding out the attack.

One implication of the findings summarized in tables 3.12–15 is that the management of a crisis that might erupt into an *inadvertent nuclear war* or *mistaken nuclear preemption* (based on false or exaggerated warning or on mistaken assumptions about leaders' intentions) looms as a larger challenge than the sizing of nuclear force reductions or even the mixture of offenses and defenses—should permissive technology present itself.[29] Even apart from nuclear war the danger of nuclear-strategic coercion might be overestimated by a power with vulnerable forces and/or command and control systems. The larger the gap between forces' performances on high as opposed to normal alert, or between forces launched on warning compared to riding out the attack, the more accident prone the system becomes.

Conclusions

The interior text of this chapter has anticipated most of the conclusion, but concise summary is now appropriate. First, the basic structure of nuclear-strategic deterrence, insofar as that matters nowadays, is secure between Russia and the United States. It cannot be taken for granted—foolish decision making is always a prerogative of policy makers. Barring moon walks into nuclear adventurism by Washington or Moscow, however, even defenses that are more competent than any hitherto tested cannot remove either the United States or Russia from a condition of mutual vulnerability. And this vulnerability, compared to that of the Cold War, is more statistical than substantive. It is not supported by hostile ideological intentions of the kind that would remake the deterrence equation into a mutually intolerable threat perception.

Despite the preceding reassurances, all is not well with nuclear deterrence and missile defenses between Russia and the United States. Missile defenses have become an arena for competitive public diplomacy and retrograde military thinking. The United States needs to think through the realistic military benefits to be had from deploying parts of any missile defense system in Eastern Europe. The United States also needs to consider whether missile defenses should be part of a grand bargain with Russia that includes shared technology development and diplomatic agreement as to location, command-control, and architecture. Russia, on the other hand, needs to lower its rhetorical threshold against any and all missile defense concepts advanced by the United States or NATO. After all, as Putin railed against U.S. BMD proposed for deployment in Poland and the Czech Republic, Russia was cooperating with NATO on theater missile defenses (TMD). Low bombast combined with expert discussions on this issue is recommended for missile defenses on both sides of the Atlantic.

Chapter 4

Missile Defenses in Context: Manageable Threat, Possible Opportunity

Missile defenses moved from the periphery to the center of U.S.-Russian relations in 2007. American proposals to deploy components of a missile defense system in Eastern Europe have raised questions about U.S.-Russian and NATO-Russian political relations. Missile defenses also raise military-strategic issues with regard to the stability of nuclear deterrence and reassurance in the twenty-first century. In addition, missile defenses deployed by the United States or jointly with Russia have implications for controlling the proliferation of nuclear weapons.

This chapter considers the problem of missile defenses, between the United States and Russia, as a combination of shared threat and potential reassurance. If the two states approach missile defenses as if the Cold War were still in progress, then threats will be emphasized. If, on the other hand, missile defenses are seen in Washington and Moscow as a matter of cooperative security, then ballistic missile defenses need not be incompatible with further reductions in offensive strategic nuclear forces.

Putin Poses a Challenge

Vladimir Putin and other leading Russian officials spoke emphatically in the spring of 2007 against announced U.S. plans to deploy missile defense components in Poland and the Czech Republic.[1] But Putin appeared to change course in June 2007, when he surprised President George W. Bush at the G8 meetings in Germany with an offer to cooperate in building a joint missile defense system using Russian-leased components in Azerbaijan.[2] U.S. and even Russian experts noted technical problems with Putin's proposal, including the insufficient capability of the radar in Gabala (Qabala) for performing the kinds of tracking and discrimination required for BMD intercept.

Nevertheless, Putin continued with expressions of interest in U.S.-Russian cooperation on missile defenses during his meetings with President Bush at

Kennebunkport, Maine, in late June and early July. He said at a July 2 press conference that he was ready to expand on his proposal for a shared missile defense system that would take Russian-U.S. relations to "an entirely new level" of cooperation.[3] Putin's revised plan would modernize the radar in Azerbaijan and add another missile warning and detection system being constructed in southern Russia.[4] In addition, he offered to open "an ABM information exchange center" in Moscow and recommended the creation of a parallel "analytical center in a European capital city, for instance, Brussels."[5]

Putin's choice of Brussels was no coincidence. He was obviously attempting to enlarge the political discourse on BMD to include NATO Europe along with Russia and the United States. His preferred forum for broadening BMD consultations was the NATO–Russia Council. Also offering the carrot of political inclusiveness and the possibility of taking U.S.-Russian relations to a higher level of cooperation, First Deputy Prime Minister Sergei Ivanov stated that if the United States accepted Putin's proposals, it would change "the configuration of international relations."[6] Ivanov told journalists in Tashkent on July 4 that BMD cooperation, along the lines of Putin's proposal, would lead to technology exchange and political cooperation: "A new space for trust will emerge. We may establish strategic partnership."[7]

For his part President George W. Bush maintained a positive atmosphere between the two heads of state despite his advisors' technical and political doubts about the Russian proposal. Part of Russia's incentive was undoubtedly to head off any BMD deployments in Poland and the Czech Republic unless these technologies were incorporated within a broader missile defenses architecture and within a NATO-Russia framework, not under unilateral American control. Bush indicated no willingness to bypass the deployments in Poland and in the Czech Republic. Expert groups were to study further possible cooperation between the United States and Russia or Russia and NATO on missile warning information exchange and BMD.

President Putin was not the only skeptic with respect to the details of Bush-proposed missile defense deployments. The U.S. Congress weighed in with various concerns about technical and political aspects of the proposed BMD deployments in Poland and the Czech Republic.[8] In June 2007 the U.S. House of Representatives passed legislation reducing funds in the fiscal 2008 defense authorization bill for construction of the interceptor missile sites in Poland and for deployment of the X-band radar in the Czech Republic. The U.S. Senate Armed Services Committee, for its part, decided to delay funding for the European BMD sites. In its report on the defense authorization bill, the committee cited Russia's opposition to East European deployments and indicated that funding for deployment should follow talks between the two governments.

In addition, the committee expressed concern that NATO had neither officially endorsed nor rejected the proposed missile defense deployments on its territory.[9]

Congress also expressed concern about the proposed timing of proposed deployments and its coordination with the pace of technology development. The U.S. Missile Defense Agency (MDA) estimated that construction and deployment could not begin until the Czech Republic and Poland ratified agreements with the United States. Such actions "would not take place before 2009."[10] The Senate Armed Services Committee reported (presumably based on MDA testimony) that the interceptor to be deployed in Poland "has not yet been developed or tested, and is not currently planned to be flight-tested until 2010."[11]

Additional doubt was expressed by the Senate committee with respect to Bush administration threat estimates relative to the requirement for BMD in Europe. Lt. Gen. Henry A. Obering III, U.S. Air Force, director of the Missile Defense Agency, had previously testified before the committee, "Right now, experts are saying that Iran will not have an ICBM until the 2010–2015 time frame."[12] However, the Senate committee doubted whether Iran would pose a significant threat even by 2015. "There is uncertainty about whether Iran will have such long-range missiles, or nuclear warheads that could work on such missiles, by 2015," it noted.[13]

Missile Defense in Perspective

Putin's proposal and congressional skepticism about missile defenses fit into a larger context that stretches back to the Cold War. Although Russia and the United States have a politically nonhostile relationship (reaffirmed by both governments at the Kennebunkport summit, where they pledged continued consultation and cooperation in reducing their numbers of deployed strategic nuclear weapons), their relationship was more geopolitically competitive under Putin that it was during the 1990s.

Russia's military and larger security establishment includes people with a Cold War mentality with respect to U.S. missile defenses. They identify U.S. missile defenses with Reagan's "Star Wars" system (SDI), which was designed in their view to win the Cold War by technological overthrow of mutual deterrence. Moscow's military conservatives also distrust the enlargement of NATO that has, since the end of the Cold War, pushed its borders closer to Russia and enlarged its membership to twenty-six countries. The combination of possibly viable U.S. missile defenses, deployed on the former territory of the Soviet-allied Warsaw Pact and within operational reach of Russia, causes hard-liners among the *siloviki* to doubt American reassurances that European BMD are intended to deter and deflect missile threats from the Middle East.

The doubts of members of Congress about the effectiveness of U.S. missile defense technology, notwithstanding the political arguments for or against BMD deployments, can also be traced back to Cold War origins. Ever since the ABM debates of the 1960s and 1970s in American politics, critics of missile defenses have charged that the technology promises more than it delivers. In addition, Cold War and later skeptics have contended that antimissile defenses are over-matched against the offensive striking power of long-range ballistic missiles armed with nuclear warheads. The paradoxical logic of deterrence that provided the dominant rationale for U.S. arms control policy during the Cold War was that even if missile defenses worked technologically, they would be politically destabilizing. By this logic "successful" nationwide missile defenses deployed by one side would deny to the other side its "assured retaliation" or "assured destruction," thereby decreasing deterrence and arms control stability.[14]

The demise of the Soviet Union, the end of the Cold War, and the attacks of 9/11, according to some, have changed the political-military and technology contexts relative to missile defenses.[15] As to the political context, the threat of nuclear or other weapons of mass destruction attack is posed primarily by rogue states or nonstate actors such as terrorists. While these state and nonstate actors may be "beyond deterrence" as a cost-benefit proposition (depending on their motives), the challenge their attacks pose to evolving BMD systems may not be as one sided as that posed by Cold War offenses against available defenses. According to this reasoning, states today, compared to the Cold War years, face a higher probability of nuclear deterrence failure, but defense technology is more equal to the task of interception of attacking missiles and war-heads against probable aggressors.

Furthermore, current proponents of BMD systems would contend that missile defenses provide both societal protection and some supplemental deter-rence. Even rogue states contemplating a nuclear first strike might pause if they expected any such attacks to be exercises in futility against superior defenses. The first strike would serve only to antagonize the victim without causing sig-nificant damage. However, there is also the aspect that defenses can be used against retaliatory strikes as well as against first strikes. A first striker supported by missile defenses might then be emboldened to attack, counting on its BMD to negate the defender's retaliation. Thus political intentions are compelling as to the purpose for which missile defense or other technologies will be used: War is still war, and strategy, strategy, per Clausewitz.

U.S., Russian, or other missile defenses, whether viewgraph systems or actual deployments, also have implications for the pace and character of nuclear weapons proliferation.[16] Arguably the spread of nuclear weapons, limited during the Cold War to a small number of major powers, is on the verge of escaping international control. This judgment is not uncontroversial. Optimists about nuclear proliferation would point to North Korea's agreement with the United States, Russia, China, Japan, and South Korea signed in February 2007.

In this agreement North Korea promised to shut down its nuclear reactor at Yongbyon within sixty days and to admit international inspectors to verify compliance. In return the DPRK was to receive an emergency shipment of fuel oil from the United States, China, Russia, and South Korea. This first phase of the agreement accomplished the freezing of North Korea's plutonium-based weapons program but left for future discussion its suspected uranium-enrichment program and other aspects of its nuclear capabilities. Some experts suggested that as of February 2007, North Korea already had accumulated sufficient fissile material to assemble between six and ten nuclear weapons.[17]

It remained to be seen whether North Korea would follow through with a more complete accountability for its nuclear weapons programs that was sufficient to satisfy the international community.[18] Verifiable and enforceable nuclear disarmament of North Korea would remove one member of President George W. Bush's "axis of evil" from the list of rogue states that were judged as either nuclear capable or nuclear aspiring. Presumably this might also weaken the U.S. case for nationwide BMD deployments, although other candidate rogues existed. With the defenestration of the Saddam Hussein regime in Iraq and the denuclearization of North Korea, the focus of U.S. and allied attention to emerging nuclear "states of concern" would shift to Iran.

Estimates of the speed with which Iran might deploy missiles of intercontinental-range and nuclear warheads vary within the government and among outside experts.[19] Regardless of the disagreements about specifics, the United States and allied governments are agreed that the acquisition of nuclear weapons by Iran would be a setback to peace and security in the Middle East. Britain, France, and Germany have taken the initiative within the European Union to negotiate with the regime in Tehran, supported by the UN Security Council and International Atomic Energy Agency. The policy consensus about the undesirability of Iranian nuclear weapons also appears to include Russia, although Russia has its own economic interests in Iran, as does China. Thus Russia and China have preferred a go-slower approach to UN sanctions against Iran than the EU triumvirate or the Security Council.

Iran's nuclear ambitions have, as noted above, backed into the issue of nuclear arms control and nuclear arms race stability in Europe. The United States fears that longer-range Iranian missiles could eventually reach military, economic, or population targets in NATO Europe. Having acquired and deployed nuclear weapons together with longer-range missiles, Iran could coerce states into compliance with its demands or deny the United States and its allies access to various theaters of operations contiguous to Iranian territory. Thus without having fired a shot in anger, an Iranian nuclear threat-in-being would raise the stakes in any diplomatic confrontation between the regime in Tehran and the United States, NATO Europe, or regional adversaries, including Israel.

The possible emergence of a nuclear armed Iran shows how the issue of cooperative security in Europe and in the Middle East is directly linked to the U.S.-Russian problem of post–Cold War nuclear stability. Russian political support is necessary inside and outside of the UN Security Council in order to contain Iranian nuclear ambitions. To obtain this cooperation the United States must reassure Russia that it has no interest in nuclear superiority with the intent of coercing Russia or using NATO as a vehicle for undermining the Russian regime. Missile defenses, if deployed, cannot have their Cold War flavor of competition for nuclear superiority but must emerge from an environment of U.S.-Russian security cooperation.

Analysis and Methodology

The United States and Russia are required, according to SORT (the Moscow Treaty) of May 2002, to reduce their numbers of operationally deployed nuclear weapons on intercontinental launchers to within the range of 2,200–1,700 warheads. The deadline for accomplishing these reductions in offensive nuclear weapons is the end of December 2012. The Bush administration preferred to negotiate SORT according to a broad framework instead of a set of detailed specifications and restrictions. Each side has "freedom to mix" its forces among land-based, sea-based, and airborne launchers, and prior START I limits on multiple-warhead missiles were superseded by SORT. The SORT approach provided Russia with more flexibility by permitting the preservation of one or more of its multiple-warhead ICBMs.

The United States has not deployed a missile defense system since the ill-fated Safeguard BMD site was demobilized by Congress in 1975. The Soviet Union and then Russia deployed several versions of missile defenses to protect the national capital and command centers around Moscow, but these systems would have been overwhelmed by Cold War and later U.S. forces. Further inhibiting Russia from deploying missile defenses has been its technological lag behind the United States in military information systems and in funding for defense research and development, especially in the 1990s. Under Putin, Russia has improved its economic performance, and the defense sector has benefited from this improvement, including modernization for the strategic and other nuclear forces.[20]

Nevertheless, Russia, like the Soviet Union during the 1980s, fears that an arms race in missile defenses would be a loser for the Kremlin, as it would be competing against the larger U.S. defense budget and U.S. defense technology innovation. All indications are that Russia would prefer to modernize its offensive nuclear forces and rely on countermeasures to overcome any U.S. defenses.

The SORT agreement leaves undecided the status of U.S. or Russian strategic nuclear forces beyond 2012.[21] Indeed, from a legal standpoint, it becomes obsolete at the very moment that it goes into effect. SORT provides for no verification protocols other than national technical means; the protocols carried forward under START I expire in 2009. Both the Bush and Putin administrations have indicated that they would prefer to maintain the SORT limits on offensive forces well beyond 2012, but the preferences of their successors after 2008 are unknown and unconstrained.

For reasons of economy or strategy, Russia might opt for limits on strategic nuclear weapons below the SORT ceilings—if the United States would agree to similar limits. A less expensive nuclear force would free additional funds for modernizing and otherwise improving Russia's conventional military. Russia's conventional forces took a big hit in virtually all categories of military capability during the 1990s: equipment, training, modernization, and quality of recruits.[22] In addition to their lack of resources and personnel for modern wars against peer competitors or even ambitious regional powers, Russia's armed forces are also inhibited by hidebound doctrine and retro definitions of their probable opponents. Russia's higher military echelons include those who remain fixated on NATO as the enemy of choice, and the Russian armed forces leadership has been slow to adapt its training and temperament to the new requirements for fighting terrorists and unconventional wars.[23]

Procedures and Data

Given the preceding context of political, military, and economic factors, the use of SORT-constrained limits for Russian and U.S. strategic nuclear force projections is at least a reasonable point of departure. For purposes of this analysis each state has been assigned four hypothetical SORT-limited forces for the period 2012–20. Russia's forces include a balanced triad, a dyad of ICBMs and SLBMs without bombers, a dyad of land-based missiles and bombers without SLBMs, and a force of strategic land-based missiles. U.S. forces include a balanced triad, a dyad of ICBMs and SLBMs without bombers, a dyad of submarine-launched missiles and bombers without ICBMs, and a force of strategic sea-based missiles. These forces are not predictions of what might actually happen; they are heuristic devices to highlight various aspects of the analysis.

The performances of the various Russian and U.S. forces are compared according to the numbers of second-strike surviving and retaliating warheads provided by each force under the following operational conditions of alertness and launch procedures: (1) generated alert and launch on warning (GEN-LOW), (2) generated alert and riding out the attack (GEN-ROA), (3) day-to-day alert and launch on warning (DAY-LOW), and (4), day-to-day alert, riding out the attack (DAY-ROA). In general, one might expect that the progression from 1 to 4 would result in decreasing numbers of surviving and retaliating warheads, but this is not always the case. Much depends on the size and character of the attack and the performance of the defender under various conditions.

We will examine the performances of these forces without defenses and then consider how well they would do with defenses added to the equation.[24] The character of future defenses is a technological unknown. Therefore I created strawman defenses with one of three levels: a single-layered defense capable of intercepting 25 percent of second-strike retaliating warheads, a two-tiered defense capable of intercepting 50 percent of the retaliating warheads, and a three-layered defense, capable of intercepting 75 percent of retaliating warheads. Of course in the "real world" of actually deployed and functioning defenses, the estimation of their performance against responsive offenses with countermeasures becomes much more complicated to accomplish—even in testing, apart from actual hostilities.[25]

Tables 4.1 to 4.5 summarize these scenarios for Russian and U.S. forces under deployment limits of 2,200 warheads. Table 1 summarizes both states' prewar nuclear weapons. In table 4.2 Russian and U.S. forces are compared by type of force and operational posture according to the numbers of surviving and retaliating warheads provided by each. In table 4.2 no defenses are assumed to exist on either side. Tables 4.3 to 4.5 introduce defenses into the equation. In table 4.3 each state is assigned defenses capable of intercepting 25 percent of second-strike retaliating warheads. Table 4.4 provides similar information to that appearing in table 4.3, but each state's defenses can now intercept 50 percent of retaliating warheads. In table 4.5 the defenses are improved again, and U.S. and Russian BMD can now intercept three-fourths of retaliating warheads. Thus the sequencing from tables 4.3 to 4.5 crudely measures the progression of improved outcomes that the United States or Russia might obtain by deploying one-layered, two-layered, and three-layered defenses (terminal only, terminal plus midcourse, and terminal plus midcourse and boost-phase defenses, respectively).

Several preliminary findings suggest themselves based on these data. First, the nuclear revolution has not been repealed in the post–Cold War world, even at greatly reduced U.S. and Russian force levels compared to Cold War norms.

TABLE 4.1. TOTAL DEPLOYED STRATEGIC WEAPONS, 2,200 LIMIT

	UNITED STATES			
	BALANCED TRIAD	No ICBMS	NO BOMBERS	ALL SLBMs
ICBMs	300	0	300	0
SLBMs	1,344	1,680	1,848	2,184
Air	512	520	0	0
	RUSSIA			
	BALANCED TRIAD	NO BOMBERS	No SLBMs	ICBMs ONLY
ICBMs	800	1,300	1,300	2,020
SLBMs	528	660	0	0
Air	840	0	820	0

TABLE 4.2. SURVIVING AND RETALIATING WEAPONS VS. NO DEFENSES, 2,200 LIMIT

	UNITED STATES			
	BALANCED TRIAD	No ICBMS	NO BOMBERS	ALL SLBMs
GEN-LOW	1,732	1,740	1,767	1,769
GEN-ROA	1,489	1,740	1,524	1,769
DAY-LOW	999	912	1,273	1,185
DAY-ROA	756	912	1,030	1,185
	RUSSIA			
	BALANCED TRIAD	NO BOMBERS	No SLBMs	ICBMs ONLY
GEN-LOW	1,760	1,705	1,476	1,818
GEN-ROA	1,169	911	682	684
DAY-LOW	806	1,277	1,170	1,818
DAY-ROA	115	170	117	182

TABLE 4.3. SURVIVING AND RETALIATING WEAPONS VS. DEFENSES, 25 PERCENT EFFECTIVE, 2,200 LIMIT

	UNITED STATES			
	BALANCED TRIAD	No ICBMS	NO BOMBERS	ALL SLBMs
GEN-LOW	1,392	1,400	1,325	1,327
GEN-ROA	1,210	1,400	1,143	1,327
DAY-LOW	750	684	955	889
DAY-ROA	567	684	772	889

TABLE 4.3 *CONT*. SURVIVING AND RETALIATING WEAPONS VS. DEFENSES, 25 PERCENT EFFECTIVE, 2,200 LIMIT

	RUSSIA			
	BALANCED TRIAD	NO BOMBERS	No SLBMs	ICBMs ONLY
GEN-LOW	1,473	1,278	1,184	1,364
GEN-ROA	1,030	683	588	513
DAY-LOW	604	958	878	1,364
DAY-ROA	86	128	88	136

TABLE 4.4. SURVIVING AND RETALIATING WEAPONS VS. DEFENSES, 50 PERCENT EFFECTIVE, 2,200 LIMIT

	UNITED STATES			
	BALANCED TRIAD	No ICBMS	NO BOMBERS	ALL SLBMs
GEN-LOW	1,053	1,059	883	885
GEN-ROA	931	1,059	762	885
DAY-LOW	500	456	636	593
DAY-ROA	378	456	515	593
	RUSSIA			
	BALANCED TRIAD	NO BOMBERS	No SLBMs	ICBMs ONLY
GEN-LOW	1,186	852	891	909
GEN-ROA	891	455	494	342
DAY-LOW	403	638	585	909
DAY-ROA	57	85	59	91

TABLE 4.5. SURVIVING AND RETALIATING WEAPONS VS. DEFENSES, 75 PERCENT, EFFECTIVE, 2,200 LIMIT

	UNITED STATES			
	BALANCED TRIAD	No ICBMS	NO BOMBERS	ALL SLBMs
GEN-LOW	713	719	442	442
GEN-ROA	652	719	381	442
DAY-LOW	250	228	318	296
DAY-ROA	189	228	257	296

TABLE 4.5 *CONT.* SURVIVING AND RETALIATING WEAPONS VS. DEFENSES, 75 PERCENT, EFFECTIVE, 2,200 LIMIT

	RUSSIA			
	BALANCED TRIAD	NO BOMBERS	No SLBMs	ICBMs ONLY
GEN-LOW	899	426	599	455
GEN-ROA	751	228	400	171
DAY-LOW	201	319	293	455
DAY-ROA	29	43	29	45

Both states' SORT-constrained forces retain the capability to provide for assured retaliation and the inflicting of unacceptable societal damage. This is emphatically the case without defenses, but it is also true with defenses added.[26] Russia's "day-to-day alert, riding out the attack" forces are less survivable than others, but Russia is unlikely to be in that posture during a crisis—if ever. (But see below for more on this case.)

Second, force structures and operational postures do matter. They matter because they influence the probability of accidental or inadvertent nuclear war as well as the tendency for leaders to jump through windows of opportunity or fear. Thus, for example, U.S. forces are more survivable than are Russian forces within the same deployment ceilings. The reason for this higher survivability of U.S. forces is the more reliable performance of the U.S. sea-based deterrent. Russia's ballistic missile submarine force went into the doldrums in the 1990s and is only now bringing into fruition newer generations of submarines and missiles. As well, Russia's long-range bomber force (less survivable than sea-based ballistic missiles but more survivable than land-based missiles deployed in silos) lags its American counterpart in providing for numbers of surviving and retaliating warheads.

Third, the performance of Russia's forces under the most pessimistic conditions of alertness and launch readiness (day-to-day alert, riding out the attack) is a possible cause for concern. Although war between the two states under any foreseeable political conditions appears impossible, the appearance of singular vulnerability in this category could contribute to greater Russian reliance on generated alert or prompt launch during a crisis. Russia can improve the performance of its forces in this category by making itself less dependent on land-based missiles through improvements in its submarine and bomber forces.

Fourth, the hypothetical forces other than U.S. and Russian "balanced triads" are not mere excursions into fantasy. They show that both states could be more imaginative in devising force structures that would provide for equal or better performance in war but at lower risk of accidental/inadvertent war or of excessive dependency on forward leaning crisis management. Some out-of-the-box thinking about force structures might induce leaders in the United States or Russia to consider one or more of the options below (the author does not necessarily endorse any or all of these).

United States

First, the United States could shift to a dyad of sea-based and bomber forces, eliminating the ICBM force. It could substitute air- and sea-launched strategic cruise missiles for the ICBM force.

Second, conventional instead of nuclear warheads could be deployed on part or all of the U.S. ICBM force. Current Department of Defense plans call for the United States to deploy some ballistic missile submarines with conventional instead of nuclear warheads. The purpose is to create a long-range conventional strike option without the collateral damage of nuclear weapons. The objective is admirable, but the ICBM force is better used for this purpose. SLBM trajectories might be confused with a U.S. first strike against Russian forces or state territory. In addition, the American SSBN fleet is the backbone of the strategic nuclear retaliatory force—not only in terms of survivable firepower but also in terms of flexible operations and deployment.

Third, the United States might eventually deploy a family of strategic non-nuclear UAVs (unoccupied aerial vehicles) with lockdown-shootdown capabilities for loitering over distant targets and hitting them with timely precision fires, including hardened and deeply buried targets such as command bunkers and WMD storage sites. These strategic nonnuclear UAVs (SNUAVs, or "snoo-avs") would provide a long-loitering, reconnaissance-strike capability during crises and would reduce dependency on the prompt or delayed use of nuclear weapons.

The United States could deploy missile defenses in synch with further reductions in offensive nuclear weapons, providing reassurance to Russia that U.S. BMD was not intended as a checkmate move against Russia's deterrent. If missile defenses or components are deployed in Europe, Russia should be brought into the conversation and the option of making use of Russian advanced air defense missile technology should be included.

When possible U.S.-Russian and Russian-NATO cooperation on missile defense technology—and notwithstanding political obstacles, on future BMD deployments—should be encouraged. Shared information from joint early warning centers, and more transparency with regard to Russian and U.S. alerts, are recommended for building trust and for improving crisis stability.

Russia

Russia could improve capabilities of sea-based and bomber deterrents and rely less on silo-based ICBMs, the vulnerability of which raises the risk of crisis instability. Russia's new Topol-M land-based missile can be deployed in mobile or fixed basing modes. Mobile missiles, to the extent that supporting infrastructure is affordable, offer additional increments of first-strike survivability compared to silo-based missiles. Mobile ICBMs could also be combined with land-based ballistic missiles of shorter ranges or cruise missiles (see below).

Further, Russia could emphasize theater instead of intercontinental-range nuclear forces in future modernization. Its nuclear "deterrent" can affect the United States by holding NATO Europe or parts of strategic Asia at risk. Russia could maintain a downsized, mini-triad of intercontinental nuclear launchers while increasing its theater and shorter-range ballistic and cruise missiles. For example, Russia might abrogate the INF Treaty and deploy a new generation of long-range intermediate nuclear forces, including both nuclear and conventionally armed missiles.[27]

Shifting the emphasis in nuclear force modernization from intercontinental to theater or shorter-range ballistic (or cruise) missiles would be more consistent with Russian military doctrine under Putin, acknowledging the option of nuclear first use in a variety of circumstances other than a war with the United States.[28] Some Russian analysts have also noted that the use of nonstrategic nuclear weapons may be a more believable and therefore more practical option:

> It is far from always advisable to perform missions of deterring and repelling aggression using only strategic nuclear weapons. Under certain conditions the most effective regional deterrence can be ensured by means which on the one hand would be powerful enough to inflict significant damage on the aggressor and thereby to carry out the real threat, and on the other hand not so powerful that the effect of self-deterrence and of their nonuse arises.[29]

As Jacob W. Kipp has noted, Russian debates over the most appropriate response to U.S. National Missile Defense proposals "became entangled in the issue of nonstrategic nuclear weapons" as early as the latter years of the Clinton administration.[30] As well, the highly visible power struggle between Igor Sergeev, the former defense minister, and Anatoliy Kvashnin, the former chief of the General Staff under both President Yeltsin and President Putin, was in part driven by the efforts of Kvashnin to diminish the role of nuclear forces (including, presumably, tactical and other nonstrategic nuclear forces) and to increase the strategic centrality and budgetary support for conventional forces.[31]

However, from an arms control standpoint, if Russia goes in this direction—greater reliance on theater or shorter-range nuclear systems—it will become more important for Russia to improve its accounting, safety, and security for fissile materials and to accept more transparency about its inventories of tactical and theater nuclear weapons than hitherto.

Flanked by a vanguard of improved operational-tactical and theater nuclear systems (as above), Russia could invest additional funds in the modernization of its conventional forces. Conventional force modernization would lower the nuclear threshold. Much needs to be done. Putin has urged the General Staff and Ministry of Defense to transition from a largely conscript military to one that relies more heavily on contract soldiers—especially in elite units that would be used against terrorists or in rapid deployments, or both. However, contract soldiers are more expensive than conscripts, so to accomplish this military reform—including less tolerance of the hazing of new recruits and higher pay for junior officers so that more will reenlist—would be required. In addition, much of the equipment in Russia's military is shopworn and badly in need of replacement or repair. Finally, troops need to spend more time in realistic training exercises using their assigned tanks, planes, and ships, and with nonscripted outcomes allowed as possibilities (unlike in the former Soviet style).[32]

Russia might take some of its ICBM force off ready alert and even download some of its land-based missile warheads into storage. Warheads from de-alerted or downloaded land-based missiles could be replaced by newer submarine-launched missiles and warheads or by newly acquired theater systems. This point and the second point under the subhead "Russia" above might seem to allow Russia greater compellence against U.S. European allies in order to provide more reassurance to Americans against crisis instability or deliberate attack. But the impression of divisible deterrence on this issue, as between the United States and NATO Europe, is mistaken. The Soviet Union tried to create this escalation firebreak between the American homeland and the territory of U.S. NATO allies in Europe in the latter 1970s, when it deployed the long-range INF SS-20 systems targeted on the European theater of military actions.

The Soviets were unsuccessful in dividing NATO on this point, however, and NATO responded with counterdeployments (Pershing II ballistic and long-range cruise missiles) targeted on Russia. *Politics* then and now determines whether the nuclear hostage status of Europe and North America can be torn into separate compartments. If NATO holds together politically, then Russian theater nuclear force modernization does not threaten Europe's survival any more than hitherto. If, on the other hand, NATO lacks political cohesion, then Russia can perhaps exploit the seams in the alliance and make use of nuclear blackmail to drive some members of NATO into appeasement. But to what end? Unlike the situation during the Cold War, Russia now embraces capitalism and guided democracy, albeit with reservations, and neither needs nor wants a global confrontation with the United States and the West. Only if Russia falls prey to internal anarchy is it likely to see nuclear brinkmanship as a strategy that pays dividends—whatever the views of remaining cavemen in its military bureaucracy.

Russia might also, in recognition of the implausibility of a nuclear war with the United States, agree to offensive arms reductions down to the level of a truly "minimum deterrent" force (say, 1,000 operationally deployed warheads on each side). The concept of minimum deterrence deserves more serious consideration that it gets from military bureaucracies in Washington and in Moscow. With 1,000 warhead forces deployed, the United States and Russia would remain ahead of other existing (or aspiring) nuclear powers.

A post-SORT arms reduction agreement down to 1,000 warheads could have an escape clause in case a peer competitor arose who posed a danger of deploying an essentially equivalent force. There would be plenty of time for Russia and the United States to react, in that eventuality. Meanwhile, Russia's minimum deterrent could deploy some 400 survivably based warheads on land-based missiles, some 300 on submarines, and another 300 on bombers. The United States could deploy 400 or so on submarines, 300 on bombers, and another 300 on land-based missiles (this assumes that both states remain with a balanced triad of forces). Of course, the "survivability" of the various launchers and warheads would not be identical, but all should be more survivable than silo-based ICBMs now are.

A post-SORT minimum deterrent would require more verification than the present SORT arrangement beyond national technical means of surveillance. Some may also object that a smaller force will deny to military planners options for counterforce attacks on certain kinds of military and other targets should deterrence fail. But once deterrence has actually failed, who would care?

Conclusions

This chapter has covered a considerable number of issues, and the major conclusions are as follows. First, there is no repeal of mutual deterrence on offer between the United States and Russia, for at least two reasons. The first reason is that neither possesses, nor will possess under SORT constraints, a first-strike capability with high confidence of avoiding unacceptable retaliation.

The second, more important reason is that there are no political issues dividing the United States and Russia worth a war—any war, let alone nuclear war. This situation should continue unless both states bungle diplomacy to a degree as yet unseen.

Second, U.S. missile defenses will not destabilize the post–Cold War relationship between the United States and Russia for at least four reasons. First, U.S. defenses will build capability incrementally. As U.S. defenses improve, Russia will have the opportunity to offset those defenses with active and other countermeasures (including military-technical means such as penetration aids and decoys or political measures such as coercing American allies to bring pressure on the United States). Second, U.S. missile defenses will not remove the United States from its nuclear hostage condition unless, and until, the United States acquires a space-based, boost-phase intercept BMD that can defend itself, or be defended against, attack by ASATs. Third, Russia, not the United States, is in Europe. If necessary, Russia can squeeze the orange pips in Europe to create juice in American policy making. And Russia's options in Europe are not limited to military ones: Russia can also turn off the gas. Fourth, and finally, the United States needs Russia to balance against a rising China with aspirations to dominate Asia economically and militarily. And Russia also needs the United States for the same reason. And both need China to balance against each other, when necessary. It's still Kissinger's world.

Chapter 5

Nuclear Disarmament: Can the United States and Russia Lead the Way?

Is the abolition of nuclear weapons a pipe dream of scientists and policy analysts or a feasible alternative to the nuclear allergy that has now overlapped
the millennium and passed its sixty-year mark?[1] Getting rid of these ulti-
mately genocidal weapons will not be easy, but it is not impossible. Political
will matters, as do available alternatives for states with deterrence and defense
requirements. In addition, nuclear disarmament cannot be accomplished on
speed dial or in cyberspace. Complicated negotiations among and within
nuclear armed states, together with voluntary or enforced restraint by other
states, can be expected between "here" and "there."

Finding a way from nuclear plenty to nuclear scarcity requires a plan
for nuclear restraint. Part of any plan for international nuclear restraint will
demand leadership by the United States and Russia. In this chapter I consider
one possible step toward nuclear restraint that could be a building block for
eventual abolition or near-abolition of long-range (intercontinental) nuclear
forces. As the Chinese proverb holds, the longest journey begins with a single step. Could Russia and the United States live with strategic nuclear forces
lower than the Moscow Treaty levels—even as low as 1,000 or 500 operationally
deployed nuclear weapons—and meet their security requirements? If so, what
implications might follow for the possible taking of other steps in the direction
of nuclear near-abolition or even ultimate disarmament?

A Maze of Policy and Strategy Issues

Expert voices among current and former policy makers, in addition to various
commentators from other walks of life, are moving toward affirmation of the
political and military irrelevance of nuclear weapons.[2] There are various reasons for this, including changes in dominant military technology and in prevailing attitudes among political leaders, military planners, and mass publics.

However, in the "real world" of political action, aims as grandiose as the abolition of nuclear weapons are realized not all at once but in stages. A first step would be acknowledgment by the United States and Russia of their leading roles and responsibilities in nuclear arms control and disarmament. This responsibility for leadership rests in Washington and in Moscow for a number of reasons.

First, the United States and Russia together account for some 95 percent of the nuclear weapons that now exist. Second, the United States and the Soviet Union, and then Russia as the Soviet nuclear successor, embraced nuclear weapons as the instruments of choice for defining great-power status during and even after the Cold War. Third, the United States and Russia have a Cold War and post–Cold War history of conducting negotiations on nuclear arms control. This experience taught important lessons about diplomacy, verification, trust, and other matters related to reducing the risk of nuclear war.

Fourth, and perhaps most important now among reasons why Moscow and Washington should take the lead in nuclear arms reductions, is the connection between the size of the U.S. and Russian arsenals and the incentive structure for further nuclear proliferation. Simply put, the United States and Russia cannot credibly call for restraint on the part of other nuclear powers in limiting the growth of their nuclear weapons inventories or deployments without setting an example themselves. In addition, the United States and Russia are obligated by the nuclear Non-Proliferation Treaty, along with other nuclear powers, to work toward the eventual disarmament of nuclear armed states— themselves included. An example of "do as I say, not as I do" by the leading nuclear powers only encourages nonnuclear states with larger political aspirations to go nuclear.

There is some good news with respect to the United States and Russia and their shared commitment to at least partial denuclearization. The Strategic Offensive Reductions Treaty of May 2002 requires the United States and Russia to reduce their numbers of operationally deployed nuclear weapons on intercontinental launchers (hereafter "strategic nuclear weapons") to between 2,200 and 1,700 force loadings by the end of calendar year 2012.[3] In addition, under the U.S. Nunn-Lugar program Russia and other former Soviet states have been provided with American funding and expertise to help safeguard and dismantle their stockpiles of nuclear and other WMD, together with related materials and delivery systems.[4]

On the other hand, there is a large agenda of unfinished business with respect to U.S. and Russian nuclear weapons deployments. First, the SORT agreement contains no built-in verification procedures. Second, the agreement more or less expires on the date of its fulfillment. What comes next is indefinite.

Third, the political auguries, between the United States and present-day Russia, are not necessarily favorable for further reductions in strategic nuclear forces. In fact, if the course of Russian-American relations in Vladimir Putin's and George W. Bush's second terms continues into the presidencies of their successors, nuclear arms control may be only one casualty of conflicting national security trajectories.

One reason for these conflicting trajectories is Russia's increased assertiveness under Putin compared to his predecessor, Boris Yeltsin. Russia's improved economy and stronger state under Putin have restored the self-confidence of its political and military leadership. In contrast to the 1990s, when Russia lurched from one economic setback to another, this century has witnessed steady economic growth based primarily on energy resources. In turn this economic growth has helped Putin to convert the already powerful office of president of Russia into a hyper-powered executive position capable of controlling regional governments and imposing central discipline on the decision making process in Moscow.

Putin's style of management has taken advantage of these and other fortuitous economic and political circumstances in order to advance his objectives. In particular the "power ministries" of military, security, and law enforcement have gained influence under Putin, and they are seeded with former *siloviki*, including members of Putin's former St. Petersburg "mafia" during his years in the former Soviet KGB. The power ministers, in turn, are interlocked with financial interests or operate as virtual financial oligarchs in their own right.[5] With cronies in the power ministries as a permanent coercive base, Putin has solidified his grip on Russia as a modernizing autocrat with enough self-confidence to dictate his choice of presidential successor in 2008 (while assuming the position of prime minister with a possible return to the presidency in 2013).

Other reasons for Putin's assertiveness with regard to U.S national security policy have to do with the views of Russia's leadership about trends in international politics related to security issues. Putin regards the United States as unacceptably dominant in global relations to the exclusion of other powers' interests and concerns, including those of Russia. The Russian president surprised attendees at the Munich security conference in February 2007, when he complained that the world was now unipolar: "One single center of power. One single center of decision making. This is the world of one master, one sovereign."[6]

Putin's pique over unipolarity was a generalized indictment, but it was also motivated by certain specific issues. Among these specific stimuli of Russian security angst was the United States' announced plan to deploy components of a missile defense system in Poland and in the Czech Republic. Another contentious issue was the apparently open-ended nature of NATO enlargement, including the possible extension of membership offers to Ukraine and Georgia. Even if they failed to fulfill the requirements for NATO membership, Ukraine and Georgia were seen by the Kremlin as cockpits of Western meddling in Russia's "near abroad" and former Soviet security space in order to promote democracy—Western style.

Following his philippic at Munich, over the next several months Putin was most specific about his missile defense complaints. Russia has, of course, viewed the George W. Bush administration plans and actions with regard to nationwide ballistic missile defense with wariness from the beginning of Bush's presidency. The Bush administration abrogated U.S. commitment to the ABM Treaty of 1972, a cornerstone of U.S.-Soviet nuclear arms control during the Cold War, and the United States began deployment of a limited nationwide BMD system in 2004 and has plans to expand it. Those plans apparently now include deployments of BMD interceptors in Poland and radars in the Czech Republic. Putin, addressing a Moscow meeting on October 12, 2007, with U.S. Secretary of State Condoleezza Rice and Secretary of Defense Robert Gates, appeared almost scornful in his appraisal of U.S. missile defense plans and in his warning that American perseverance would have diplomatic costs in Russia: "Of course we can sometime in the future decide that some anti-missile defense system should be established somewhere on the moon. But before we reach such arrangements we will lose the opportunity for fixing some particular arrangements between us."[7]

Putin's reactions have been hot and cold with respect to the possibility of U.S.-Russian cooperation on the issue of missile defense. A number of presidential and other official Russian statements about U.S. missile defenses during the spring of 2007 were emphatically negative.[8] Military experts specifically emphasized the determination of Russian weapons designers to produce new versions of offensive missiles or reentry vehicles that could circumvent any antimissile defenses that the United States chose to deploy.[9] On the other hand, Putin surprised Bush at the G8 meetings in Germany in June 2007 by offering to cooperate in building a joint BMD system with Russian-leased components in Azerbaijan.[10] The Russian president expanded and modified his plans for cooperative U.S.-Russian and NATO-Russian BMD deployments over the next several months, including his favorable presentation of this idea at the Kennebunkport summit in July.[11]

Some of Putin's posturing about missile defense could be contributory to his self-positioning in the spring and summer of 2007 for parliamentary elections later in the same year and the presidential election in the spring of 2008. Putin's high-profile nationalism and portrayal of a muscular Russianism (including his own chest-exposed photo shoots) play well with Russian voters, who already accord him on the order of a 70 percent approval rating. On the other hand, not all of Putin's objections to U.S. missile defenses deployed in Europe are motivated by domestic political consumption. The United States' missile defenses in Europe resonate unfavorably in Russia because they are linked to other issues, including NATO enlargement and revision of the CFE Treaty. The latter agreement dates from the Cold War and required amendments to adjust to the post-Soviet world, but Russia and NATO have disagreed about the timing of their compliance with the amended conditions. Putin temporarily suspended Russian compliance with the treaty in July 2007 pending resolution of some of Russia's complaints about the amended pact, using planned U.S. BMD deployments in Europe as the justification.

In reality CFE is a corpse rotting in the parlor, awaiting a decent burial on account of its obsolescence. There is a more serious connection between U.S. missile defenses in Europe and NATO enlargement, about which post-Soviet Russia feels betrayed. Former Soviet president Mikhail Gorbachev was persuaded during the George H. W. Bush administration to acquiesce to the unification of Germany along with German membership in NATO as part of the way station toward a peaceful end to the Cold War. In turn the Soviet Union claims to have received verbal assurances from the United States that NATO would not enlarge its membership eastward. Obviously this pledge, if made, has not been fulfilled: NATO enlargement since the end of the Cold War has been a steady movement of commitments and capabilities closer to the Russian border. The original NATO of sixteen nations now incorporates some twenty-six members and, under its various partnership programs, could conceivably extend its membership farther into former Soviet security space.

In principle if Russia and the United States are no longer ideological enemies, as were the United States and the Soviet Union, then the enlargement of NATO virtually to the border of Russia (actually, to the border if Kaliningrad is taken into account) should provoke no consternation from Russians. In international relations, apart from textbooks, principle must also take into account power relationships. NATO enlargement reflects the reality that states and alliances do what they can get away with. Under President Bill Clinton and President George W. Bush, NATO enlargement represents for the West a validation of its vision for a Europe from the Atlantic to the Urals that is democratic and based on market economics. For Russia such a Europe poses issues of power as well as principle, and the power equation is not necessarily favorable.

Despite the ups and downs of its economy since the end of the Cold War, Russia aspires to great-power status. Its geographical span across the breadth of Eurasia and its long borders also create enormous challenges for its international and domestic security. Russian and Soviet history teach hard lessons about the vulnerability of Russia's western borders to invaders across the centuries, including marquee performers such as Charles XII of Sweden, Napoleon Bonaparte, and the German Wehrmacht. Russia's history can be used tendentiously by its hawks and unrequited military troglodytes, of course. NATO has no plan and no intention to invade Russia. That, however, is beside the point. Russia does not fear a premeditated NATO attack. Rather, it fears the comparative obsolescence of its standing as a military great power, especially in Europe. A Russia that is not feared in Europe, or at least respected for its military power and potential, may not be loved either.

In present circumstances this places the question of nuclear arms control with respect to Russia in a position of some delicacy. Russia's conventional military forces are inferior to those of NATO in size and in capability, especially in the information-led domains of C4ISR and long-range precision strike. Therefore, Russian political leaders and defense experts feel that they need to maintain a nuclear force essentially equivalent to that of the United States—although they disagree about exactly what "equivalent" means. Some would be satisfied with any force that provided for assured retaliation: a second-strike capability inflicting unacceptable societal damage after any enemy surprise attack. Others would prefer not only an assured retaliation capability for deterrence but also a more versatile and adaptive force that could engage in limited and selective attacks.[12] Russian military doctrine reportedly envisions the possible use of operational and tactical nuclear weapons in order to reestablish escalation dominance and escalation control in a conventional war within Russian state territory or near its borders and posing a strategic threat to Russia.

Russia's conventional inferiority relative to NATO and its reliance on nuclear weapons for major power status contribute to the definition of sufficiency in strategic nuclear forces. Russia no longer requires, as the Soviet Union sought to do, military-strategic parity with the United States across the entire spectrum of nuclear weapons and delivery systems. In addition, the U.S.-Russian political relationship is one in which neither state anticipates the onset of a major war involving the use of nuclear weapons against the state territory of the other. Sufficiency for Russia therefore lies in the direction of fewer rather than more weapons compared to the highly competitive deployments of the Cold War years.

Russia's political relationship with NATO is also different from that of the Soviet Union during the Cold War. NATO has expanded its membership since the end of the Cold War, but a larger membership is a mixed political and military blessing. Since the alliance works by consensus, obtaining shared agreement on policy and strategy becomes more complicated as the number of members expands. One could observe this process at work during NATO's deliberations on whether to use force to compel Serbia to withdraw its forces from Kosovo in 1999. The complexity of NATO's decision-making process caused problems in defining its political objective and other difficulties in carrying out military missions. As to the latter, the definition and approval of air-strike packages and targets became overly complicated. Too many cooks delayed completion of the menu in good time. As a result a more streamlined process was adopted which disallowed delaying tactics or vetoes for most states whose forces were not directly involved. The complexity of NATO's decision making on Kosovo also embroiled relations between the supreme allied commander, Gen. Wesley Clark, located in Brussels, and the Pentagon. Both the secretary of defense and the chairman of the Joint Chiefs of Staff (JCS) were at loggerheads with General Clark over a variety of issues; in fact, at one point the JSC chairman ordered Clark to stop appearing on television.

Thus a geographically expanded NATO is not necessarily a more threatening NATO relative to Russia. American and allied NATO policy planners during the Cold War worried about whether a consensus could be obtained for nuclear first use under the conditions of a conventional force attack by the Soviets and Warsaw Pact allies that was going unfavorably for NATO. Under current conditions NATO is less dependent on nuclear first use during any conflict in Europe than it would have been during the Cold War. The obtaining of any consensus for nuclear first use would be even harder now than then. In fact, NATO might have difficulty obtaining consensus behind a "second use" of nuclear weapons if the situation of first use were one of ambiguous political ownership or confused military circumstances.[13]

The preceding summary of political and military circumstances between the West and Russia leads to an important conclusion about the role of U.S. and Russian nuclear weapons in the new world order. They are less likely to serve credibly as weapons of military utility, even for deterrence, as opposed to symbols of great-power status and as claim checks for the right to participate in high-end diplomacy within or outside of Europe. If that conclusion is warranted, then analysts might usefully take the next step and ask whether both Russia and the United States could meet their national security requirements for the nuclear deterrence mission with significantly fewer weapons than those permitted under the Moscow Treaty of 2002. The analysis presented in the next section offers a partial answer to the question whether a below-SORT strategic condominium could suffice for Russia and the United States.

Methodology

In this section two below-SORT forces for Russia and for the United States are hypothesized and then statistically interrogated. In the first case each state is assigned a triad of land-based missiles, sea-based missiles, and bombers within an upper limit of 1,000 operationally deployed strategic nuclear warheads. This force will stand in as a candidate "minimum deterrent" force. In the second case Russia and the United States will each be assigned a triad of forces within the lower limit of 500 operationally deployed warheads. The second level will represent a "micro deterrent" force. For each state decisions about future deployments are notional and not necessarily predictive of actual deployments. Nevertheless, judgments put forward here are "in the ballpark" with respect to political and military feasibility and past experience.[14]

The strategy of analysis proceeds in three phases. First, the numbers of surviving and retaliating second-strike warheads for Russia and for the United States are calculated for each force size. These calculations are made for each of four different force structures for the United States and Russia. The various U.S. forces are (1) a balanced triad of land-based, sea-based, and air-delivered weapons, (2) a dyad without ICBMs, (3) a dyad without bombers, and (4) a force composed entirely of SLBMs. For Russia the optional force structures include (1) a balanced triad of land- and sea-based missiles and bombers, (2) a dyad without bombers, (3) a dyad without SLBMs, and (4) a force composed entirely of ICBMs.

In addition, the results of these nuclear exchanges are also modeled for each of four conditions of operational readiness and launch doctrine: (1) strategic nuclear forces are on generated alert and launched on warning of attack, (2) forces are on generated alert and ride out the attack before retaliating, (3) forces are on day-to-day alert and launched on warning, and (4) forces are on day-to-day alert and ride out the attack. In principle the numbers of surviving and retaliating warheads for each state should be maximized in the "generated alert, launch on warning" condition, minimized in the "day-to-day alert, ride out the attack" posture, and fall into an intermediate zone in either the "generated alert, riding out the attack" condition or in the "day-to-day alert, launch on warning" posture.

However, this principle does not always apply in practice, depending on the actual kinds of forces deployed and their performances relative to those of their opponents. It is also the case that Russian and U.S. forces might be in different operational conditions at the same phase of a nuclear crisis. Added to the complexity of the situation is that different arms of service have technical or other biases toward specific kinds of doctrines. For example, ballistic missiles forces have the advantage of promptness in delivery once launched, but they lack the flexibility of recall that bombers have. On the other hand, the ability of bomber forces to survive is highly dependent on early warning in order to scramble a survivable portion of the force. Survivable bombers are flexible and can deliver a variety of munitions: gravity bombs, air-launched cruise missiles (ALCMs), and short-range attack missiles (SRAMs). Ballistic missile submarines are highly survivable and flexible in their deployments, but communications with the submarines under anything approaching wartime conditions pose many uncertainties.

U.S. nuclear declaratory policy for most of the Cold War was that of second-strike retaliation. Thus the canonical analyses of nuclear attacks assumed a U.S. "generated alert, riding out the attack" posture during a crisis or war with the Soviet Union. American analysts and government officials did not agree about the Soviets' proclivities in this regard. The Soviets were usually thought to be dependent on "launch on warning" for their ICBM force, but their proclivities for operating other arms of service were less remarked upon. Some experts questioned whether either the Cold War United States or the Soviet Union could really have waited to ride out a nuclear first strike by the other and then retaliate—on account of the vulnerability of the two states' nuclear command and control systems.[15]

Some readers may ask at this point, Why go through this analysis when your object is to get past the self-referential logic of deterrence by past practice and into a more disarmed, and less dangerous, nuclear world? It's a fair question, and the answer requires specification.

First, it is important to work through the data, imperfect as they are, because we have (thankfully) only models of two-sided nuclear wars. One does this for the same reason that officers and planners throughout history have studied maps, conducted staff rides and mock battles, and gathered "on-the-ground" intelligence prior to war. One does what one can. Especially in the case of nuclear war, the object is to avoid war by convincing prospective opponents of its suicidal and self-defeating nature. However, this is not automatically accomplished. Leaders are not all risk averse, and military briefers can have their own institutional or professional agendas (for example, a bias toward preemption in order to safeguard military capability).

A second reason to go through the pertinent numbers is to acknowledge their limitations as much as their significance. Nuclear wars are virtual wars, and therefore the outcomes of models are virtual estimates about virtual wars. For that reason, humility in the face of the uncertainties attendant to the climate of war, as described by Clausewitz and others, is especially pertinent to the problem of foresight in nuclear war.[16] Moreover, although the uncertainties and imponderables attached to nuclear *war* are not necessarily the day-to-day preoccupations of defense ministries and military chiefs of staff, the issues related to nuclear *deterrence*, and to the *avoidance* of accidental or inadvertent nuclear war, are certainly so. Theorists can escape into their armchairs from this concern with the "what ifs" of deterrence and inadvertent nuclear war, but politicians and generals are required to look into the abyss—if only to get to a better place.

Third, if the Cold War demonstrated anything, it showed that nuclear arms control and disarmament are not accomplished in one grand gesture—as in, for example, universal adoption of the 1946 Baruch Plan for international control of nuclear materials. A step-by-step process of getting from the present to the future will require painstaking negotiations among governments and their respective general staffs. Nuclear arms reductions and progress in nonproliferation will have to go through this same process of one step, two steps. Getting to "no nukes" or virtually no nukes requires the careful building of consensus among nuclear armed states. Russia and the United States will have to lead before others will follow.

Data Analysis

Tables 1–3 summarize the data and findings for the Russian and U.S. 1,000-warhead forces. Table 5.1 shows the Russian and U.S. preattack forces. In table 5.2 the numbers of U.S. and Russian second-strike, retaliating warheads are summarized for each of four conditions of alertness and/or launch doctrine.[17]

Table 5.3 adds an additional dimension to the profile: ballistic missile defenses. In the simulation in table 5.3, each state is equipped with defenses capable of deflecting or destroying 50 percent of the other side's retaliating missile warheads. Defenses this good are not available now and may not be available for many years—if ever. Nevertheless, a notional 50 percent provides a conservative estimate against which pessimists can benchmark the performances of offensive retaliatory forces.

Tables 5.4–6 summarize the data and findings for the Russian and U.S. 500-warhead levels. Table 5.4 shows the Russian and U.S. prewar forces, table 5.5 summarizes the numbers of surviving and retaliating second-strike warheads by category of alertness and launch protocols, and table 5.6 shows the effect of defenses that intercept 50 percent of each side's retaliating second-strike warheads.

The tables suggest a number of findings. First, either the 1,000-warhead force or the 500-warhead force ("mini" or "micro") provides the United States and Russia with a number of surviving and retaliating warheads sufficient to inflict unacceptable societal damage on the attacker. For example, without

TABLE 5.1. TOTAL DEPLOYED STRATEGIC WEAPONS, 1,000 LIMIT

	BALANCED TRIAD	NO ICBMS	NO BOMBERS	ALL SLBMS
UNITED STATES				
ICBMs	300	0	300	0
SLBMs	392	686	686	980
Air	308	314	0	0

	BALANCED TRIAD	NO BOMBERS	NO SLBMS	ICBMS ONLY
RUSSIA				
ICBMs	440	530	470	980
SLBMs	264	456	0	0
Air	288	0	530	0

TABLE 5.2. SURVIVING AND RETALIATING WEAPONS, 1,000 LIMIT

	BALANCED TRIAD	NO ICBMS	NO BOMBERS	ALL SLBMS
UNITED STATES				
GEN-LOW	812	785	826	794
GEN-ROA	569	785	583	794
DAY-LOW	483	372	642	532
DAY-ROA	240	372	399	532

	BALANCED TRIAD	NO BOMBERS	NO SLBMS	ICBMS ONLY
RUSSIA				
GEN-LOW	820	846	809	882
GEN-ROA	504	458	469	210
DAY-LOW	439	551	423	882
DAY-ROA	61	85	42	88

TABLE 5.3. SURVIVING AND RETALIATING WEAPONS VS. DEFENSES, 1,000 LIMIT

	BALANCED TRIAD	NO ICBMS	NO BOMBERS	ALL SLBMS
UNITED STATES				
GEN-LOW	518	507	413	397
GEN-ROA	397	507	291	397
DAY-LOW	241	186	321	266
DAY-ROA	120	186	200	266

TABLE 5.3 *CONT.* SURVIVING AND RETALIATING WEAPONS VS. DEFENSES, 1,000 LIMIT

	Russia			
	BALANCED TRIAD	NO BOMBERS	NO SLBMs	ICBMs ONLY
GEN-LOW	515	423	598	441
GEN-ROA	357	229	428	105
DAY-LOW	219	275	212	441
DAY-ROA	30	42	21	44

TABLE 5.4. TOTAL DEPLOYED STRATEGIC WEAPONS, 500 LIMIT

	United States			
	BALANCED TRIAD	NO ICBMS	NO BOMBERS	ALL SLBMs
ICBMs	120	0	108	0
SLBMs	196	294	392	490
Air	184	204	0	0
	Russia			
	BALANCED TRIAD	NO BOMBERS	NO SLBMs	ICBMs ONLY
ICBMs	190	307	250	500
SLBMs	120	192	0	0
Air	180	0	250	0

TABLE 5.5. SURVIVING AND RETALIATING WEAPONS, 500 LIMIT

	United States			
	BALANCED TRIAD	NO ICBMS	NO BOMBERS	ALL SLBMs
GEN-LOW	401	387	415	397
GEN-ROA	304	387	327	397
DAY-LOW	214	160	310	266
DAY-ROA	117	160	222	266
	Russia			
	BALANCED TRIAD	NO BOMBERS	NO SLBMs	ICBMs ONLY
GEN-LOW	399	432	407	450
GEN-ROA	286	224	294	86
DAY-LOW	190	307	225	450
DAY-ROA	27	43	23	45

TABLE 5.6. SURVIVING AND RETALIATING WEAPONS VS. DEFENSES, 500 LIMIT

UNITED STATES				
	BALANCED TRIAD	No ICBMS	No BOMBERS	ALL SLBMs
GEN-LOW	268	268	207	198
GEN-ROA	219	268	164	198
DAY-LOW	107	80	155	133
DAY-ROA	59	80	111	133
RUSSIA				
	BALANCED TRIAD	No BOMBERS	No SLBMs	ICBMs ONLY
GEN-LOW	265	216	295	225
GEN-ROA	209	112	238	43
DAY-LOW	95	154	113	225
DAY-ROA	13	22	11	23

defenses for either state, U.S. 1,000-warhead preattack forces, with a balanced triad, provide for a maximum of 812 and a minimum of 240 surviving and arriving warheads; the comparable Russian 1,000-warhead force provides for a maximum of 820 and a minimum of 61 retaliators. For the U.S. 500-warhead force the range of surviving and retaliating warheads for a balanced triad force is from a high of 401 to a low of 117; for the Russian balanced triad force, it ranges from a high of 399 to a low of 27 warheads.

These findings require some additional interpretation, however. It would be unlikely that either Russia or the United States would be caught so unprepared by the outbreak of war following a nuclear crisis that their forces would be on day-to-day alert and riding out the attack (although the case must be included for benchmark purposes). More likely would be the condition in which both states' forces were on generated alert and either launched on warning or after riding out a first strike. In either instance, only the Russian "ICBMs only" force structure, and within the lower deployment ceiling of 500 warheads, provides fewer than *several hundred* surviving and retaliating warheads.

Second, when defenses are added to the equation, the fundamentals do not change but some marginal effects are apparent. Defenses equally capable of intercept do not necessarily have symmetrical consequences for the two states. Russia's retaliatory performance under conditions of day-to-day alert and riding out the attack, against U.S. defenses, results in a range of surviving and retaliating warheads from a high of 44 to a low of 21 (for the 1,000-warhead force) or a range from a high of 23 to a low of 11 warheads (for the 500-warhead force). Thus both Russia's "mini" and "micro" forces are threatened asymmetrically in this posture, increasing the pressure on Russian planners for hair-trigger responses if forced to deal with a crisis on this basis. Admittedly, this is a worst case, but Russia may be more concerned to plan against this worst case than the United States on account of Russia's greater dependency on land-based missiles compared to the U.S. emphasis on more survivable submarine-launched ballistic missiles.

Third, the "big picture" with or without defenses is this. Micro and mini U.S. and Russian forces are possible and adequate to the narrow mission of nuclear deterrence and the broader mission of nuclear suasion. However, it should not be assumed that the controlling of U.S.-Russian "vertical" proliferation and the reduction of their deployed strategic nuclear forces to mini or micro forces will necessarily constrain "horizontal" proliferation in the form of new nuclear weapons states. A great deal else must be done to prevent other states from joining the nuclear club, including a global effort to secure and/or destroy existing stockpiles of fissile materials, strengthening the nuclear NPT and its inspection regime, and minimizing the "drivers" that might interest nonnuclear states in going nuclear. These drivers include the expectation that nuclear weapons will bring security, enhance prestige, promote science and technology, and create favorable coalitions in domestic politics.[18]

Conclusions and Thinking Outside the Box

The United States and Russia could reduce their deployed strategic nuclear warheads substantially below the Moscow Treaty limits without compromising their deterrent credibility. Either a mini or a micro force could suffice, especially if international nuclear life were only a two-way nuclear street. Unfortunately it is not. Other nuclear powers exist and more may be in the offing over the next decade or so. Therefore, putting Moscow and Washington on a diet, with respect to nuclear weapons and long-range delivery systems, is a necessary but insufficient condition for success in nonproliferation.

Furthermore, sub-SORT reductions in Russian and U.S. strategic nuclear forces, especially below the level of "mini" forces, will require restraint on the part of other existing powers. The United States and Russia will be reluctant to cross the threshold from 1,000-warhead to 500-warhead forces because both value their nuclear superiority relative to third parties. And Russia in turn values the symbolism and prestige of its nuclear successor status with regard to the former Soviet Union. Thus restraint in the growth of other nuclear forces, and perhaps even reductions, will be required. China presents an important unknown in this regard.

Missile defenses excited Vladimir Putin in 2007 and have caused Russians (and Soviets) considerable angina in the past. But missile defense technology is still on the nursery slopes of military maturity relative to the tasks expected of it. It will be decades before missile defenses capable of intercepting and destroying massive attacks of many hundreds of weapons (or more) can be deployed. More feasible are limited national or theater missile defenses that can deter or defeat light attacks (tens of weapons or fewer) from rogue states or powers with small nuclear arsenals.

For the United States and Russia, therefore, missile defenses should not be a "war stopper" for further reductions in offensive nuclear weapons. In fact, under the right political conditions (politics rules, as Clausewitz emphasized!), limited BMD could support a defense-protected build-down of American and Russian long-range, offensive nuclear weapons. Mutual defense deployments might require some scientific and military cooperation between the two sides, but so what? There are few if any technological mysteries nowadays that do not soon migrate from the source of origin to potential competitors. Another Manhattan Project, in terms of prolonged secrecy, defies gravity in the Internet and information age.

There is something to be said for innovative thinking about arms control structures that might also contribute to nonproliferation by encouraging tighter linkage between vertical and horizontal disarmament. One possibility would be a U.S.-Russian Security Plan for Arms Control and Non-proliferation (SPAN) worked out collaboratively by their respective defense and foreign ministries. The two states could develop a specific shared agenda for nuclear arms reductions and nonproliferation initiatives, together with action plans for implementation and pertinent timetables. SPAN could also serve as a Russian and U.S.-sponsored leadership forum for international consultation and education about the most important issues having to do with the nuclear arms race.

In addition, and thinking more expansively, Russia, the United States, and NATO could also collaborate on a "northern alliance for nuclear restraint" that encouraged arms reductions and nonproliferation. Under this umbrella of government and government-supported private initiatives, additional research would be sponsored on topics such as nonproliferation, arms control, environmental issues related to nuclear weapons and peaceful uses of nuclear energy, and pacific settlement of disputes involving at least one nuclear armed state. The same governments could also support research and development toward the discovery of new nonnuclear weapons, including those for long-range precision strike, which could substitute for nuclear weapons. Disconnecting nuclear weapons from logical missions, or at least making nuclear weapons less than optimal for those missions compared to alternatives, would encourage the view that military status and respect lie in avoiding rather than embracing nuclear forces for security.

Chapter 6

Nuclear Proliferation in Asia: Risks and Opportunities

The potential spread of nuclear weapons among states in Asia is a major threat to regional and global peace and security in the twenty-first century. Nuclear proliferation in Asia not only raises the probability and cost of wars among states but also invites nuclear hand-offs to terrorists or other nonstate actors with grievances aplenty and bad manners. In addition, nuclear turbulence in Asia is a back door to the reawakening of instability in Europe, otherwise politically and militarily stable.

In this chapter I put forward a "thought experiment" about a possible but not inevitable nuclear future in Asia. I project to the year 2020 or shortly thereafter. Are deterrence stability, crisis stability, and arms race stability even conceivable, let alone possible, in a multipolar nuclear Asia? The political context of an Asian nuclear arms race is obviously different from the political context that surrounded U.S.-Soviet competition throughout the Cold War. The consequences of variations in the performances of various forces may be more significant for crisis and arms race stability in an eight-sided arms competition compared to the two-way street of the Cold War.

Policy Problems and Issues

U. S. policy has been to support the nuclear Non-Proliferation Treaty requiring nonnuclear state subscribers to the treaty to abjure the option of nuclear weapons. Nonnuclear states have, under the NPT, the right to develop a complete nuclear fuel cycle for peaceful purposes (generating electricity, for example). States adhering to the NPT are required to make available their facilities and infrastructure for scheduled or challenge inspections by the International Atomic Energy Agency (IAEA). The IAEA has a mixed track record; depending on the cooperation or resistance of the regime in question, inspectors may obtain an accurate roadmap of a country's nuclear program or be misled. In Iraq, for example, regular IAEA inspections prior to 1991 failed to detect the complete size and character of Saddam Hussein's efforts to develop nuclear weapons.

U.S. intelligence has also performed erratically in ascertaining the extent of WMD, including nuclear, activities in potential proliferators. The CIA assured President Bush and his advisors that the presence of large quantities of WMD in Iraq in 2003 was a "slam dunk," but no WMD were found by inspectors after the completion of Operation Iraqi Freedom and the ousting of Hussein from power. The CIA apparently was taken by surprise in 1998 by the Indian and Pakistani near-simultaneous detonations of nuclear weapons followed by announcements in New Delhi and Islamabad that each was now an acknowledged nuclear power. The U.S. government signed an agreement with North Korea in 1994 freezing its nuclear development programs, but in 2002 North Korea unexpectedly denounced the agreement, admitted it had been cheating, and marched into the ranks of nuclear powers.

The difficulties in containing the spread of nuclear weapons and delivery systems are only compounded by the possibility that materials or technology could find its way into the hands of terrorists—to deadly effect. Reportedly al-Qaeda has tried to obtain weapons-grade material (enriched uranium and plutonium) and assistance in assembling both true nuclear weapons and radiological bombs (conventional explosives that scatter radioactive debris). Nuclear weapons are in a class by themselves as weapons of "mass destruction"; a miniature nuclear weapon exploded in an urban area could cause much more death and destruction that either biological or chemical weapons similarly located.

In addition to the plausible interest of terrorists in nuclear weapons, there is also the disconcerting evidence of nuclear entrepreneurship resulting in proliferation. The A. Q. Khan network (revolving around the scientist who was the prime mover behind Pakistan's nuclear weapons program) of Pakistani and other government officials, middlemen, scientists, and nondescripts trafficked for several decades in nuclear technology and know-how. The Khan network, described as a Wal-Mart of nuclear proliferation, apparently reached out and touched North Korea, Libya, and Iran, among others.[1] States seeking a nuclear start-up can save enormous time and money by turning to experts in and out of government for help, and the knowledge how to fabricate nuclear weapons is no longer as esoteric as it was in the early days the atomic age.

In response to 9/11 and to the possible failure of nuclear containment in Asia and the Middle East, the Bush administration has sought to reinforce traditional nonproliferation with an interest in preemptive attack strategies and missile defenses. U.S. superiority in long-range, precision weapons makes preemption technically feasible provided the appropriate targets have been identified. U.S. policy guidance apparently also allows for the possible use of nuclear weapons in preemptive attack against hostile states close to acquiring their own nuclear arsenals.[2] Missile defenses are further behind the curve compared to deep strike, but the first U.S. national missile defense deployments took place in 2004 under the Bush administration commitment to deploy defenses based on several technologies against rogue state or terrorist attacks. Preemption strategies and defenses are controversial in their own right.[3] For present purposes, however, they are simply talismans of U.S. government awareness and acknowledgment that containment and deterrence can no longer complete the antiproliferation toolkit.

Uncertainty about the rate of nuclear weapons spread in future Asia is in contrast to the comparative stability of the Cold War experience. During the Cold War nuclear weapons spread from state to state at a slower rate than pessimists projected. In part this was due to the bipolar character of the international system and nuclear preeminence of the Soviet Union and the United States over other contenders. Both superpowers discouraged horizontal proliferation among other state actors, even as they engaged in vertical proliferation by creating larger and more technically advanced arsenals. In addition, the NPT and the regime it established contributed to limitation in the rate of nuclear weapons spread among states that might otherwise have gone nuclear.[4]

The end of the Cold War and the demise of the Soviet Union have moved the zone of political uncertainty, and the interest in WMD and missiles, eastward across the Middle East, South Asia, and the Pacific basin.[5] The states of North America and Western Europe, pacified or at least debellicized by an expanded NATO and a downsized Russia, regard nuclear weapons as dated remnants of the age of mass destruction. The most recent revolution in military affairs has created a new hierarchy of powers based on the application of knowledge and information to military art.[6] Nuclear and other WMD are, from the standpoint of postmodern Westerners, the military equivalent of museum pieces, although they are still dangerous in the wrong hands.

On the other hand, major states in Asia, and in the Middle East within the range of long-range missiles based in Asia, see nuclear weapons and ballistic missiles as potential trumps. The appeal of nuclear weapons and delivery systems for these states is at least threefold. First, they enable "denial of access" strategies for foreign powers who might want to interfere in regional issues. U.S. military success in Afghanistan in 2001 and in Iraq in 2003 only reinforced this rationale of access denial via WMD for aspiring regional hegemons or nervous dictators. Second, nuclear weapons might permit some states to coerce others who lack countermeasures in the form of deterrence. Israel's nuclear weapons, not officially acknowledged but widely known, have appealed to Tel Aviv as a deterrent against provocative behavior by Arab neighbors and as a possible "Samson" option on the cusp of military defeat leading to regime change.

Third, nuclear weapons permit states lacking the resources for advanced technology, conventional military systems to stay in the game of declared major powers. Russia is the most obvious example of this syndrome. Without her nuclear arsenal, Russia would be vulnerable to nuclear blackmail, or even to conventional military aggression, from a variety of strategic directions. Russia's holdover deterrent from the Cold War, assuming eventual modernization, guarantees Moscow military respect in Europe and makes its neighbors in Asia more circumspect.

North Korea is another example of a state whose reputation and regard are enhanced by its possible deployment of nuclear weapons and potential deployment of long-range ballistic missiles. Absent a nuclear capability, North Korea is a politically isolated outlaw state with a bankrupt economy that would receive almost no international respect. But as an apparent nuclear power, North Korea has played nuclear poker with a five-nation coalition attempting to disarm its program by peaceful means: the United States, Russia, Japan, China, and South Korea.

In an agreement signed with those five powers in February 2007, North Korea promised to shut down within sixty days its nuclear reactor at Yongbyon and to admit international inspectors into the DPRK to verify compliance. For taking this step North Korea was to receive an emergency shipment of fuel oil from the United States, Russia, China, and South Korea. The first phase of this pact thus froze the North Korean plutonium-based weapons program but left for future discussions its suspended uranium-enrichment program. In September 2007 North Korea agreed to declare and disable all of its nuclear programs by the end of calendar year 2007.[7]

Failure to contain proliferation in Pyongyang could spread nuclear fever throughout Asia. Japan and South Korea might seek nuclear weapons and missile defenses. A pentagonal configuration of nuclear powers in the Pacific basin (Russia, China, Japan, and the two Koreas—not including the United States, with its own Pacific interests) could put deterrence at risk and create enormous temptation toward nuclear preemption. Apart from actual use or threat of use, North Korea could exploit the mere existence of an assumed nuclear capability in order to support is coercive diplomacy. As George H. Quester has noted:

> If the Pyongyang regime plays its cards sensibly and well, therefore, the world will not see its nuclear weapons being used against Japan or South Korea or anyone else, but will rather see this new nuclear

arsenal held in reserve (just as the putative Israeli nuclear arsenal has been held in reserve), as a deterrent against the outside world's applying maximal pressure on Pyongyang and as a bargaining chip to extract the economic and political concessions that the DPRK needs if it wishes to avoid giving up its peculiar approach to social engineering.[8]

A five-sided nuclear competition in the Pacific would be linked, in geopolitical deterrence and proliferation space, to the existing nuclear deterrents of India and Pakistan and to the emerging nuclear weapons status of Iran. An arc of nuclear instability from Tehran to Tokyo could place U.S. proliferation strategies into the ash heap of history and call for more drastic military options, not excluding preemptive war, defenses, and counterdeterrent special operations. In addition, an eight-sided nuclear arms race in Asia would increase the likelihood of accidental or inadvertent nuclear war because (1) some of these states already have histories of protracted conflict; (2) states may have politically unreliable or immature command and control systems, especially during a crisis involving a decision for nuclear first strike or retaliation (unreliable or immature systems might permit a technical malfunction that caused an unintended launch or a deliberate but unauthorized launch by rogue commanders); and (3) faulty intelligence and warning systems might cause one side to misinterpret the other's defensive moves to forestall attack as offensive preparations for attack, thus triggering a mistaken preemption.

Thus far I have discussed the problem of an Asian nuclear arms race as an abstract, albeit sufficiently alarming, problem. In the sections to follow, I want to pin down the concept by detailed interrogation of one hypothetical scenario: an eight-sided nuclear polygon of force structures and therefore of probable operational performances in deterrence, in crisis management, and, if necessary, in war.

Comparative Deployments and Outcomes

What would a nuclear arms race in Asia look like after the second decade of the present century? If proliferation in Asia is successfully contained or rolled back by politics or by war, speculation becomes irrelevant. Therefore we will assume a more pessimistic future: Proliferation is not contained. The second or third decade of the twenty-first century witnesses an eight-sided nuclear club: Russia, China, Japan, North Korea, South Korea, India, Pakistan, and Iran. Although proliferation is not contained under this set of assumptions, it does not automatically result in war. The assumption that nuclear weapons can spread among

these states without war will be questioned by some, and with some justification. For example, the United States has declared that an Iranian or a North
Korean nuclear capability is presently unacceptable; the former must be pre-
vented and the latter must be rolled back. And some experts would surely argue
that China would never accept a Japan armed with nuclear weapons.

On the other hand, the rollback of North Korea's nuclear program is not a
certainty; a complicated international bargaining process may leave the DPRK
as a standing nuclear power with a tradeoff including more glasnost on the part
of the regime, a willingness on the part of Pyongyang to adhere to some international arms control agreements, and economic assistance from the United
States and other powers to help rebuild North Korea's moribund economy. As
for the Iranian nuclear case, both Israel and the United States have obliquely
threatened preemption (presumably with conventional weapons) against Iran's
nuclear infrastructure and against any nuclear-capable military forces. But the
costs of carrying out the threat of preemption against Iran must be factored
into the equation. Iran is a large state and cannot be conquered and occupied
by outside powers, unlike Iraq. Iran could therefore reconstitute any destroyed
nuclear power plants or other infrastructure. An additional consideration is
political. An Israeli preemption against Iran becomes a recruitment poster for
another holy war by jihadists against Israel. Iran has been one of the major
sponsors of Hezbollah and other groups that have carried out past terror attacks
in Palestine. An Israeli preemption against Tehran might reignite the intifada
or otherwise destabilize the peace process headed toward political devolution
and Palestinian self-rule.

The point is that many uncertainties loom, and the exclusion of any specific candidate state from the future nuclear club is not automatic. Therefore
we will include all eight in the analysis and assign to them notional forces. As
a benchmark we assume that the older and newer nuclear forces are deployed
within an agreed limit comparable to the agreed ceilings of the Moscow Treaty
between the United States and Russia: a ceiling of 2,200 warheads on launchers of "strategic" or intercontinental range with freedom to mix various types
of launch platforms among land-based, sea-based, and air-launched weapons.
Given the geography of the situation, however, it is not necessary for some states
to have missiles or aircraft of transcontinental range in order to inflict strategic, that is, catastrophic and decisive, damage on one or more adversaries. Thus
nuclear-capable missiles of intermediate or medium range, and bombers with
comparable combat radii, might qualify as strategic launchers, depending on
who is actually threatening, or shooting at, whom. For analytical purposes, we
will simply stipulate that "ICBM" or "bomber" could also include ballistic missile or fixed-wing aircraft of less-than-transcontinental range. (Cruise missiles

are omitted from this analysis for purposes of simplification, but the reader should be alerted that as cruise missiles become smarter, stealthier, and more widely available, they could be a preferred weapon for some states if capped with nuclear charges compared to ballistic missiles.)

States in the analysis include Russia, China, India, Pakistan, North Korea, South Korea, and Japan.[9] Some might object to the inclusion of Japan, whose current policy abjures any nuclear weapons capability. However, unless North Korea's nuclear arsenal is verifiably dismantled, incentives for South Korea or Japan to go nuclear increase, especially if North Korea deploys additional ballistic missiles of longer range.

Table 6.1 summarizes the forces deployed and available to the various state parties, under the agreed (formal or tacit) ceiling of 2,200 warheads.[10] Each nation would have to plan for the likelihood that only a portion of its forces would survive a nuclear first strike, retaliate, and arrive at their assigned targets. The relationship between each state's initially deployed forces and its survivable and retaliating forces is summarized in table 6.2. In addition, the numbers of surviving and retaliating warheads are grouped by the alert status and launch doctrines for each military. Forces may be on either of two alert statuses (generated or day alert), and they may be planning for prompt or delayed launch after attack.

Several findings of significance are already apparent, and some are counterintuitive for advocates of nonproliferation. From the standpoint of deterrence stability, there is no clear metric by which one can say that "so many additional nuclear powers equate to such-and-such a decline in deterrence." First, it is not impossible for a many-sided nuclear rivalry, even one as regionally robust as this case is, to be stable. Provided it has the resources and the technical know-how to do so, each state could deploy sufficient numbers of "first-strike survivable" forces to guarantee the "minimum deterrent" mission and perhaps the "assured destruction" mission as well.

TABLE 6.1. TOTAL DEPLOYED STRATEGIC WEAPONS, ASIA, 2,200 LIMIT

	RUSSIA	JAPAN	PRC	DPRK	ROK	INDIA	PAKISTAN	IRAN
Land-based weapons	1,300	50	510	250	200	500	250	390
Sea-based weapons	288	240	288	48	32	224	64	192
Air-delivered weapons	492	280	280	192	304	350	144	220

TABLE 6.2. SURVIVING AND RETALIATING WEAPONS, ASIA, 2,200 LIMIT

	RUSSIA	JAPAN	PRC	DPRK	ROK	INDIA	PAKISTAN	IRAN
GEN-LOW	1,762	444	896	404	410	842	382	667
GEN-ROA	709	403	483	201	264	477	179	392
DAY-LOW	1,326	175	615	251	167	441	235	382
DAY-ROA	273	135	202	49	19	59	28	51

Both "minimum deterrence" and "assured destruction" are terms of art that overlap in practice. Assured destruction (or assured retaliation) forces are second-strike forces sufficient under all conditions of attack to inflict "unacceptable" societal damage. Unacceptable varies with the recipient of the damage and depends on cultural values and political priorities. But it would be safe to assume that the decapitation of the regime and the loss of at least 25 percent of its population and/or half its industrial base would satisfy the requirements of assured destruction for "rational" attackers (defining "rationality" is a separate problem; see below).

Minimum deterrence is a standard presumably less ambitious than assured destruction: It requires only that the defender inflict costs on the attacker that would create enough pain to make the gamble of an attack insufficiently appealing. During the Cold War, for example, the French nuclear retaliatory forces were not sufficient by themselves to deter a Soviet attack on NATO, but they might have deterred nuclear blackmail against France separately by threatening Moscow with the prospect of "tearing an arm off," or destroying several Soviet cities.

To see the preceding arguments more clearly, let us compare the outcomes for two sets of operational assumptions. First, in table 6.3 we summarize the performances of each state's forces under the most favorable operational conditions: The retaliator has forces on generated alert and decides in favor of prompt launch. This maximum condition for each state's forces is compared to the minimum condition of alertness and launch readiness, summarized in table 6.4.

Some of the states' forces perform more effectively than others do. Much depends on force mix as well as alertness and launch protocols. States more dependent on land-based missiles in fixed basing modes as opposed to submarines and bombers will find themselves more dependent on prompt as opposed to delayed launch for survivability. And bombers are not nearly as assuredly survivable as submarines. On the other hand the complexity of operating sub-

TABLE 6.3. MAXIMUM RETALIATION, GEN-LOW, 2,200 LIMIT

	RUSSIA	JAPAN	PRC	DPRK	ROK	INDIA	PAKISTAN	IRAN
Land-based weapons	1,170	45	459	225	162	405	225	351
Sea-based weapons	233	194	233	39	26	181	52	156
Air-delivered weapons	359	204	204	140	222	255	105	160

TABLE 6.4. MINIMUM OR ASSURED RETALIATION, DAY-ROA, 2,200 LIMIT

	RUSSIA	JAPAN	PRC	DPRK	ROK	INDIA	PAKISTAN	IRAN
Land-based weapons	117	5	46	23	16	41	23	35
Sea-based weapons	156	130	156	26	3	18	5	16
Air-delivered weapons	0	0	0	0	0	0	0	0

marine missile forces is daunting; ballistic missile firing submarines require advanced construction techniques, sophisticated command-control systems, and highly educated officers and enlisted personnel. Political reliability is also necessary. Submarine forces cause problems for dictatorships because once at sea, captains and crews can resist micromanagement better than land-based forces can. The Soviet Union attempted to solve this problem during the Cold War by assigning special political officers to each boat, watching over the political reliability of the captain and crew and having to acquiesce to any orders that required other than routine business.

Nor should the complexity of operating bombers as nuclear retaliatory forces be underestimated. Bombers have the advantage that they can be scrambled, or even launched, to signal firm intent but then recalled short of attack. They are less first-strike survivable than submarines, but more so than silo-based missiles. Bombers also have men in the loop who have considerable discretion once they are in flight and en route to "fail-safe" points prior to final attack confirmation. Bombers would probably exist in so many varieties among the various states that no single standard of readiness, flight training, or technological performance would serve as an adequate basis for deterrence planning. A number of states included in our analysis might still rely on tactical fighter-bombers instead of "true" special-purpose strategic bombers for the delivery of nuclear munitions by air-to-ground missiles or gravity bombs. As "slow flyers" compared to missiles, bombers pose less of a threat of preemptive attack provided early warning is obtained (the quality of air defenses throughout the region and among our states of interest varies considerably).

The preceding discussion is only the tip of the iceberg, however. The stability of the Asian balance of terror rests more on the political intentions of the actors than it does on the characteristics of their forces. Their forces can support a policy of adventurism and brinkmanship or one of adherence to the political status quo and "live and let live," or a range of policies in between. In international systems terms stability is enhanced when the power of states favoring the status quo exceeds the power of states or other actors in favor of systemic overthrow. The "status quo" here refers to the existing number of major actors, their relative military and other power positions, and the polarities that create tension and possible conflicts among them. These matters can be unpredictable and surprising even for heads of state and military planners whose business it is to avoid systemic surprise. As an example, the process by which the July crisis of 1914 avoided diplomatic resolution and led the great powers into World War I involved preexisting alliance commitments, ill-considered diplomatic demarches, and inappropriate military plans highly dependent on rapid mobilization and deployment immediately prior to war. Leaders saw hasty mobilization as a deterrent, but overlapping mobilizations, combined with political alarms in late July and early August, created a vortex of suspicion that leaders seeking an "out" were unable to control.

Although the projection of past events into future scenarios is always perilous, something like the July 1914 crisis in Europe could erupt in Asia once nuclear weapons have been distributed among eight states and in numbers sufficient to tempt crisis-bound leaders. National, religious, or other cultural hatreds could be combined with the memory of past wrongs and the fear of preemptive attack. This could occur not only between dyads of states but between alliances, as it did on the eve of World War I. Coalitions might form among a nuclear-armed China, Pakistan, North Korea, and Iran—lined up against Russia, Japan, South Korea, and India. This would be an alignment of market democracies of various stripes against dictatorships or authoritarian regimes of sorts. Another possibility would be conflicts between dyads within or across democratic and dictatorial coalitions, such as rivalry between Japan and China, between the two Koreas, or between India and Pakistan. Russia might find itself in bilateral competition or conflict with China or with Japan. Iran might use its nuclear capability for coercion against U.S. allies such as Saudi Arabia or Israel, drawing American political commitments and military power directly into a regional crisis. And China might coerce or attack Taiwan with the same result.

Measuring Stability and Sensitivity

We noted previously that decisions for war or nuclear blackmail will probably be driven by political variables more than military ones. Nevertheless, even in the case of nuclear forces which are intended more for coercion than for actual use, it can matter a great deal how they are deployed, and operated, short of war. The deployments and operational modes for nuclear forces may seem as if they are "hard" or "objective" facts, and to some extent they are: whether weapons are to be land or sea based, how many warheads or reentry vehicles are carried by a particular missile, and so forth. On the other hand nuclear force deployments and operational characteristics also have subjective properties. Weapons, launchers, and command-control protocols "communicate" intentions with respect to the probable or possible behaviors of states and their leaders, intentions that might not be correctly interpreted or understood by other states. During a crisis in which one or more states contemplate the possibility of nuclear attack, countries will not only listen to one another's diplomatic statements but also watch what the other fellow is doing, including his military capabilities and maneuvers, for clues about his future behavior.

How could one estimate the delicacy or sensitivity of states' nuclear forces to the risk of a mistaken preemption or other hasty decision for nuclear war? One approach would be to compare the various states' survivable and retaliating warheads under the following exigent conditions: *prompt launch stability* under conditions of "generated" versus "day" alert and *generation stability* under conditions of prompt or delayed launch. In tables 6.5–8 we summarize the results of those comparisons.

Table 6.5 shows the differences among the states' performances in generation stability while riding out the attack (delayed launch) or in launching on warning (prompt launch). In table 6.6 the states' performances in prompt launch stability on day alert compared to generated alert are summarized. For example, in table 6.5 Russia's generation stability under conditions of delayed launch is 39 percent. In table 6.6 Russia's generation stability under prompt launch is 75 percent. The difference measures how much more Russia depends on prompt launch for survivability when its forces are not already on high alert.

Although the data summarized in tables 6.5–8 are based on notional forces only, they offer important insights about the kinds of systems states might deploy and their consequences. In order to make these insights clearer, we have

TABLE 6.5. GENERATION STABILITY, ROA, 2,200 LIMIT.

	RUSSIA		JAPAN		CHINA		NORTH KOREA		SOUTH KOREA		INDIA		PAKISTAN		IRAN	
	No defenses		No defenses		No defenses		No defenses		No defenses		No defenses		No defenses		No defenses	
	Russian forces		Japanese forces		PRC forces		DPRK forces		ROK forces		Indian forces		Pakistan forces		Iranian forces	
	DAY-ROA	GEN-ROA	DAY-ROA	GEN-ROA	DAY-ROA	GEN-ROA	DAY-ROA	GEN-ROA	DAY-ROA	GEN-ROA	DAY-ROA	GEN-ROA	DAY-ROA	GEN-ROA	DAY-ROA	GEN-ROA
Land-based weapons	117	117	5	5	46	46	23	23	16	16	41	41	23	23	35	76
Sea-based weapons	156	233	130	194	156	233	26	39	3	26	18	181	5	52	16	156
Air-delivered weapons	0	359	0	204	0	204	0	140	0	222	0	255	0	105	0	160
All	273	709	135	403	202	483	49	201	19	264	59	477	28	179	51	392
Stability	39%		33%		42%		24%		7%		12%		15%		13%	

TABLE 6.6. GENERATION STABILITY, LOW, 2,200 LIMIT.

	RUSSIA		JAPAN		CHINA		NORTH KOREA		SOUTH KOREA		INDIA		PAKISTAN		IRAN	
	No defenses		No defenses		No defenses		No defenses		No defenses		No defenses		No defenses		No defenses	
	Russian forces		Japanese forces		PRC forces		DPRK forces		ROK forces		Indian forces		Pakistan forces		Iranian forces	
	DAY-ROA	GEN-ROA	DAY-ROA	GEN-ROA	DAY-ROA	GEN-ROA	DAY-ROA	GEN-ROA	DAY-ROA	GEN-ROA	DAY-ROA	GEN-ROA	DAY-ROA	GEN-ROA	DAY-ROA	GEN-ROA
Land-based weapons	1,170	1,170	45	45	459	459	225	225	162	162	405	405	225	225	351	351
Sea-based weapons	156	233	130	194	156	233	26	39	5	26	36	181	10	52	31	156
Air-delivered weapons	0	359	0	204	0	204	0	140	0	222	0	255	0	105	0	160
All	1,326	1,762	175	444	615	896	251	404	167	410	441	842	235	382	382	667
Stability	39%		33%		42%		24%		7%		12%		15%		13%	

TABLE 6.7. PROMPT LAUNCH STABILITY, DAY, 2,200 LIMIT.

	RUSSIA No defenses Russian forces		JAPAN No defenses Japanese forces		CHINA No defenses PRC forces		NORTH KOREA No defenses DPRK forces		SOUTH KOREA No defenses ROK forces		INDIA No defenses Indian forces		PAKISTAN No defenses Pakistan forces		IRAN No defenses Iranian forces	
	DAY-ROA	GEN-ROA	DAY-ROA	GEN-ROA	DAY-ROA	GEN-ROA	DAY-ROA	GEN-ROA	DAY-ROA	GEN-ROA	DAY-ROA	GEN-ROA	DAY-ROA	GEN-ROA	DAY-ROA	GEN-ROA
Land-based weapons	170	1170	5	45	46	459	23	225	16	162	41	405	23	225	35	351
Sea-based weapons	156	156	130	130	156	156	26	26	3	5	18	36	5	10	16	31
Air-delivered weapons	0	0	0	0	0	0	0	0	0	0	0	0	0	0	0	0
All	273	1326	135	175	615	896	49	251	19	167	59	441	28	235	51	382
Stability	39%		33%		42%		24%		7%		12%		15%		13%	

TABLE 6.8. PROMPT LAUNCH STABILITY, GEN, 2,200 LIMIT.

	Russia		Japan		China		North Korea		South Korea		India		Pakistan		Iran	
	No defenses		No defenses		No defenses		No defenses		No defenses		No defenses		No defenses		No defenses	
	Russian forces		Japanese forces		PRC forces		DPRK forces		ROK forces		Indian forces		Pakistan forces		Iranian forces	
	DAY-ROA	GEN-ROA	DAY-ROA	GEN-ROA	DAY-ROA	GEN-ROA	DAY-ROA	GEN-ROA	DAY-ROA	GEN-ROA	DAY-ROA	GEN-ROA	DAY-ROA	GEN-ROA	DAY-ROA	GEN-ROA
ICBM	117	1,170	5	45	46	459	23	225	16	162	41	405	23	225	76	351
SLBM	233	233	194	194	233	233	39	39	26	26	181	181	52	52	156	156
Air	359	359	204	204	204	204	140	140	222	222	255	255	105	105	160	160
All	709	1,762	403	444	483	896	201	404	264	410	477	842	179	382	392	667
Stability	40%		91%		54%		50%		64%		57%		47%		59%	

deliberately set up an artificial situation in which total force sizes are more or less similar (except for Russia) across states. In the "real world" of Asian nuclear arms races, one danger is that richer states, like wealthier U.S. baseball teams, will outspend their rivals into nuclear bankruptcy and deploy forces intimidating by sheer size.

Regardless of force size, force characteristics and operational assumptions make a considerable difference for crisis and arms race stability. Most states in Asia will depend on land-based missiles and/or bomber-delivered weapons as the bulwark of their deterrents. Few if any will be capable of operating fleets of ballistic missile submarines as does the United States. Thus countries in Asia dependent on ICBM or intermediate-range/medium-range ballistic missiles will rely on alerted forces and prompt launch to guarantee survivability. Hair triggers may be more the rule than the exception. In addition, many of the land-based missiles available to Asian powers for use as "strategic" launchers will be of medium or intermediate range—theater, as opposed to intercontinental, missiles. These theater-range missiles will have shorter flight times than true ICBMs, allowing less time for the defender's launch detection, decision making, and response. Errors in launch detection, in the estimation of enemy intentions, and in choice of response are more likely with shorter than longer-range missiles.

The high dependency of Asian forces on land-based missiles will be compounded by command and control systems that may be accident prone or politically ambiguous. In democratic states, political control over the military is guaranteed by checks and balances and by constitutional fiat. In authoritarian polities, the military may operate as a political tool of the ruling clique or it may be an autonomous political force subject to intrigue and coup plotting. The possibility of political overthrow or military usurpation during a nuclear crisis would not be ruled out in systems lacking constitutional or other political safeguards. The danger is not only that of Bonapartism on the part of disgruntled officers but also the danger of panic in the face of nuclear threats and an institutional military bias for getting in the first blow in order to maximize the possibility of military victory and avoid defeat.

The performance of forces in our illustrative and hypothetical case is also influenced by the command and control systems that connect political and military leaders with force operators and with one another. Although command and control variables have not been built into the model, the implications for command decision making, and for the problem of control during crisis management, are clear enough. The forces most dependent on land-based ballistic missiles show the most discrepancy between hair-trigger and slow-trigger responses. On the other hand, states with balanced forces such as Russia, or with major reliance on sea-based as opposed to land-based missiles (Japan), are comparatively less reliant on jumpy warning and fast firing. If hair-trigger responses are necessary for survivability, then policy makers and commanders will have few minutes in which to make life-and-death decisions for entire societies. And missiles of theater or shorter range offer even fewer minutes of decision time than ICBMs, whose intercontinental reach requires twenty minutes or so from silo to silo.

Faced with this analysis states might decide to supplement vulnerable and potentially provocative land-based ballistic missiles with cruise missiles. Cruise missiles can be based in various environments on land, at sea, and in the air. They can be moved on relatively short notice and can attack from various azimuths with high accuracy. Other states cannot have failed to notice the United States' use of cruise missiles to great effect during the Persian Gulf War of 1991 and in punitive strike campaigns throughout the 1990s, as well as during Operation Enduring Freedom in Afghanistan and in Operation Iraqi Freedom in 2003. Cruise missiles can be fitted with conventional or nuclear warheads; the choice obviously depends on the target and mission, and on the decision whether to arm the missile with nuclear or nonnuclear munitions, which affects its operational range. But it is certainly conceivable that various states in our mix will turn to ALCMs, sea-launched cruise missiles (SLCMs), and ground-launched cruise missiles (GLCMs) as weapons of choice for high priority conventional or nuclear missions. The absence of air defenses of any consequence, in many states, invites their opponents to explore this option if they can.

The analysis here also underlines the truth of the old saying that "everything old is new again." The end of the Cold War did not repeal the nuclear revolution, although it did make deterrence calculations more complicated. It remains the case that nuclear weapons are in a class by themselves: Very small numbers can produce historically unprecedented destruction and social chaos almost anywhere. States in our example showed, for a variety of force structures, meaningful percentage differences based on three variables: their mix of land, sea, and airborne launch platforms; their levels of alert; and their respective launch proclivities.

What is important about these differences is *not* the numbers and percentages, however, but the possible effect of leaders' *perceptions* that higher alerts and faster launches are necessary in order to avoid catastrophic defeat should war occur. There are no "winnable" nuclear wars depicted here, nor would there be even if agreed levels among the powers were reduced to several hundreds of warheads.[11] The danger is that a war might begin not so much from deliberation as from desperation, from states feeling that their nuclear deterrents were threatened and they were therefore coerced to make a yes-no decision on a time line that permits neither reflection nor appropriate vetting of the information at hand.

Conclusions

There is little good news on offer with regard to nuclear weapons in Asia, notwithstanding the 2007 agreement with North Korea that may (hopefully) contain and then dismantle its nuclear weapons capability. Spreading nuclear weapons in Asia do not automatically yield a catastrophic outcome. Stability of a regional balance of terror resides mainly in the policies of states and in the intentions of their leaders. On the other hand, to assume continuation of Cold War nuclear stability under the pressure of a nuclear potlatch in Asia is to indulge in unaffordable optimism. Regional rivalries, including ethnonationalist and religiously inspired disagreements, combine dangerously with weapons of mass destruction from the standpoint of international security and stability.

States' nuclear forces may be deployed and operated with more or less sensitivity to the problem of provocative crisis behavior. Asian states with high dependency on land-based missiles for their retaliatory forces may find their freedom of action constrained by the "lose or use" quality of these launchers. Coupled to command-control and warning systems with insufficient fidelity, ballistic missiles armed with nuclear weapons invite irrevocable decisions based on insufficient evidence and desperate hopes. And on account of their shorter flight times compared to intercontinental missiles, theater- or shorter-range ballistic missiles may have greater potential for triggering inadvertent or accidental nuclear war.

The role of ballistic missile defenses in this context of unknown missile and WMD, including nuclear, proliferation in Asia is a composite of Clausewitz's description of the climate of war: danger, exertion, uncertainty, and chance.[12] Both road-tested nonproliferation measures (including existing treaty regimes such as the NPT) and counterproliferation measures (including missile defenses and the threat of preemption) will be candidate options for future policy makers' toolkits.[13] Against the new nuclear forces of smaller states, theater or nationwide BMD may pose some credible threat of deterrence by denial. However, missile defenses without a strategy for slowing the spread of nuclear weapons will be a paper chase of poor policy by aspiring technology.

Chapter 7

Ending a Nuclear War: Should We Even Try and Would Missile Defenses Help?

A war that is "open ended"—that has no clearly delineated geographical, political, and military goals beyond "victory"—is a war that may escalate itself indefinitely, as wars will, with one success requiring still another to insure the first one. An insistence on going all-out to win a war may have a fine masculine ring, and a call to "defend freedom" may have a messianic sound that stirs our blood. But the ending of an all-out war in these times is beyond imagining. It may mean the turning back of civilization by several thousand years, with no one left capable of signaling the victory.

—*Gen. Matthew B. Ridgway*

During the Cold War, especially in the 1980s, there were some serious efforts in the academic and policy communities to study the question how a nuclear war could end.[1] The large nuclear arsenals of the Americans and Soviets, the drift of U.S. and Soviet military thinking, and the policy related anxieties of other skeptics, all precluded closure on this question before the Cold War ended.

The subject of nuclear war termination should be reopened now. The political and technical environments relevant to starting and stopping a nuclear war are markedly different from the Cold War context. It would be a major tragedy if, in the aftermath of the first nuclear weapons fired in anger since Nagasaki, neither the United States nor other great powers had thought through how to abort a nuclear war in its early stages. For unlike the hypothetical Armageddon between the Americans and Soviets that never occurred in the last century, smaller but highly destructive nuclear wars may take place in this century.

Deterrence: How Reliable?

The first use of a nuclear weapon by one state against another since 1945 will create a tectonic shift in the expectations of policy makers and military planners worldwide. The nuclear taboo that supposedly held back the hands of crisis-bound policy makers during the Cold War and for the remainder of the twentieth century will have been shattered.[2] Left in its place will be uncertainty and the plausible expectation that a first use may be followed by retaliation and further escalation. Of course, a nuclear power could choose to attack or coerce a nonnuclear state. Such a one-sided attack could bring condemnation from the international community and responses from allies of the victim—including those with nuclear weapons.

We all assume that the probability of a nuclear war is related, in some unquantifiable but definable way, to the numbers of states with nuclear weapons and to the friendliness or animosity in their relations. Of particular interest are the numbers and kinds of states with basically status quo orientations to the existing international order compared to the numbers and kinds of states with antisystemic or revisionist goals.

The problem of containing proliferation among "rogue" or other revisionist actors was actually a two-part one. The first part was what to do with additional state actors having become nuclear capable. The second aspect was the valid concern that rogue nuclear powers might pass nuclear technology or know-how to nonstate actors, including terrorists. It was known, for example, that al-Qaeda even before 9/11 had attempted to acquire nuclear weapons-grade material. The United States and other countries with large coastlines and national territories were vulnerable to various attacks by WMD, including chemical, biological, radiological, or nuclear weapons.

Optimists about the probable consequence of further nuclear weapons spread among states might argue, as some have done, that deterrence would still work in the future as it presumably had done during the Cold War. The optimism was very much based on after-the-fact hindsight that we survived the Cold War without accidentally or deliberately setting off a U.S.-Soviet nuclear exchange leading to a global catastrophe. People living through the Cold War and its various crisis, especially the Cuban Missile Crisis, had a somewhat less deterministic view about the success of deterrence. Even if Cold War deterrence was as overdetermined as optimists supposed, deterring terrorists and other nonstate actors from nuclear adventurism was another task altogether.

We will leave the problem of deterring nonstate actors for another study, assuming for the moment that "deterrence" as a robust concept applies at all to the problem of preventing terrorist attacks. The objective of deterring rogue or other states is sufficiently challenging for Western planners and policy makers. Some government officials and others concerned about the behavior of rogue actors have concluded that they are, in all likelihood, beyond the grasp of rational deterrence strategies. At least rogues might not be amenable to military persuasion by the U.S. or Western model of rational deterrence.

The U.S. model of deterrence rationality emphasizes the calculation of costs and benefits attached to various alternative courses of action. Decision makers choose the alternative with the smallest anticipated cost and the largest potential benefit relative to other available alternatives. Deterrence theory is thus one aspect of public choice theory, and as such it works only within a limited frame of reference or "bounded rationality." Within this framework, adversaries are assumed to have accurate information about one another's goals, alternatives, and positive or negative weights assigned to various options.

The vulnerabilities of this model of analysis applied to the real world of nuclear crisis management are serious and potentially deadly.[3] It is not so much that deterrence theory is more deficient in the abstract compared to other possible approaches to conflict management. The challenge lies in applying the abstract logic to a myriad of concrete situations. The specific circumstances of a crisis are important in understanding how it tumbled into a war. Once deterrence has failed (presumably) and war has broken out, the course of battle influences the options remaining for policy makers and commanders who wish to stop the war sooner instead of later.

It is a mistake to suppose that an outbreak of war is necessarily the result of deterrence failure. An adversary may be bent on attack come what may. Thus the motives and mind-sets of possible enemies are as important as are their capabilities for determining whether, and when, they might attack. History is full of wars begun under assumptions about enemy intentions and capabilities that were later proved, by the test of battle, to have been fallacious. Attackers have not infrequently begun wars against states with greater military capabilities. Often the attackers in question doubted the resolve of the defenders. In other instances, states misperceived one another's intentions relative to war because they failed to comprehend essential aspects of the other side's strategic culture, military planning priorities, or "art of war." Wars undertaken by leaders who get one or more of these things wrong are sometimes referred to as "accidental" or "inadvertent" (usually by political scientists who favor these concepts, less often by historians who are more skeptical).

Deterrence during the Cold War, at least in U.S. academic discourse and public policy analysis, was in constant danger of overstretch. For some analysts and policy makers it became a talisman that substituted for hard data or serious thought. Deterrence was also sometimes substituted for policy instead of for military strategy (separate problems, but related). The "domino theory" by which U.S. military escalation of its commitment to the war in Vietnam was justified is one example of deterrence (and its twin, credibility) having been stretched across the conceptual and geographical fault lines that separated war in Europe from war in Asia.

It would be premature to declare that aspiring nuclear powers including "rogue" states are "beyond deterrence" in the sense of existential deterrence. But deterrence will certainly operate differently in the twenty-first century compared to the Cold War. One reason for this is related to nuclear proliferation. Nuclear weapons were the hallmarks of great powers that were, during the Cold War, mostly content with the geopolitical status quo. Future nuclear-aspiring or nuclear-capable states, on the other hand, may be revisionists with regard to their international policy objectives. In fact, the very term "rogue" or "state of concern" implies as much: The rogue is only roguish from the standpoint of those who favor the existing system and its parameters. Those who wish to overturn the system might regard rogues as heroes. In the eighteenth century American and French revolutionaries were rogues against the established order, and now their successor states are part of it.

Another question raised about deterrence is whether it can apply to heads of state, military leaders, or terrorists whose motives are apocalyptic or otherwise nonrational. Of course, this begs the question: What is a rational motive?[4] We will not get into this matter judgmentally. Suffice it to say that one state's rationality may be another's irrationality, but the distinction is not clinical. Individuals who are clinically suspect may nevertheless make clear decisions on behalf of their states in troubled times; indeed, many have done so. Rationality has to do with the logic of means-ends connections: Is the state acting in a way that maximizes its likelihood of success or minimizes its probability of failure?

In a crisis between two nuclear powers, the difficulty rises because the decision logics or "rationalities" of the two sides are interdependent. Each has a sequence of moves that may be more, or less, logical in reaction to the move of the other. This interdependency of moves and motives is what makes nuclear or other crises so hard to manage. Imagine a two-dimensional chess game with the players blindfolded and with each side permitted a finite number of mistakes (say, two wrong moves) before the players and the board are blown to smithereens. The example is not fatuous: President John F. Kennedy and Premier Nikita Khrushchev played something like this during the Cuban missile crisis.

Principles of Escalation Control

As related to the problem of ending a nuclear war, theories of escalation control have several key propositions on offer. All are controversial, but none is self-evidently impossible. First, even nuclear war, however destructive, would involve political goals—at the outset, at least. Second, states and leaders can be expected to recognize certain rules of the road about fighting and ending wars, despite cultural and national differences. Third, although time pressures and the military planning process impose constraints on escalation control for war termination, success is not precluded in practice.[5] With reference to defensible Cold War views of this matter, Paul Bracken has argued, "The assumption of robustness with respect to time pressures and planning rigidities is supported by the certainty that in a nuclear crisis each nation's top leader would be at the helm, overriding bureaucratic obstacles of delay and omission."[6]

The idea of ending a nuclear war already in progress implies that deterrence can be applied to the problem of limiting a war as well as preventing it. A nuclear war is a failure of deterrence that has already happened. Worse, however, would be for the various parties to the conflict to continue firing until their arsenals had been exhausted or all major cities destroyed. Getting combatants to the bargaining table after the shock of nuclear combat would not be easy. Unless the war had been started by mistake, say, an accidental launch or a rogue commander, important issues of state would be in dispute. In addition, the anger of survivors at the consequences of nuclear attacks on their society would be difficulty for governments to manage. Survivors' demands for retaliation and revenge might overwhelm policy makers' efforts to arrange cease-fires or surrenders.

The termination of a nuclear war, as in any war, has both military-tactical and politico-strategic aspects.[7] The tactical situation on the battlefield is obviously important. After the early nuclear attacks have taken place, each side may have surviving forces. The surviving forces are bargaining assets that can be used in negotiating a cease-fire or peace agreement. Even a few surviving forces on either side can threaten to inflict a great deal of societal destruction on the other, and its leaders might prefer to negotiate instead of continue fighting. However, in the chaos attendant to nuclear war, even a "small" regional war by Cold War standards, leaders and their military advisors might not have reliable information about the status of the enemy's forces and command-control systems.

Command-control systems present an anomaly to planners who might want to leave the door open for intrawar deterrence and nuclear war termination. On one hand, in traditional military thinking based on experience in conventional war fighting, attacking command-control and communications systems makes perfect sense. It is an efficient way to destroy the opponent's military cohesion and coordination. Attacks on the enemy's brain and central nervous system, as were carried out during Operation Desert Storm, are important "force multipliers" that can be used to win a war in good time and save both friendly and enemy casualties.

But in a nuclear war the destruction of enemy political or military command and control systems would almost certainly exacerbate the problem of ending the war, and at two levels. At the tactical level the destruction of military control systems would cut the nuclear retaliatory forces and their commanders into separate pieces. Each piece would be programmed to continue firing and fighting unless otherwise directed to stand down. However, the stand-down orders might never reach the relevant field commanders having custody of nuclear weapons, nor those authorized to fire them (who might be the same people, but not necessarily). Thus "outliers" in the nuclear military chain of command might not hear, or want to hear, cease-fire orders.[8]

Destruction of the main political center of the opponent might paralyze its civilian leadership and make it impossible for the president or prime minister, or other surviving cabinet officials, to gain secure and reliable control over the armed forces.[9] Consider, for example, an Iranian attack on Israel, or a Pakistani strike against India, that "succeeded" in decapitating the heart of the enemy's political leadership. Effective control over the armed forces of the attacked states would almost certainly pass directly to the military and other security organs. The surviving political leadership in Tel Aviv and in India would at least temporarily be the prisoners of fast moving events and asserted military imperatives. It would take considerable time, and at least the appearance of an interim cease-fire, before anything like "normal" relationships between politicians and the armed forces were reestablished.

Assessment of the viability of command-control systems under the stress of nuclear or other WMD attacks is made difficult by the scarcity of reliable information in the public record. It might be supposed, for example, that each state or government has official, written arrangements for delegation of political office and for devolution of military command during crisis and war. But this assumption could be mistaken for nuclear-aspiring or new nuclear states. Even if written protocols exist, they may not be adhered to or correspond to reality once the shooting starts. Furthermore, the delegation of political authority and the devolution of military command-control may differ in important ways.

We do know something about the U.S. systems for political delegation and military devolution of command. The American Presidential Succession Act and various other legislative enactments, as well as constitutional requirements, clarify both nonemergency and emergency procedures for answering the question, Who is in charge if the president is killed or disabled? The military chain of command, although it begins with the presidential center, is not identical to the political one. The wartime devolution of military command proceeds from the president, to the secretary of defense, and then to the regional or functional combatant commanders (through the Joint Chiefs of Staff). This system ensures that even if the political decision center is paralyzed by a surprise attack, the military commands authorized to retaliate can do so in a timely manner. These command and control arrangements were worked out over many years of Cold War trial and error. They were, and are, intended to provide a solution for the oxymoronic requirement that forces "never" be fired without appropriate authorization but "always" respond promptly when authorized missions are required.[10]

In the early years of the nuclear age, U.S. policy makers and military leaders struggled to define a rule set for the control of nuclear weapons in peacetime and for the management of nuclear forces during crisis and war. As is well known, the Truman administration initially assigned custody over atomic weapons to a civilian agency. The weapons could only be released to the military by presidential order. As this became impracticable in the missile age, systems were required for dispersing weapons to the military while maintaining them in secure storage and proof against accidental or unauthorized use. In addition, land-based, sea-based, and air-launched weapons required platform-specific protocols; aircraft could surge to "fail-safe" points and wait for confirming orders before proceeding to attack. Missiles, on the other hand, were not subject to recall. Their launch was an irrevocable decision for war.

New Challenges in Escalation Control

The details of U.S. and Soviet Cold War force operations, including command and control, are not important here. Enough has been presented to make the point that only over considerable time, and as a result of much trial and error on the part of operators and analysts, were these systems established as reliable against usurpers or accidents and as responsive to authorized commands. The "lessons learned" by the Americans and Soviets in this regard have not necessarily been passed along to future generations of nuclear-capable states. The extent to which some existing nuclear powers, to say nothing of future ones, accept the idea of deterrence based on second-strike capability, as opposed to preemption, is unclear. Nor are the relationships among the highest levels of political and military command with regard to the alerting of forces in crisis or the employment of forces in war altogether clear for states such as Pakistan and North Korea. The manner in which custody of nuclear weapons along with the authority to fire them has been delegated to field commanders in India, Pakistan, Israel, or North Korea is a closely guarded secret.

Once nuclear weapons had been fired in anger in South or Northeast Asia or in the Middle East, would political leaders be able to maintain continuing control over force employment, targeting, and termination decisions? States with small inventories of weapons, especially if they were first-strike vulnerable, might follow the logic of "use them or lose them" and expend rapidly their existing arsenals. On the other hand, even smaller states might want to maintain some forces in reserve in order to avoid nuclear blackmail in the postattack phase of a war. A small residue of survivable forces, perhaps tactical missiles or nuclear-capable aircraft of limited range, could be the difference between an imposed surrender and a negotiated peace.

In order for negotiations between an India and Pakistan, or Israel and a nuclear Iran, to take place after the nuclear threshold had been crossed, leaders in firm control of their nuclear forces would be prerequisite. Leaders would have to survive the early attacks, communicate with their nuclear forces, and impose targeting restraints or even nuclear cease-fires. These steps to expedite negotiation might not be possible. Rogue commanders once enabled to fire nuclear weapons, and having observed unprecedented destruction on their own country, could resist cease-fires and become bent on revenge or holocaust. The delegation of nuclear release authority having been made from senior politicians and military commanders to force operators, retrenchment and "putting the genie back in the bottle" would call for wartime commanders to put professional obligations and the military chain of command ahead of personal agendas and motives. Some might, and some might not.

Nor is this problem one that has been entirely done away with among "mature" nuclear powers. Russia in the 1990s was an economic basket case. As its economy lagged, its conventional military forces became cash starved and operationally deprived of oxygen. Consequently, Russia became primarily dependent on its nuclear weapons, especially its long-range weapons, for deterrence of major nuclear *or* conventional attacks on its state territory. Russia's position in the 1990s was like NATO's during the Cold War: presumed inferiority in conventional forces and therefore an acknowledged reliance on nuclear weapons to cover more bets. In addition, Russia's missile warning and control systems deteriorated, including its satellite and ground-based radar networks, after the fall of the Soviet Union. Russia's nuclear weapons complex and its nuclear scientific establishment were also casualties of its free-falling economy. The United States established programs of military assistance to Russia in the 1990s in order to improve Russia's handling of nuclear materials and weapons, including accurate accounting and safe storage and dismantlement.

The previous sentence marks an ironic turn of events. The U.S. government is now the largest "investor" in Russian nuclear safety and security. The concern in Washington is no longer, as during the Cold War, the prospect of a deliberate Soviet nuclear attack but of Russian loss of political or military control that leaves nuclear weapons and launchers in the hands of regional warlords. This subject is almost taboo in official diplomatic circles, but interestingly, the topic of Russian breakup or deconstruction into a plurality of regional entities is the subject of much speculation among Russians. Russian media and polling organizations frequently sample public opinion on this issue, and about a third of Russians generally regard the possibility of a breakup of post-Soviet Russia as more than trivial. The question, in such an event, is whether the split would be a case of gradual and consensual political devolution or whether it would be more like a nasty divorce or a civil war.

The current administration of President Dmitri Medvedev and Prime Minister Vladimir Putin has made clear its intent to resist any regionalization or other dismemberment of Russia. Putin's firm opposition to Chechen terrorism and insurgency and his absolute *nyet* to the demand for political autonomy or independence for that troubled region have been consistent and emphatic: There will be no departure from Russia by means of armed resistance. U.S. policy is that Russia should, indeed, hold together, for a major breakup of Russia would destabilize the entire central Eurasian subcontinent with ripple effects to the west, east, and south. An immediate concern about a fissiparous Russian polity would be the consequences for the command and control over its nuclear weapons and launch platforms.

The United States and its allies have been there once before. In the immediate aftermath of the Soviet breakup, the post-Soviet states of Ukraine, Belarus, and Kazakhstan were suddenly numbered among the world's nuclear powers. The fates of their respective nuclear arsenals were up for grabs, and various heads of state in these countries sought to play the nuclear card for economic assistance or for the temporary prestige it might bring them. U.S. policy was to establish Russia as the logical and legal successor state to the Soviet Union for the purpose of controlling nuclear weapons and forces. Otherwise, dispersal of nuclear weapons among post-Soviet states could lead to chaos, including the unauthorized distribution of nuclear weapons and weapons-grade materials among terrorists. After considerable political wheeling and dealing in the early 1990s that involved the United States, Russia, and the new trio of nuclear powers, agreement was reached for the forces of Ukraine, Belarus, and Kazakhstan to be "returned" to Russia (standing in for the former Soviet Union) or dismantled.

Russia's nuclear weapons deployed for use on intercontinental missiles or long-range bombers are, according to Russian officials, under secure storage and control in peacetime. (Weapons-grade or other nuclear materials, including vast stores of uranium and plutonium, are another matter. American and other nonproliferation experts remain concerned about leakage from Russia's nuclear weapons complex or other sources of nuclear or radiological materials. This is a separate, albeit important, subject.)[11] In the nearest approximation to a nuclear crisis during the 1990s, the launch of a Norwegian scientific rocket in January 1995 was temporarily confused by Russian warning systems with a possible U.S. missile launch from a ballistic missile submarine. Russian nuclear forces were alerted. President Boris Yeltsin, together with his defense minister and chief of the General Staff, used for the first time in the post–Cold War era their nuclear "footballs," the briefcases that accompany the head of state and his principal military advisors. Russian tracking of the missile trajectory eventually established that its path was headed out toward sea and away from Russian territory.[12]

It turned out that the "Black Brant" missile launch that temporarily alarmed the Russians had been the result of a diplomatic snafu. The Norwegian government had notified the Russian Foreign Ministry months in advance of the planned rocket launch and its purpose: gathering scientific data on the aurora borealis. But the communication got lost in the Russian bureaucracy and never made it to the desks of the responsible officials in the Russian armed forces and defense ministry.

The preceding resume of concerns about mature nuclear powers is not intended to single out Russia but to caution against casual acceptance of the assumption that "rogues" or new nuclear states would be more likely to start a war, and less willing to end a war short of Armageddon, than long-standing nuclear powers would be. Of course, the larger and more diverse arsenals of the major powers give them options for controlling conflict and for intrawar deterrence, compared to smaller powers. And even at lower levels of force size, the qualities of forces and their operational parameters are partial determinants of their ability to maintain political and military control during a nuclear war.

That having been said, the decisions for prolonging or ending a war are very subjective ones based on the motives and personalities of leaders and the moods of publics that have been subjected to attacks. An additional variable for any state engaged in a nuclear war will be the policy-making process in that state: how power and influence are distributed among office holders and politically influential persons. We have some ideas about how the process of national security decision making would work in the United States, Britain, France, China, and Russia because these polities have been studied extensively by insiders and outsiders.

But what power shifts would take place after war began in India, Pakistan, North Korea, or Iran? North Korea is virtually opaque to U.S. intelligence. Pakistan is a government under siege from jihadists whose influence extends into its military and intelligence organs. The regime in Tehran is torn between traditionalist ayatollahs with visceral hatred for the United States and Israel and modernizers who would prefer to focus on economic development and gradual social change. India is the world's largest democracy and a remarkably stable one, but under the stress of a nuclear attack, the relationship between its military and its government might undergo drastic change, compared to its peacetime condition. Recall that one Indian prime minister during the Cold War was assassinated by several of her own official bodyguards.

For that matter, what could we expect from an American president in the aftermath of a nuclear attack on U.S. soil by a rogue or other state? U.S. history is not inspiring of confidence that cool heads would prevail and that government would seek to manage a conflict toward "victory" at the lowest possible level of destruction or to negotiate an agreed peace. U.S. reaction to 9/11 was instructive; not only terrorists everywhere but also regimes that aided terrorists were placed into the cross-hairs of American vengeance. Al-Qaeda deserves all the opprobrium it received, but the point here is a different one. Americans and their political leaders are not, by temperament and training, accustomed to dealing out military punishment in measured doses. The likely reaction to a nuclear attack even by terrorists on U.S. soil would be an elite and public demand for a Carthaginian peace.

This and the two preceding sections have discussed only some of the problems attendant to ending a nuclear war. I have not emphasized technical problems or military doctrine, but issues related to the nexus between politics and warfare, that is, strategy. In the next section I will interrogate the issue of nuclear war termination by modeling some of the possibilities, using alternative future U.S. and Russian forces for the development of insights and hypotheses.

Modeling Nuclear War Termination

The dynamics of ending a nuclear war resist rigorous modeling for two reasons: (1) no two-sided nuclear war has ever been fought, and (2) the complexity of nuclear operations, unrestrained by efforts to limit the war in duration and intensity, is sufficiently challenging for any researcher. Even more complicated would be the effort to fight and limit a nuclear war at the same time.

Nevertheless, this is precisely what leaders would attempt to do, unless they had taken leave of their political and military senses. Fighting for honor or revenge, or even more apocalyptic motives, with nuclear weapons is a luxury that only stateless terrorists can afford. Leaders of governments have a responsibility to their states and societies. By whatever chain of events a nuclear war had gotten started, it would be imperative to shut it off as soon as political will could be exerted in that direction.

The possibility that heads of state would *not* just throw up their hands and passively await Armageddon once nuclear war had begun was a controversial offering on the plates of policy makers and analysts during the Cold War. The major reason for resistance to the study of nuclear war termination was the massive size of U.S. and Soviet arsenals. It was simply assumed that even a "small" nuclear exchange involving the two Cold War superpowers would leave their societies with unacceptable, and perhaps irreparable, damage. And indeed a nuclear war in which several thousand warheads exploded on the American or Russian heartlands, the result of so-called counterforce attacks, would have created a postattack, prehistoric residue that only novelists could imagine.

On the other hand, in the twenty-first century the possibility of limiting nuclear war to less than Armageddon is not only a hypothetical one. A regional nuclear war on the Korean peninsula or the Indian subcontinent would be a holocaust for the immediate victims, but it would not necessarily inflict catastrophic damage on the planet. In addition, the equation has changed considerably between the Americans and Russians in the twenty-first century compared to the Cold War condition of self-annihilating forces.

Under the constraints of the Moscow Treaty of 2002 the United States and Russia may deploy a maximum of 2,200 warheads on intercontinental missiles and long-range bombers. The treaty regulates only weapons actually deployed, and it does not require reductions to the agreed warhead ceilings to be symmetrical in character. Each side is to proceed according to its own "freedom to mix" among launch platforms, so long as the designated ceiling is not exceeded. The United States or Russia may, of course, choose to deploy fewer than the maximum number of warheads.

With initially deployed forces of 2,200 warheads or fewer, the United States and Russia will not have the redundant forces of the Cold War ("overkill") to compensate for poor decisions about strike planning, targeting, and other aspects of force management. With more than 10,000 warheads deployed on strategic launchers by each side during the early 1980s, for example, either the United States or Russia could have launched a highly destructive counterforce first strike against the other, retained a reserve force for follow-on countercity attacks, or withheld sufficient forces to deter a third party from intervening in the conflict (e.g., China, the UK, or France).

Restricted to the smaller forces of the Moscow Treaty regime, the United States and Russia must plan with more care for a postattack world before committing themselves to strikes against one another. Consider the arithmetic. A U.S. first strike against Russian counterforce targets (land-based missiles, submarine bases, bomber bases, and associated military command-control) or a Russian first strike against the United States of a similar nature would require about 1,000 fast flying warheads on ICBMs or SLBMs. The second striker would require a similar number of warheads to put at risk the unused portion of the first striker's force. Both would be left with a residue that might be "essentially equivalent" to the remaining weapons of its opponent. But the "remaining" forces would offer fewer options for postattack coercion against one another, or against third parties, compared to the Cold War forces.

To illustrate these points, I will generate hypothetical Russian and U.S. forces for the upper and lower bounds of the Moscow Treaty (2,200 and 1,700 deployed warheads). Each country will be assigned variable force structures. In the first step of the analysis I compare the performances of the various forces in a simple attack model: Each side absorbs a counterforce first strike. I calculate the surviving warheads for each force under four conditions of alertness and launch readiness: (1) generated alert, launch on warning, (2) generated alert, ride out the attack, (3) day-to-day alert, launch on warning, and (4) day-to-day alert, ride out the attack. For the United States I generate the following alternative force structures: (1) a balanced triad of land-based, sea-based, and air-delivered weapons, (2) a dyad of land- and sea-based forces only (no bombers), (3) a dyad of sea-based and bomber forces only (no ICBMs), and (4) a force entirely based on SLBMs. Russian forces in the analysis are (1) a balanced triad, (2) a dyad without bombers, (3) a dyad without SLBMs, and (4) a force entirely based on ICBMs.

Analysis

The results of the first step in the analysis are summarized in tables 7.1–4 for Russia and tables 7.5–8 for the United States.* The findings suggested by the data in tables 7.1–8 offer pertinent insights into the management of forces for intrawar deterrence and war termination of the following kind. First, from the perspective of deterrence prior to the outbreak of war, any of these force structures can guarantee "unacceptable damage" or assured retaliation against the opponent's society. Within the higher (2,200) or lower (1,700) deployment ceilings, each state remains in a nuclear hostage condition to the other. Second, while there are some advantages especially for Russia in higher alert levels and prompt launch doctrines, the marginal gain in military effectiveness is offset by the higher risk of dependency on "hair-trigger" responses.

*Tables in this chapter are based on a model originally developed by Dr. James J. Tritten and adapted by author. Dr. Tritten is not responsible for any data, analysis, or arguments in this study.

TABLE 7.1. SURVIVING AND RETALIATING WEAPONS, RUSSIAN BALANCED TRIAD, 2,200 AND 1,700 LIMITS

	2,200 DEPLOYED	1,700 DEPLOYED
GEN-LOW	612	554
GEN-ROA	510	462
DAY-LOW	408	369
DAY-ROA	306	277

TABLE 7.2. SURVIVING AND RETALIATING WEAPONS, RUSSIA, NO BOMBERS, 2,200 AND 1,700 LIMITS

	2,200 DEPLOYED	1,700 DEPLOYED
GEN-LOW	668	573
GEN-ROA	556	477
DAY-LOW	445	382
DAY-ROA	334	286

TABLE 7.3. SURVIVING AND RETALIATING WEAPONS, RUSSIA, NO SLBMs, 2,200 AND 1,700 LIMITS

	2,200 DEPLOYED	1,700 DEPLOYED
GEN-LOW	390	336
GEN-ROA	325	281
DAY-LOW	260	225
DAY- ROA	195	169

TABLE 7.4. SURVIVING AND RETALIATING WEAPONS, RUSSIA, ICBMs ONLY, 2,200 AND 1,700 LIMITS

	2,200 DEPLOYED	1,700 DEPLOYED
GEN-LOW	413	582
GEN-ROA	344	485
DAY-LOW	275	388
DAY-ROA	207	291

Note: Depending on the actual mix of platforms deployed, more surviving RVs may result from a smaller initial deployment (1,700 vs. 2,200).

TABLE 7.5. SURVIVING AND RETALIATING WEAPONS, U.S. BALANCED TRIAD,
2,200 AND 1,700 LIMITS

	2,200 DEPLOYED	1,700 DEPLOYED
GEN-LOW	843	653
GEN-ROA	702	544
DAY-LOW	562	436
DAY-ROA	421	327

TABLE 7.6. SURVIVING AND RETALIATING WEAPONS, UNITED STATES,
NO BOMBERS, 2,200 AND 1,700 LIMITS

	2,200 DEPLOYED	1,700 DEPLOYED
GEN-LOW	1,087	802
GEN-ROA	906	669
DAY-LOW	724	535
DAY-ROA	543	401

TABLE 7.7. SURVIVING AND RETALIATING WEAPONS, UNITED STATES,
NO ICBMs, 2,200 AND 1,700 LIMITS

	2,200 DEPLOYED	1,700 DEPLOYED
GEN-LOW	989	799
GEN-ROA	824	666
DAY-LOW	659	533
DAY-ROA	494	400

TABLE 7.8. SURVIVING AND RETALIATING WEAPONS, UNITED STATES,
SLBMs ONLY, 2,200 AND 1,700 LIMITS

	2,200 DEPLOYED	1,700 DEPLOYED
GEN-LOW	1,219	948
GEN-ROA	1,016	790
DAY-LOW	813	632
DAY-ROA	609	474

Third, as the numbers of forces come down, the qualities of forces matter more. With the plurality of forces that the Cold War permitted, it seemed self-evident to American and Soviet planners that a triad of land-based, sea-based, and bomber-delivered weapons was the most preferred force structure. A triad of launch platforms, compared to a dyad or monad, complicated the attack calculus for any first striker. But with smaller total forces, reduced to 2,000 or so deployed warheads, every platform must be justified on the grounds of intrinsic cost effectiveness, such as its survivability and penetration capability per unit. In this regard, the high survivability of ballistic missile submarines compared to bombers and land-based missiles makes them more appealing as forces shrink. SSBNs can launch weapons other than ballistic missiles and can, if necessary, be used as first-strike counterforce weapons.

Fourth, from the standpoint of intrawar deterrence and conflict management, submarines and bombers are more flexible than ICBMs, especially silo-based ICBMs. Bombers can be recalled after launch, and submarines can escape detection from satellite or other surveillance. But even road mobile land-based missiles are a high risk for prompt destruction, given the reconnaissance and location technology available today to attackers. What can be seen can be hit, and what can be hit can be destroyed—even with conventional weapons. In fact, it might be possible for some ICBMs to be loaded with conventional instead of nuclear warheads for use in "prenuclear" first strikes, as demonstrative attacks that would threaten pieces of the other side's deterrent without crossing the nuclear threshold or causing mass casualties.

Fifth, although not measured in this model, the substitution of nuclear armed cruise missiles on board surface ships and submarines might be justified as a "fourth" arm of the nuclear-capable "quadrad." In this model, some ICBMs would remain nuclear armed and others would carry conventional warheads. The nuclear warheads offloaded from ICBMs could be assigned to SLCMs that would be relatively more mobile and survivable compared to their land-based counterparts. Eventually the United States might prefer to retire its land-based missile force entirely. The George W. Bush administration has already opened the door to a more flexible construction of U.S. strike forces with its concept of a "new triad" consisting of nuclear and nonnuclear long-range attack forces, antimissile defenses, and improved defense infrastructure for the support of nuclear and nonnuclear forces.

In the second part of the analysis let us consider in more detail what would happen if the United States and Russia were unable to cease hostilities after their first wave of attacks. In this application of the model each has already fired its first salvo, either as a preemptive attack or in retaliation. The United States and Russia now launch most of their remaining forces, keeping a small reserve for each side. Moscow and Washington make this decision to continue fighting despite the likelihood that carrying destruction into this extended stage will kill many more of their citizens and destroy additional societal values. Not only that, but continuation of nuclear war into successive waves of attacks would reduce Moscow and Washington to second-rate postwar nuclear powers.

Tables 7.9–16 summarize the results for Russia and for the United States of the second wave of attacks. The remaining forces for each side are tabulated for each of the U.S. and Russian force structures and for each condition of alertness and launch readiness. Tables 7.9–12 summarize the results for Russian forces, and tables 7.13–16 for U.S. forces.

The outcomes summarized in tables 7.9–16 confirm preceding arguments about the merits of various force structures relative to one another. Sea-based and bomber forces offer more survivability and flexibility than do land-based forces and therefore would seem to be the weapons of choice for future deterrence. Furthermore, "air" forces of the future will almost certainly be "aerospace" forces that include space planes for conventional or nuclear deep strike. The justification for large missile parks during the Cold War was that U.S. or Soviet ICBMs would have to be attacked promptly in war and by numerous and redundant strikes. By attracting so many warheads on land-based forces, each side would have more sea-based and bomber-delivered weapons would survive to retaliate.

In addition to the findings that are consistent across both ranges of tables, some observations specific to the summaries in tables 7.9–16 are pertinent here. Even after having absorbed first waves of attack, the United States and Russia can still do considerable, even "unacceptable," further damage to one another. In fact, their situation following the first wave of strikes leaves Russia and the United States with a security dilemma comparable to that of currently "medium" nuclear powers such as Britain, China, or France. The United States and Russia, after having suffered initial nuclear attacks as posited here, would still be major players at the nuclear table and would have "on paper" forces that still exceeded those of third parties. However, taking into account the damage suffered by each to its forces *and* society, Russia and the United States would now be essentially equivalent to medium nuclear powers of the first decade of this century.

And the decision to continue their fighting, once war had begun, from "World War III" into "World War IV" would risk toppling them into small- instead of medium-power status, into the ranks of India, Pakistan, and Israel, for example. Thus hawks in Moscow and in Washington might side with doves in either capital in order to stop a war that had begun by failed crisis management or inadvertent means. As bad as World War III would be, World War IV would only inflict additional and superfluous harm. And as the data in tables 9–16 show, each side would retain considerable, and lethal, forces after its initial

TABLE 7.9. SURVIVING AND RETALIATING WEAPONS, RUSSIAN BALANCED TRIAD, EXTENDED WAR PHASE, 2,200 AND 1,700 LIMITS

	2,200 DEPLOYED	1,700 DEPLOYED
GEN-LOW	220	237
GEN-ROA	183	197
DAY-LOW	147	158
DAY-ROA	110	118

TABLE 7.10. SURVIVING AND RETALIATING WEAPONS, RUSSIA, NO BOMBERS, EXTENDED WAR PHASE, 2,200 AND 1,700 LIMITS

	2,200 DEPLOYED	1,700 DEPLOYED
GEN-LOW	248	219
GEN-ROA	206	182
DAY-LOW	165	146
DAY-ROA	124	109

TABLE 7.11. SURVIVING AND RETALIATING WEAPONS, RUSSIA, NO SLBMs, EXTENDED WAR PHASE, 2,200 AND 1,700 LIMITS

	2,200 DEPLOYED	1,700 DEPLOYED
GEN-LOW	130	126
GEN-ROA	109	105
DAY-LOW	87	84
DAY-ROA	65	63

TABLE 7.12. SURVIVING AND RETALIATING WEAPONS, RUSSIA, ICBMs ONLY, EXTENDED WAR PHASE, 2,200 AND 1,700 LIMITS

	2,200 DEPLOYED	1,700 DEPLOYED
GEN-LOW	135	286
GEN-ROA	112	238
DAY-LOW	90	191
DAY-ROA	67	143

TABLE 7.13. SURVIVING AND RETALIATING WEAPONS, U.S. BALANCED TRIAD, EXTENDED WAR PHASE, 2,200 AND 1,700 LIMITS

	2,200 DEPLOYED	1,700 DEPLOYED
GEN-LOW	403	313
GEN-ROA	336	261
DAY-LOW	268	209
DAY-ROA	201	157

TABLE 7.14. SURVIVING AND RETALIATING WEAPONS, UNITED STATES, NO BOMBERS, EXTENDED WAR PHASE, 2,200 AND 1,700 LIMITS

	2,200 DEPLOYED	1,700 DEPLOYED
GEN-LOW	496	362
GEN-ROA	413	302
DAY-LOW	330	241
DAY-ROA	248	181

TABLE 7.15. SURVIVING AND RETALIATING WEAPONS, UNITED STATES, NO ICBMS, EXTENDED WAR PHASE, 2,200 AND 1,700 LIMITS

	2,200 DEPLOYED	1,700 DEPLOYED
GEN-LOW	486	397
GEN-ROA	405	331
DAY-LOW	324	265
DAY-ROA	243	199

TABLE 7.16. SURVIVING AND RETALIATING WEAPONS, UNITED STATES, SLBMS ONLY, EXTENDED WAR PHASE, 2,200 AND 1,700 LIMITS

	2,200 DEPLOYED	1,700 DEPLOYED
GEN-LOW	573	446
GEN-ROA	478	372
DAY-LOW	382	297
DAY-ROA	287	223

attack had been made—and these forces would be important bargaining coun-
ters for war termination. However bad the mess already created, what would be
the point of continuing attacks into the weeks and months needed to track
down roaming submarines, relocated bombs, and perhaps suicide squads of
commandos armed with portable nuclear devices smuggled onto ships or
across land and capable of wreaking havoc for years?

Would missile defenses change the essential outcomes in the tables? To
ascertain this I assign various estimates of U.S. and Russian missile defense
effectiveness against "postattack" retaliatory strikes (as in step two of the preceding analysis). Defenses are assigned one of four values: They intercept successfully 20, 40, 60, or 80 percent of incoming warheads. These values are
merely intended to establish a range; they are not point predictions of future
BMD effectiveness. In order to simplify the analysis in this phase, retaliatory
strikes are based on the assumption of intermediate retaliation: second-strike
retaliation after riding out the attack. In the unreal "real world" of postattack
nuclear war, we acknowledge that trigger fingers might be jumpier than this,
but the second-strike ride-out assumption is consistent with the behaviors of
states that still hoped, however fitfully, to stop the war with some forces and
societies still intact. And with defenses, postattack nuclear war termination
might be less of a pipe dream. But how much less?

In tables 7.17–24 the effectiveness of defenses against retaliatory strikes in
this phase is summarized as follows. Phase I defenses intercept 20 percent of
the attackers (allow 80 percent leakage), Phase II defenses intercept 40 percent
(allow 60 percent leakage), Phase III defenses intercept 60 percent (allow 40
percent leakage), and Phase IV defenses intercept 80 percent (permitting 20
percent leakage).

The results of this phase of the analysis give some comfort to those who
would prefer to see defenses deployed. The same numbers caution against the
assumption that nuclear war can be made politically tolerable or socially acceptable. It requires defenses of very high effectiveness, about 80 percent or better,
before the numbers of retaliating warheads are reduced to two figures instead of
three. Even in that eventuality social destruction will be horrific, although not
necessarily precluding regime survival. In addition, it matters during a nuclear
war, as well as prior to the outbreak of war, what mix of launchers and weapons
have been deployed. Moral philosophers might not care, and understandably so,
but military planners would do well to note some of the preceding numbers.

For example, if defenses have been deployed, especially in the face of
war-driven offensive force attrition, it becomes more important to have sea-
based as opposed to land-based and airborne delivery systems at hand. Submarine-launched ballistic missiles will be the queens of the war termination

TABLE 7.17. SURVIVING AND RETALIATING WEAPONS VS. DEFENSES OF VARIABLE EFFECTIVENESS, RUSSIAN BALANCED TRIAD, 2,200 AND 1,700 LIMITS

	2,200 DEPLOYED	1,700 DEPLOYED
Phase I defenses	147	158
Phase II defenses	110	118
Phase III defenses	73	79
Phase IV defenses	37	39

TABLE 7.18. SURVIVING AND RETALIATING WEAPONS VS. DEFENSES OF VARIABLE EFFECTIVENESS, RUSSIA, NO BOMBERS, 2,200 AND 1,700 LIMITS

	2,200 DEPLOYED	1,700 DEPLOYED
Phase I defenses	165	146
Phase II defenses	124	109
Phase III defenses	83	73
Phase IV defenses	41	36

TABLE 7.19. SURVIVING AND RETALIATING WEAPONS VS. DEFENSES OF VARIABLE EFFECTIVENESS, RUSSIA, NO SLBMs, 2,200 AND 1,700 LIMITS

	2,200 DEPLOYED	1,700 DEPLOYED
Phase I defenses	87	84
Phase II defenses	65	63
Phase III defenses	44	42
Phase IV defenses	22	21

TABLE 7.20. SURVIVING AND RETALIATING WEAPONS VS. DEFENSES OF VARIABLE EFFECTIVENESS, RUSSIA, ICBMs ONLY, 2,200 AND 1,700 LIMITS

	2,200 DEPLOYED	1,700 DEPLOYED
Phase I defenses	90	191
Phase II defenses	67	143
Phase III defenses	45	95
Phase IV defenses	22	48

TABLE 7.21. SURVIVING AND RETALIATING WEAPONS VS. DEFENSES OF VARIABLE
EFFECTIVENESS, U.S. BALANCED TRIAD, 2,200 AND 1,700 LIMITS

	2,200 DEPLOYED	1,700 DEPLOYED
Phase I defenses	268	209
Phase II defenses	201	157
Phase III defenses	134	104
Phase IV defenses	67	52

TABLE 7.22. SURVIVING AND RETALIATING WEAPONS VS. DEFENSES OF VARIABLE
EFFECTIVENESS, UNITED STATES, NO BOMBERS, 2,200 AND 1,700 LIMITS

	2,200 DEPLOYED	1,700 DEPLOYED
Phase I defenses	330	241
Phase II defenses	248	181
Phase III defenses	165	121
Phase IV defenses	83	60

TABLE 7.23. SURVIVING AND RETALIATING WEAPONS VS. DEFENSES OF VARIABLE
EFFECTIVENESS, UNITED STATES, NO ICBMs, 2,200 AND 1,700 LIMITS

	2,200 DEPLOYED	1,700 DEPLOYED
Phase I defenses	324	265
Phase II defenses	243	199
Phase III defenses	162	132
Phase IV defenses	81	66

TABLE 7.24. SURVIVING AND RETALIATING WEAPONS VS. DEFENSES OF VARIABLE
EFFECTIVENESS, UNITED STATES, SLBMs ONLY, 2,200 AND 1,700 LIMITS

	2,200 DEPLOYED	1,700 DEPLOYED
Phase I defenses	382	297
Phase II defenses	287	223
Phase III defenses	191	149
Phase IV defenses	96	74

chessboard, and added to defenses they offer a coercive bargaining advantage to the side that is more competent in SLBMs and BMD. The finding has political and military implications for Russia. Russia's navy is a wasting asset and will take years, if ever, to rebuild to major maritime power status. If, in addition, Russia lags the United States in missile defenses, then Russia faces a two-sided competition that puts its planners and negotiators at a distinct disadvantage—in peace or war. Knowing this, Russia's diplomatic options might emphasize accommodation with, as opposed to confrontation against, the United States in major crises.

In August 2005 Russia and China carried out their first large-scale, combined military exercise of the new century—in China. The scenario for the exercises was officially described as counterterrorism. But the script was clearly aimed at a possible PRC incursion against Taiwan or as an access denial exercise against the United States. The political message was that Russia and China were tiring of U.S. military hegemony, especially as it was playing out in the Far East. Fair enough: power invites either bandwagoning or balancing, and the Sino-Russian military entente was obviously influenced by U.S. power projection into Central Asia since 2001.

On the other hand it needs reminding that this game of military bluffmanship is a very different business when nuclear powers, as opposed to nonnuclear ones, are engaged in muscle flexing. Ending a nuclear war is not something that any of the powers has scripted very well, and in the case of Russia and China, it is not even clear whether their leaders understand the concept. On the evidence, a failure of deterrence would be followed in Beijing or in Moscow by a decision for a traditional war fighting instead of a fighting-while-negotiating approach. The war ends when the supply of bombs runs out. So the United States needs to take care in planning for nuclear war limitation or termination; the adversary's worldview is a matter of some strategic importance.

Conclusions

Nuclear war termination was controversial during the Cold War, and for different reasons it will continue to be so. Contemplation of the "awfulness" of nuclear war is certainly not to be expected of most politicians or publics, apart from the now-ubiquitous fears of nuclear terrorism after 9/11. But apart from terrorism, states still have the responsibility for world order, and peace making does not stop after war has begun. Political leaders and military planners in nuclear armed and other leading states need to think through, before the fact of deterrence failure, what the "downstream" steps would be. Military machines should not be permitted to run on nuclear autopilot.[13]

The preceding illustrations do not constitute a prediction but a template for considering some aspects of the problem of nuclear conflict termination. We have used U.S. and Russian forces because we know something about how each state has operated its nuclear forces during peacetime and in crises—and because they have committed themselves to structural and operational arms control through the year 2012. Finally, the diversity of U.S. and Russian launch platforms, even at lower levels of force size, holds implications for smaller nuclear power and for nuclear-aspiring but currently nonnuclear states.

Missiles do not fire themselves. The management or prevention of nuclear proliferation is made harder by the uncertainty about relationships between politicians and their militaries in countries that are only notional democracies, or even less democratic than that. How will arrangements for delegation of authority and nuclear enablement for deterrence or war fighting be handled in a future nuclear armed Iran or Egypt or, for that matter, in nuclear-capable North Korea and Pakistan? Opacity in these matters is not reassuring, and dictatorships have a way of appearing solid on the outside, but brittle on the inside, once the fertilizer hits the oscillator of crisis and war. Nuclear weapons could spread into the hands of small and lethal Ottomans or Austro-Hungarians, circa 1910: tottering and dithering, seeking glory in self-destruction, and dragging others into the maelstrom before their policy-making processes could abort military determinism and lust for revenge.

Conclusion

Missile Defense and U.S.-Russian Nuclear Strategy

A number of conclusions can be drawn from this study. First, missile defense technologies are, relative to their twentieth-century predecessors, certain to improve. We are more than sixty years beyond the invention of the long-range ballistic missile and the beginning of the nuclear age. Second, new missile defenses, in the hands of Americans, Russians, or others, will not eliminate the need for nuclear deterrence and arms control in the future, nor will they create a "defense-dominant" world. Offenses will be mixed with defenses in more complex patterns than hitherto—deterrence by denial will complement deterrence by threat of unacceptable retaliation. Third, politics rules the roost. States' intentions will dominate their decisions whether to deploy missile defenses and for what purposes: for increasing deterrence stability, for hedging against rogue state or unauthorized attacks, or for supporting diplomatic maneuvering and coercive diplomacy.

Fourth, missile defenses will be of little value in a world in which nuclear proliferation is unconstrained or in a region where political hostility is permitted to overtake sensible deterrence and nuclear restraint. Faith in deterrence, nuclear or otherwise, and with or without missile defenses is misplaced; history is unkind to optimists.[1] Fifth, the United States and Russia must establish a favorable context for nuclear security in the coming world order that includes (1) reducing their long-range nuclear forces well below those ceilings permitted under SORT; (2) drastically reducing, if not eliminating, U.S. and Russian nuclear weapons that require prompt launch for survivability; (3) acting in concert with other powers to keep nuclear weapons out of the hands of revisionist powers that have already crossed, or soon will cross, the threshold of nuclear weapons capability; (4) collaborating on national missile defense and TMD, along with NATO, structured and tasked against rogue attacks from outside of Europe; and (5) making particular efforts to discourage nuclear weapons spread in Asia and the Middle East; missile defenses may be part of that story, if they are not provocative of offensive countermeasures that exacerbate regional arms races.

This study cannot resolve all the controversy surrounding U.S. and Russian nuclear deterrence and arms control policies in a possible, and increasingly plausible, world of nuclear plenty. Its more modest objective is to establish some benchmarks for defining the requirements for nuclear deterrence, arms control, proliferation, and missile defenses in the new world order. Within that framework, researchers, policy analysts, and government officials can interrogate various models for specific questions about how much is enough for deterrence or, if deterrence fails, for retaliation—with or without defenses. These are contentious issues, and the fog of analysis will grow larger as nuclear and other WMD spread among more international actors. Some perspective is also useful that brings together issues of policy and strategy with assumptions about technology. For improved technology is no guarantee of greater success in strategy, or in policy: Strategy is a hard business, and policy harder still, requiring marginal tradeoffs among various outcomes that leave domestic politics in turmoil and military historians shaking their heads.

Background and Pertinent Concepts

Stability during the Cold War was, in causal terms, overdetermined. The United States and the Soviet Union dominated military-strategic competition; other powers were reduced to playing allied or supporting roles. In addition, nuclear weapons were the trumps of world politics. But they were trump cards of a peculiar sort. In order to get them across oceans and land masses to their intended destinations in good time, they had to be flown in long-range aircraft or launched aboard missiles. As ballistic missiles became the delivery systems of preferred choice, the superiority of offensive technologies for warfare enforced the supremacy of defensive strategy. Antiballistic missile and air defenses remained primitive and ineffective compared to offensive delivery systems from the early years of the nuclear age until the end of the twentieth century.

Both the Americans and the Soviets, throughout the years of their Cold War military competition, sought to escape this paradox of shared nuclear peril. If either side could have deployed a preclusive defensive system capable of negating the other side's retaliatory strike, the first side could have had a plausible first-strike capability. As such, it could have imposed its will without war. U.S. and Soviet leaders feared such an eventuality, but science and technology fell short of overturning the "nuclear revolution." From the 1970s through the end of the Cold War, U.S. and Soviet leaders accepted the fact, if not the desirability, of mutual deterrence and "mutual assured destruction," although the Soviet Union never preferred "assured destruction" as a declaratory policy.

U.S. military planners and policy makers struggled to escape this nuclear stalemate and to provide a way to make nuclear weapons usable apart from threatening Armageddon. Various U.S. presidents sought limited nuclear options and other escapes from having to choose between engaging the entire strategic nuclear war plan and conceding the issue to the opponent. Approaches to the control of escalation during a nuclear war were considered, from the beginning of the Kennedy administration through the Carter administration. President Reagan, aghast at the possibility that the United States could face total annihilation without any capability to destroy attacking missiles in flight, called for a research and development program leading to the eventual deployment of national missile defenses. Scaled-down versions of BMD continued during the administrations of President George H. W. Bush and President Bill Clinton.

The World Turned Upside Down

The end of the Cold War and the demise of the Soviet Union made irrelevant the global competition between communism and capitalism. Instead of ideological conflicts rooted in superpower interests and European ideologies, new axes of disagreement grew up among state and nonstate actors. Even prior to the end of the twentieth century U.S. intelligence organs and defense planners recognized that new threats arose from rogue "states of concern," from terrorists, and from the anarchic fallout of failed states. State and nonstate actors in the twenty-first century sought to acquire weapons of mass destruction, including nuclear ones, for purposes of blackmail or destruction. Terrorist attacks on U.S. soil and elsewhere during the 1990s were premonitory of the global reach of al-Qaeda and other amorphous but relentless groups that sought nuclear and other WMD. The devastation of 9/11, bad as it was, could have been worse with nuclear or radiological weapons.

In addition to the possibility of stateless entities with WMD, the spread of nuclear and other WMD among states outside of Europe and not under the control of the United States or Russia created anxieties in Washington and in Moscow. India and Pakistan went officially nuclear after offsetting series of tests in 1998. North Korea expelled UN weapons inspectors in 2003, having abrogated the Framework Agreement intended to constrain further development of its nuclear infrastructure, and in 2005 the DPRK finally acknowledged what U.S. intelligence already knew: Pyongyang had deployed one or more assembled nuclear weapons.[2] North Korea's weaponized status, combined with its apparent plans to deploy intermediate and longer-range ballistic missiles, presented a potential threat to Japan and a proximate threat to U.S. forces stationed there and in South Korea. Fortunately, under a 2007 agreement with the United States,

South Korea, Russia, China, and Japan, North Korea agreed to open its nuclear infrastructure for inspection and eventual dismantlement.[3]

The possibility of further proliferation in Asia, in response to the acknowledged or obvious nuclear statuses of India, Pakistan, and North Korea, could not be ignored.[4] Nuclear weapons could appeal to South Korea or even to Japan. In addition, the Middle Eastern and south Asian politico-military template was complicated by the imminence of an Iranian nuclear capability unless Tehran was persuaded to reverse course by U.S. and European pressure. Israel might try to preempt an Iranian decision to go nuclear, although its official policy in the spring of 2005 was to support U.S. and European coercive diplomacy to that effect. Nuclear weapons could make North and South Asia (including parts of the Middle East from which nuclear-capable missiles could reach into Asia) a geostrategically crowded neighborhood: Russia, China, North Korea, South Korea, Japan, India, Pakistan, and the United States could all have vital interests and nuclear forces to support those interests.

The Bush Security Strategy

The George W. Bush administration National Security Strategy emphasized that the threat from rogue states or terrorists in possession of weapons of mass destruction requires rethinking of Cold War assumptions about deterrence. The direction that post–Cold War revisionism should take is far from obvious, however. The concept of assured retaliation by survivable retaliatory forces as one component of stable deterrence, as opposed to the entire basis of military-strategic relationships among major powers, is likely to endure into the twenty-first century. Populations will remain hostage to the effects of mass destruction weapons, including those delivered by terrorists. Protection of populations through active and passive defenses may improve, compared to Cold War standards. But population protection can never be absolute, and small numbers of nuclear weapons can inflict large amounts of societal destruction.

The potential of nuclear weapons as vehicles for mass destruction has more than intuitive appeal. It has been well documented, and it is as necessary for strategic as for humanitarian purposes to remind ourselves of nuclear uniqueness. The locution "weapons of mass destruction" in which nuclear, biological, and chemical weapons are conflated along with "dirty bombs" (conventional explosions designed to scatter radioactive debris but not involving true nuclear fusion or fission) is misleading. Nuclear weapons are a case apart from the others in that "WMD" category. For example, the Natural Resources Defense Council published in 2001 a study that included "assured destruction" calculations for many of the world's largest countries.[5] The study used highly

---

TABLE C.1. NUMBER OF 475-KT WEAPONS REQUIRED TO THREATEN 25 PERCENT OF THE POPULATION, FOR SELECTED COUNTRIES

COUNTRY	1999 POPULATION (IN MILLIONS)	25% OF 1999 POPULATION (IN MILLIONS)	NUMBER OF WEAPONS
United States	259	65	124
Russia	152	38	51
China	1,281	320	368
United Kingdom	56	14	19
France	58	14	25
Germany	81	20	33
All NATO nations	755	189	300
North Korea	22	5–6	4
Iran	64	16	10

Source: McKinzie et al., *U.S. Nuclear War Plan*, ch. 5, p. 126.

sophisticated simulation techniques to estimate the number of 475-kiloton weapons required to threaten 25 percent of the population in each state. The results for selected states appear in table C.1.

In addition, nuclear weapons can be used to attack targets other than value targets such as cities. Preemptive or retaliatory strikes against military forces are also possible. During the Cold War, scenarios focused on massive U.S.-Soviet force exchanges involving thousands of weapons. Each side feared that the other would execute a disarming first strike against its retaliatory forces. Much of this danger was exaggerated, but it drove analysis at the margin. And although we are well past the Cold War, U.S. and Russian nuclear forces are still sized against one another's capabilities, regardless of political intentions, as the "gold standard" against which other nuclear powers are compared. The Moscow Treaty of 2002 signed by President Bush and President Putin calls for reductions in the numbers of deployed warheads on each side's strategic launchers to between 2,200 and 1,700 by 2012.[6] Although parity in numbers of weapons is important to the two sides, each is trusted, according to the protocols of the treaty, to implement its own reductions according to its own state priorities. This permissive approach to verification reflects the officially nonhostile political relations between the United States and Russia after the Cold War.

In addition to the canonical scenario of a massive U.S.-Russian nuclear exchange, it is equally or more likely that nuclear weapons in the future will be used for coercive diplomacy or in actual attacks as part of regional "access denial" strategies. In this respect the object of a North Korean or Iranian nuclear capability, for example, would be to preclude the intervention in a local conflict of U.S. or allied hostile forces. An Iraq with nuclear weapons already available on Scud launchers would have posed a very different problem for U.S. planners of Desert Storm in 1990 and 1991. The same holds true for the U.S. war to impose regime change on Iraq in 2003.

U.S. Information Dominance and Countermeasures

The United States demonstrated in the Persian Gulf War of 1991, in Afghanistan in 2001, and in the ongoing Iraq War that its full-spectrum dominance of information-based warfare, including reconnaissance-strike complexes augmented by highly specialized ground forces, confers a decisive military advantage in large-scale, conventional warfare. Simply put the United States has no peer competitor at the high end of the spectrum of war fighting capabilities. For that very reason, opponents will seek to fight "asymmetrically," or against the grain of U.S. preeminence: unconventional warfare at one end of the spectrum of destructiveness, WMD at the other.[7] Although opposite in military-destructive potential, unconventional tactics and WMD share in common the attribute of changing the equation by turning the battlefield into one of psychology more than destruction of targets.

Unconventional warfare—for example, revolution or terrorism—seeks to impose costs on the population and to demonstrate that the regime cannot protect its own citizens, thus bringing the government into contempt. The object of revolutionaries and many terrorists, other than apocalyptic ones, is not mass murder but isolation of the government from its political support in favor of an alternative supported by the insurgents. Insurgents seek to drive up the cost of maintaining law and order and to provoke disproportionate retaliation against the population at large.

In a similar fashion, the objective of states in possession of WMD is not only, or mainly, the actual carrying out of missile strikes or air attacks that might provoke retaliation against their own territory. Instead, new nuclear powers can more successfully exploit the fear of possible attacks against U.S. expeditionary forces, allies, or U.S. territory in order to induce a more cautious diplomatic and military approach to conflict resolution. North Korea over the decade from 1994 to 2004 provides a case in point. North Korea used its latent and then manifest nuclear capabilities to squeeze the United States and other major powers for economic assistance and diplomatic concessions. The United States was not worried about losing a war against North Korea, if it came to that. The risk posed by even a small North Korean nuclear force was based on its potential to coerce regional rivals, including South Korea and Japan, allied to the United States.[8] In addition, North Korea might become a nuclear Wal-Mart for terrorists.

Consideration of "access denial" strategies supported by WMD or of the possible use by terrorists of weapons of mass destruction has led the Bush administration to emphasize preemption as an option in its military-strategic planning. The prospect of a Taliban or al-Qaeda with nuclear weapons suggests that traditional strategies of retaliation after attack may fall short of the degree of persuasion required for successful deterrence. More broadly, the Bush administration has called for rethinking the entire concept of the nuclear-strategic "triad" of land-based missiles, sea-based missiles, and bomber-delivered weapons that were the basis of its Cold War nuclear force structure. The Bush Nuclear Posture Review called for a "new triad" composed of (1) nuclear and nonnuclear offensive forces, (2) active and passive defenses, and (3) improved infrastructure for reconstitution of forces in a crisis, maintaining forces at necessary levels of readiness, and providing necessary research, development, and testing to ensure against future surprises.[9]

Missile Defense Redux

With regard to missile defenses as part of the new triad, Bush strategy included abrogation of the ABM Treaty and the decision to begin deploying a national ballistic missile defense system in 2004. The DOD and its Missile Defense Agency envisioned a phased program of technology development and deployment that would include capabilities for missile intercept in the boost and post-boost, midcourse, and terminal stages of missile trajectory.[10] Candidate technologies included the airborne optical laser for boost-phase intercept, land- and sea-based midcourse intercept systems, and PAC-3 and follow-on concepts for destruction of missiles in their terminal phase after atmospheric reentry. In addition to launchers and kill vehicles, advanced development would be required for space-based reconnaissance and launch detection and for battle management, including integrated command, control, and communications. Unlike the more ambitious proposals of the Reagan years for a comprehensive missile defense system capable of defeating a massive Soviet attack, the Bush missile defense program was based on iterative technology development and deployment. Deployment of the first phase of a land-based, midcourse-intercept BMD component began in the summer of 2004 in Alaska.

Even the postmodern version of missile defense, designed against attacks from rogue states or accidental/inadvertent launches, was controversial among defense analysts and arms control experts. It was also controversial in Moscow. President Putin registered no official objection to the U.S. decisions to abrogate the ABM Treaty and to begin missile defense deployments (except in Europe). Putin and his military advisors indicated, however, that Russia would do whatever was necessary in order to maintain the viability of its nuclear deterrent.

Russia was particularly piqued in 2007 about the U.S. decision to deploy missile defense interceptors and radars in Eastern Europe and on the territory of NATO members formerly included within the Soviet-dominated Warsaw Pact. Especially in the post–Cold War climate of fiscal uncertainty and reductions in its conventional military forces, Russia was dependent entirely on its nuclear weapons for membership in the club of major military powers. Reflecting this reality, Russia's military doctrine now admits of the possibility of nuclear first use or first strike in response to large-scale conventional attack on Russian forces or vital centers.

Indeed, the U.S.-Russian nuclear relationship assumes a special importance even with the likelihood of further nuclear weapons spread in Asia and an n-sided nuclear arms race globally. Defenses that are truly effective and not just notional components of a "new triad" could place the United States and Russia, if the technologies were shared between the powers, into a twenty-first-century version of their Cold War strategic nuclear bipolarity. A shared strategic defensive space in the Northern Hemisphere against rogue attacks and accidental launches would be a daunting challenge to lesser powers, even for those with their own ballistic missile forces and nuclear weapons. Instead of having Russia outside the tent of U.S. and NATO security protection looking in, Moscow could be within the U.S. and NATO strategic security perimeter provided by active and passive defenses based on information-age principles.[11] For example, with regard to proliferation concerns about Iran and their relationship to Russian-U.S. cooperation on missile defenses, Joseph Cirincione has noted that "a joint U.S.-Russian system would deliver a powerful strategic and political blow to Iran. The cooperation would help to isolate Iran, which would now have the humiliation of having its most important political ally and nuclear technology supplier turning its military assets against it. It would also reverse the deterioration in U.S.-Russian relations, paying dividends far into the future."[12]

Cooperative Security and New Missile Defenses

This possibility of a U.S.-Russian defense dominant condominium is not as visionary as it might first appear. Information-age technology makes possible antimissile defenses on an affordable scale. The key to future missile defenses is not only in kinetic science but also in the mastery of "knowledge space" of advanced electronics and cybernetics. Advanced electronics and cybernetics provide for the sensors, data processing, communications, and command-control systems that turn "dumb" interceptors of the Cold War era into "smart" systems benefiting from the synergy of aerospace, land-based, and sea-based components. Prior to the information age, the linkage of "system of systems" elements among disparate platforms for missile intercept could not be accomplished in good time on account of the limitations of electronic and computer technology. Future systems for BMD, compared to their Cold War counterparts, will be lighter, faster, modular, and flexible—just as twenty-first-century U.S. infantry are compared to the "dogfaces" and "grunts" of the previous century.

Defenses based on information dominance will, of course, have to deal with countermeasures available to attackers. However, in this sector as well as in advanced defenses, strategy favors those who already have a head start. The United States and Russia are far ahead of other powers in the development of offensive countermeasures against ballistic missile defenses, having spent much of the Cold War working on this problem. In addition, the United States and Russia are the world's preeminent military space powers. Other states that would want to race the United States and Russia simultaneously in the realm of missile defenses or antimissile countermeasures have an uphill climb. And on the basis of prior Cold War experience (although under very different circumstances), reasonable persons could argue that a U.S.-Russian security community in Eurasia would support, although not necessarily guarantee, stability in both Europe and Asia.

U.S.-Russian security cooperation on the high ground of space and missile defenses might also expedite offensive arms reductions in both countries and the improvement of conventional forces in Russia. The latter objective, of improving the quality of Russian long-range and other conventional forces, would make Russia less reliant on threats of nuclear preemption in response to the possibility of attacks on or near its territory by nonnuclear means. Russia is a long way from being able to afford the kind of military "transformation" that the United States is now going through. But if Russia intends to lay claim to major power status in the twenty-first century, it must accomplish the modernization of its armed forces by technological innovation and by personnel policies more suited to a partly voluntary force.[13] The days of the mass army as an effective fighting force are numbered: virtually any massing of forces on a significant scale can be detected in good time and rapidly attacked by unforgiving long-range, precision strikes.

The transition from the world of mass destruction to the world of precision warfare affects the paradigm for strategic nuclear deterrence, in addition to its implications for conventional war fighting. Missile defenses, based on information principles and the mature exploration of space as a medium for peacetime and wartime missions, are over the horizon. Their deployment will end the free ride that offensive ballistic missiles have had since their creation during World War II. Along with this, the accuracies of offensive missiles will also improve, based on information-age upgrades, as will the precision of ballistic and cruise missile strikes against military and other targets.

Mature defenses therefore will not eliminate the importance of offensive first-strike or retaliation strategies and forces. Defenses and offenses will coexist as technology advances and as states' assumptions about their security dilemmas evolve. But it is important to appreciate the significance of a shift from an offense-only to an offensive-defensive competition in technology related to strategic nuclear warfare or to nuclear coercion. We have reached a moment of punctuated equilibrium: from simplicity, in assessing the requirements for nuclear coercion or retaliation, to complexity, in evolving technology for attacking with missiles and for defending against them.

Appendix: Methodological Notes

I gratefully acknowledge James Scouras and James Tritten, expert scientists and policy analysts as well as published authors on nuclear weapons and arms control, for permission to make use of their analytical models in this study.

Scouras's model AWSM@ is an enhanced Excel spreadsheet that calculates the outcomes of nuclear force exchanges and draws corresponding graphs of very high fidelity. Calculations are based on parameters established by the investigator relative to force structures and weapons performance characteristics. A sample spreadsheet is produced in table A.1; cell entries are illustrative and not necessarily actual data. I adapted the model for this study. Scouras bears no responsibility for the database or for the results and arguments herein.

For a more comprehensive explanation of this methodology with pertinent applications, see Stephen J. Cimbala and James Scouras, *A New Nuclear Century: Strategic Stability and Arms Control* (Westport, Conn.: Praeger, 2002), 25–73.

Tritten's model is also based on a spreadsheet, first developed by him during his tenure as a professor at the U.S. Naval Postgraduate School. I have modified the original model, adapted it for use as an Excel spreadsheet, and revised the database to account for changes in U.S. and Soviet (and then Russian) forces. A sample output is reproduced in table A.2 with notional numbers.

The models assist the investigator by calculating formulas and by converting calculations into graphs. The investigator is required to specify the values for force structure, numbers of forces and weapons deployed, estimated performance characteristics of weapons, and other parameters.

| US Force 1 | US | Unavailable | Balanced Triad | | | | |
Platform Name	Total Platforms	Off-line Platforms (number)	Off-line Platforms (%)	SNDVs per Platform	Warheads per SNDV	Total SNDVs	Total Warheads
MM III MK21	300	0	0.00	1	1	300	300
Total ICBM	300					300	300
Trident II	14	0	0.10	24	4	336	1344
Total SLBM	14					336	1344
B-52H	44	0	0.10	1	8	44	352
B2	20	0	0.10	1	8	20	160
Total Air	64					64	512
Grand Total	378					700	2156

TABLE A.2. TRITTEN MODEL ILLUSTRATIVE SPREADSHEET

RUSSIAN FORCES	LAUNCHERS	WARHEADS @	TOTAL WARHEADS
SS-11/3	0	1	0
SS-17	0	1	0
SS-18	50	10	500
unnamed	0	1	0
SS-19/3	30	6	180
SS-27 silo	50	1	50
subtotal fixed land	130		730
SS-25 (road)	20	1	20
SS-27 (road)	50	1	50
subtotal mobile land	70		70
subtotal land-based	200		800
SS-N-6/3	0	1	0
SS-N-8/2	0	1	0
SS-N-18/2	0	1	0
Borey/SS-NX-30 Bulava	24	3	72
Delta IV/SS-N-23	96	4	384
subtotal sea-based	120		456
Tu-95 H 6 / ALCM	20	6	120
Tu-95 H 16 / ALCM	44	16	704
Tu-160 Blackjack	12	8	96
subtotal air-breathing	76		920
Total Russian forces	396		2,176

TABLE A.2 CONT. TRITTEN MODEL ILLUSTRATIVE SPREADSHEET

U.S. FORCES	LAUNCHERS	WARHEADS @	TOTAL WARHEADS
Minuteman II	0	1	0
Minuteman III	0	1	0
Minuteman IIIA	300	1	300
Peacekeeper MX	0	10	0
subtotal land-based	300		300
Trident C-4	0	4	0
Trident D-5/W-76	0	4	0
Trident D-5/W-88	336	4	1,344
subtotal sea-based	336		1,344
B-52G gravity	0	0	0
B-52G gravity	0	0	0
ALCM		0	0
B-52H ALCM	24	12	288
B-2	20	12	240
subtotal air-breathing	44		528
Total U.S. forces	680		2,172

(Preceding data multiplied through matrix of seventeen parameters in order to produce summary descriptors, as below).

SUMMARY DESCRIPTORS	NUMBERS
Total Russian deliverable warheads	321.60
Total Russian deliverable EMT	85.04
Deliverable Russian reserve warheads	138.36
Deliverable Russian reserve EMT	155.15
Total U.S. deliverable warheads	702.43
Total U.S. deliverable EMT	212.82
Deliverable U.S. reserve warheads	343.04
Deliverable U.S. reserve EMT	187.64

Notes

Introduction: Missile Defenses in a New Nuclear Century

1. Robert Burns, "Zeroing in on a Satellite," *Philadelphia Inquirer*, February 16, 2008, A4.

2. Ibid.

3. Thom Shanker, "Missile Strikes a Spy Satellite Falling from Its Orbit," *New York Times*, February 21, 2008, http://www.nytimes.com/2008/02/01/us/21satellite.html.

4. Colin S. Gray, *Recognizing and Understanding Revolutionary Change in Warfare: The Sovereignty of Context* (Carlisle Barracks, Pa.: Strategic Studies Institute, U.S. Army War College, September 2006), is not too emphatic in his exclamation that "warfare is all about context" (15).

5. The concept of "second nuclear age" is developed and explained in Colin S. Gray, *The Second Nuclear Age* (Boulder, Colo.: Lynne Rienner, 1999), esp. 5–9. See also Keith B. Payne, *Deterrence in the Second Nuclear Age* (Lexington: University Press of Kentucky, 1996).

6. Alexander L. George, "Strategies for Crisis Management," chap. 16 in *Avoiding War: Problems of Crisis Management*, ed. Alexander L. George (Boulder, Colo.: Westview Press, 1991), 377–394, esp. 384–387. George's definition of coercive diplomacy corresponds to Thomas C. Schelling's concept of "compellence"; see Schelling, *Arms and Influence* (New Haven, Conn.: Yale University Press, 1966), 69–78.

7. On this issue, see Raymond L. Garthoff, *Deterrence and the Revolution in Soviet Military Doctrine* (Washington, D.C.: Brookings Institution, 1990), 174–185.

8. For an exemplary discussion of the problem of deterrence and rationality, see Patrick M. Morgan, *Deterrence Now* (Cambridge: Cambridge University Press, 2003), esp. 55–79.

9. Paul Bracken, *Fire in the East: The Rise of Asian Military Power and the Second Nuclear Age* (New York: Harper Collins, 1999), 40.

10. Ibid., 42–43.

11. C. J. Chivers and Mark Landler, "Putin to Suspend Pact with NATO," *New York Times*, April 27, 2007, http://www.nytimes.com/2007/04/27/world/europe/27russia.html.

12. Jim Rutenberg, "Putin Expands on His Missile Defense Plan," *New York Times*, July 3, 2007, http://www.nytimes.com/2007/07/03us/03putin.html.

13. For this distinction and authoritative discussion of the topic, see MacGregor Knox and Williamson Murray, eds., *The Dynamics of Military Revolution, 1300–2050* (Cambridge: Cambridge University Press, 2001), esp. chaps. 1, 4, and 8–10, on thinking about revolutions in warfare, about military innovations in World War I and World War II, and about implications for the future of war, and policy. Also indispensable on this topic is Colin S. Gray, *Strategy for Chaos: Revolutions in Military Affairs and the Evidence of History* (London: Frank Cass, 2002). Gray is especially useful in focusing the RMA debate on its significance for strategy, war and history: as opposed to a self-regarding intellectual preoccupation. See also Stephen Biddle's discussion of the emergence of the "modern system" of force employment in his *Military Power: Explaining Victory and Defeat in Battle* (Princeton, N.J.: Princeton University Press, 2004), esp. 1–10 and chaps. 3–4.

14. Max Boot, *War Made New: Technology, Warfare, and the Course of History, 1500 to Today* (New York: Gotham Books, 2006), esp. 455–473; citation on 463.

Chapter 1. Russian and American Nuclear Force Reductions

1. Joseph Cirincione, *Bomb Scare: The History and Future of Nuclear Weapons* (New York: Columbia University Press, 2007), 133.

2. The motives for states to acquire nuclear weapons also include technology and economics. See ibid., 47 and passim.

3. Andrei Zagorski, "Moscow Seeks to Renegotiate Relations with the West," *Russian Analytical Digest* 26 (September 4, 2007): 2–5.

4. Ibid., 3.

5. Choe Sang-Hun, "North Korea Says U.S. Will Lift Sanctions," *New York Times*, September 4, 2007, http://www.nytimes.com/2007/09/04/world/asia/04korea.html.

6. Jane M. O. Sharp, "Missile Madness," *World Today*, December 2007, http://www.theworldtoday.org, in Johnson's Russia List 2007, No. 245, November 28, 2007, http://www.cdi.org/russia/johnson/.

7. Mark A. Smith, *A Review of Russian Foreign Policy* (Shrivenham: Conflict Studies Research Centre, Defense Academy of the United Kingdom, July 2007), 1.

8. Ibid., 2.

9. Associated Press, "Missile Defense, Kosovo Are 'Red Lines' for Russia, Foreign Minister Says," *International Herald Tribune Europe*, September 3, 2007, http://www.iht.com/articles/2007/09/03/asia/russia.php.

10. Andrew E. Kramer and Thom Shanker, "Russia Suspends Arms Agreement Over U.S. Shield," *New York Times*, July 15, 2007, http://www.nytimes.com/2007/07/15/world/europe/15russia.html.

11. Rutenberg, "Putin Expands on His Missile Defense Plan."

12. Vadim Solovyev, "Report on Russian Expansion of Offer to Create Joint Missile ABM System," *Nezavisimoye Voyennoye Obozreniye*, July 15, 2007, in Johnson's Russia List 2007, No. 155, July 16, 2007, http://www.cdi.org/russia/johnson/.

13. Norman Polmar, "Improved Russian Missile Tested," June 4, 2007, Military.com website, http://www.military.com/forums/0,15240,138051.00.html; and "Russia Plans ICBM to Counter U.S. Missile Shield," Spiegel On Line International, August 6, 2007, http://www.spiegel.de/international/world/0,1518,498338.00.html.

14. Associated Press, "Russian Bombers Force U.S. Jets to Scramble," August 9, 2007, Military.com website, http://www.military.com/NewsContent/0,13319,145423,00.html.

15. For pertinent assessments, see U.S. Government Accountability Office, *Defense Acquisitions: Status of Ballistic Missile Program in 2004* (Washington, D.C.: GAO, March 2005), and Lisbeth Gronland et al., *Technical Realities: An Analysis of the 2004 Deployment of a U.S. Missile Defense System* (Cambridge, Mass.: Union of Concerned Scientists, May 2004). Challenges facing national and theater missile defenses are also analyzed in Dean A. Wilkening, *Ballistic-Missile Defence and Strategic Stability* (Oxford: Oxford University Press, 2000).

16. "Treaty between the United States of America and the Russian Federation on Strategic Offensive Reductions," May 24, 2002, in *Arms Control Today*, June 2002, http://www.armscontrol.org/documents/sort.asp/.

17. Cirincione, *Bomb Scare*, 132.

18. Wolfgang K. H. Panofsky, "Nuclear Insecurity," *Foreign Affairs*, September/October 2007, in Johnson's Russia List 2007, No. 180, August 23, 2007, http://www.cdi.org/russia/johnson/.

19. Stephen M. Walt, *Taming American Power: The Global Response to U.S. Primacy* (New York: W. W. Norton, 2005), 240.

20. Ibid.

21. Miller, quoted in Cirincione, *Bomb Scare*, 132.

22. Perle, quoted in ibid.

23. Associated Press, "Experts See Decline in Russia's Military," November 13, 2007, in Johnson's Russia List 2007, No. 236, November 14, 2007, http://www.cdi.org/russia/johnson/.

24. Force structures are the author's. Forces are notional and not necessarily predictive of actual force deployments. See also, for Russian forces, Pavel Podvig, *The Russian Nuclear Arsenal* (Stanford, Calif.: Center for International Security and Cooperation, Stanford University, and International Relations and Security Network, 2006), and Irina Isakova, *Russian Defense Reform: Current Trends* (Carlisle, Pa.: Strategic Studies Institute, U.S. Army War College, November 2006), 34–38.

25. The author gratefully acknowledges James Scouras for use of his AWSM@ model in this study. Scouras is not responsible for any of the analysis or arguments here.

For additional information on pertinent methodology, see Stephen J. Cimbala and James Scouras, *A New Nuclear Century* (Westport, Conn.: Praeger, 2002).

26. Assured destruction or assured retaliation is nukespeak for the credible threat to destroy in retaliation enough of the opponent's society and economy to make any first strike irrational by any reasonable standard. Experts differ about what is reasonable or rational, but most of that is professional wordplay. Even tens of strategic nuclear warheads directed against the major cities and infrastructure of most states would be sufficiently deterring to leaders who are operating within a cost-benefit model of rationality. For those who are not, deterrent bets are off. For diverse views on this problem, see Derek D. Smith, *Deterring America: Rogue States and the Proliferation of Weapons of Mass Destruction* (Cambridge: Cambridge University Press, 2006); Stephen J. Cimbala, *Nuclear Weapons and Strategy: U.S. Nuclear Policy for the Twenty-First Century* (London: Routledge, 2005); Gray, *Second Nuclear Age*; and Payne, *Deterrence in the Second Nuclear Age*.

27. See Richard Weitz, *Russian-American Security Cooperation after St. Petersburg: Challenges and Opportunities* (Carlisle, Pa.: U.S. Army War College, Strategic Studies Institute, April 2007), and Jennifer G. Mathers, *The Russian Nuclear Shield from Stalin to Yeltsin* (New York: St. Martin's Press, 2000).

28. This concern is expressed by Keir A. Lieber and Daryl G. Press, "The Rise of U.S. Nuclear Primacy," *Foreign Affairs*, March/April 2006, http://www.foreignaffairs. org/20060301faessay85204/keir-a-lieber-daryl-g-press/html.

29. For example, the Moscow-based *Kommersant* reported that Russia might counter the U.S. missile defense deployments in Poland and the Czech Republic by stationing nuclear weapons in Belarus. *Kommersant* cited Russia's ambassador to Belarus, Alexander Surikov, as its source. Michael Heath, "Russia Has No Need to Counter Europe Missile Shield, U.S. Says," August 31, 2007, Bloomberg.com, http://www.bloomberg. com/apps/news?pid=20601085&sid=avnR1CVYB.Cs&refer=europe.html.

Chapter 2. Missile Defenses: The Priority of Politics

1. For the technical and policy rationales for long-range missile defenses in Europe, see Patricia Sanders, *Missile Defense Program Overview for the European Union, Committee on Foreign Affairs, Subcommittee on Security and Defense* (Washington, D.C.: Department of Defense, June 28, 2007). A critical assessment of this proposal is provided in Richard Garwin, "Ballistic Missile Defense Deployment to Poland and the Czech Republic," paper presented at the Erice International Seminar, 38th Session, August 31, 2007, available at http://www.fas.org/rlg/081507BMDPe.pdf.

2. Rutenberg, "Putin Expands on His Missile Defense Plan."

3. The NATO-Russia Council was created in 2002 and replaced the Permanent Joint Council as a forum for shared discussion and decision making. See Dmitri Trenin, "NATO and Russia: Sobering Thoughts and Practical Suggestions," *NATO Review*, Summer 2007, http://www.nato.int/docu/review/2007/issue2/english/art1.html.

4. Vadim Solovyev, "Report on Russian Expansion."

5. Kramer and Shanker, "Russia Suspends Arms Agreement."

6. Polmar, "Improved Russian Missile Tested."

7. "Russia Plans ICBM to Counter U.S. Missile Shield."

8. Polmar, "Improved Russian Missile Tested."

9. "Russia Resumes Nuke Bomber Sorties," Reuters, August 9, 2007, http://www.cnn.com/2007/WORLD/europe/08/09/russia.sorties.reut/index.html.

10. Ibid.

11. Ivan Safranchuk, Moscow office director of the World Security Institute, quoted in ibid.

12. Kristin Roberts, "U.S. Offers to Keep Shield on Stand-by: Officials," Reuters, October 23, 2007, in Johnson's Russia List 2007, No. 220, October 23, 2007, http://www.cdi.org/russia/johnson/.

13. Following a U.S. expert team visit to the Russian early warning radar located in Azerbaijan in September 2007, Secretary Rice and Secretary Gates invited Russia in October to join the United States and NATO as a partner in designing and operating an antimissile system protecting all of Europe, according to press reports. See Thom Shanker, "U.S. Official Calls Russian Radar Good, but Not Exact Enough for Tracking Plan," *New York Times*, via *International Herald Tribune*, November 5, 2007, http://www.iht.com/pages/americas/index.php/.

14. Amy Knight, "Is Kremlin Infighting Destabilizing Russia? A Bitter Power Struggle among Putin's Security Chieftains May Explain Renewed Hostility against the West," *Toronto Globe and Mail*, October 16, 2007, in Johnson's Russia List 2007, No. 216, October 16, 2007, http://www.cdi.org/russia/johnson/.

15. Alexei Arbatov, "Is a New Cold War Imminent?" *Russia in Global Affairs*, July–September 2007, in Johnson's Russia List 2007, No. 175, August 16, 2007, http://www.cdi.org/russia/johnson/.

16. Ibid.

17. Ibid.

18. Ibid.

19. "Treaty between the United States of America and the Russian Federation."

20. Joint Statement, United States of America and the Russian Federation, Moscow, May 24, 2002, in *Arms Control Today*, June 2002, http://www.armscontrol.org/documents/sort.asp/.

21. Ibid.

22. Ibid.

23. Ibid.

24. U.S. and Russian officials have discussed cooperation on missile defenses since the early 1990s. U.S.-Russian discussions have emphasized national missile defenses, and NATO-Russian consultations have focused on theater missile defenses against short- and medium-range missiles. For example, Russian officials have offered to

164 NOTES TO PAGES 44–50

contribute their advanced air defense systems S-300 and S-400, the latter with some TMD capability, to a European-wide missile defense system. See Weitz, *Russian-American Security Cooperation*, 12–14 and passim.

25. Force structures are the author's. Forces are notional and not necessarily predictive of actual force deployments. See also Podvig, *Russian Nuclear Arsenal*.

26. For purposes of this part of the analysis and to simplify calculations, retaliators are assumed to be in a "generated alert, riding out the attack" posture that was canonical for U.S. analysis during the Cold War—although not necessarily an accurate representation of operational proclivities.

27. This and other factors making the task of missile defense more difficult than that of attack are noted in Andrew M. Sessler, John M. Cornwall, Bob Dietz, Steve Fetter, Sherman Frankel, Richard L. Garwin, Kurt Gottfried, Lisbeth Gronlund, George N. Lewis, Theodore A. Postol, and David C. Wright, *Countermeasures: A Technical Evaluation of the Operational Effectiveness of the Planned U.S. National Missile Defense System* (Cambridge, Mass.: Union of Concerned Scientists, April 2000), xxii and passim.

28. As Dean A. Wilkening has noted, the principal limitation of national and theater missile defense systems based on midcourse or terminal intercept is their potential vulnerability to countermeasures. Fewer countermeasures exist against boost-phase intercept but boost-phase intercept is more technically challenging. One possibility is airborne intercept. According to Wilkening: "Airborne interceptors launched from high-altitude UAVs may provide an effective and robust theater *and* national missile defense against small states such as North Korea, Iraq and possibly Iran. Moreover, this type of defence would not pose a serious threat to Russian or Chinese strategic missiles because the UAVs would have to fly directly over these countries' airspace." Wilkening, *Ballistic-Missile Defence*, 74. An interesting proposal for an air-launched, kinetic boost-phase intercept with applications for national or theater missile defenses appears in Col. Robert C. Wiegand, U.S. Air Force, *Heads, Not Tails: How Best to Engage Theater Ballistic Missile Defenses?* Occasional Paper No. 53, Center for Strategy and Technology, Air War College (Maxwell AFB, Ala.: Air University, February 2006).

29. See Wilkening, *Ballistic-Missile Defence*, 45–58.

30. The Shanghai Cooperation Organization (SCO) was formed in June 2001 by Russia, China, and the four Central Asian states of Tajikistan, Kyrgyzstan, Kazakhstan, and Uzbekistan. Its charter of June 2002 empowered the organization as a forum for interstate cooperation on security, economic, and other issues.

31. Brad Roberts, *China and Ballistic Missile Defense: 1955 to 2002 and Beyond* (Paris: French Institute of International Relations, Winter 2004), 37.

32. According to Chinese academic analyst Zhen Huang, "For the purpose of reconstructing minimum deterrence, China is not only required to keep improving

the survivability of its nuclear forces through measures such as camouflage of deployment sites, development of solid propellant and acquisition of mobile delivery systems as well as improvements in C4ISR (command, control, communications, computers, intelligence, surveillance and reconnaissance) capabilities. More critically, it is required to develop effective means to penetrate U.S. missile defense structure so as to strike at least some major cities. It is in this connection that China's nuclear force is likely to move to an initial limited deterrence capability at the strategic level." Zhen Huang, "China's Strategic Nuclear Posture by 2010: Minimum or Limited Deterrence? Likely Impact of U.S. Missile Defense," paper presented for the 8th ISODARCO-Beijing Seminar on Arms Control, Beijing, October 14–18, 2002, cited in Roberts, *China and Ballistic Missile Defense*, 38.

33. Russian-U.S. cooperation is especially important in preventing nuclear terrorism, which is not inevitable. See Graham Allison, *Nuclear Terrorism: The Ultimate Preventable Catastrophe* (New York: Times Books–Henry Holt, 2004), esp. 140–151.

34. As Colin S. Gray has noted, per Clausewitz, the political dimension of strategy "is the one that gives it meaning." Gray, *Modern Strategy* (Oxford: Oxford University Press, 1999), 29 and passim.

35. The analogy between the 1990s and Russia's original Time of Troubles in the early 1600s appears in Philip Longworth, *Russia: The Once and Future Empire from Pre-History to Putin* (New York: St. Martin's Press, 2005), 301.

Chapter 3. Deterrence and Missile Defenses: Compatible or Antithetical?

1. Associated Press, "Russia Says It Will Target European Sites if U.S. Missile Shield Proceeds," *International Herald Tribune Europe*, June 3, 2007, http://www.iht.com/articles/ap/2007/06/04/europe/EU-GEN-Russia-Putin-US.php/.

2. Ibid.

3. Associated Press, "Russia: U.S. Base Hosts May Be Targets," February 20, 2007, http://www.military.com/NewsContent/0,13319,125839,00.html.

4. Mikhail Nikolayev, "Hypersonics Will Punch Holes in American Missile Defense. Problem Is, the New Weapon Will Not Be Fielded Soon," *Nezavisimoye Voyennoye Obozreniye*, March 21, 2007, in Johnson's Russia List 2007, No. 69, March 22, 2007, http://www.cdi.org/russia/johnson/.

5. Ibid.

6. Ibid.

7. Ibid.

8. Rutenberg, "Putin Expands on His Missile Defense Plan."

9. "Putin Waiting for U.S. Response to Missile Defense Initiatives," Itar-Tass, July 3, 2007, in Johnson's Russia List 2007, No. 148, July 5, 2007, http://www.cdi.org/russia/johnson/.

10. "RF ABM Proposals May Change Configuration of Global Relations–VP," Itar-Tass, July 4, 2007, in Johnson's Russia List 2007, No. 148, July 5, 2007, http://www.cdi.org/russia/johnson/.

11. Ibid.

12. Ibid.

13. For an expansion of this point, see Dale R. Herspring, *The Kremlin and the High Command: Presidential Impact on the Russian Military from Gorbachev to Putin* (Lawrence: University Press of Kansas, 2006), 155–157.

14. On Russia's war in Chechnya from 1994 to 1996, see Stephen J. Cimbala and Peter Rainow, *Russia and Postmodern Deterrence* (Dulles, Va.: Potomac Books, 2007), 113–134.

15. Herspring, *Kremlin and the High Command*, chap. 6 is especially good on this point.

16. Ibid., 157–168.

17. For pertinent context and projections, see Podvig, *Russian Nuclear Arsenal*. See also Nikolai Sokov, *Russian Strategic Modernization: The Past and Future* (Lanham, Md.: Rowman and Littlefield, 2000), 125–155.

18. Peter Vincent Pry, *War Scare: Russia and America on the Nuclear Brink* (Westport, Conn.: Praeger, 1999). On the challenges for Russian nuclear policy and force modernization, see Rose Gottemoeller, "Nuclear Weapons in Current Russian Policy," chap. 6 in *The Russian Military: Power and Policy*, ed. Steven E. Miller and Dmitri Trenin (Cambridge, Mass.: MIT Press, 2004), 183–215, and Olga Oliker and Tanya Charlick-Paley, *Assessing Russia's Decline: Trends and Implications for the United States and the U.S. Air Force* (Santa Monica, Calif.: RAND, 2002).

19. Trenin, "NATO and Russia."

20. Ibid.

21. Ibid.

22. For background, see Alex Goldfarb with Marina Litvinenko, *Death of a Dissident: The Poisoning of Alexander Litvinenko and the Return of the KGB* (New York: Free Press, 2007), esp. 315–333. This is not, for obvious reasons, a disinterested account.

23. Vladimir Isachenkov, "Putin Orders Boost in Military, Spying," Associated Press, July 25, 2007, http://www.breitbart.com/article.php?id=D8QJQ3Q80&show_article=1&cat=0/.

24. Ibid.

25. Force structures are based on Podvig, *Russian Nuclear Arsenal*, and my estimates.

26. Human factors are vitally important, including the performance of command-control and communications systems under duress, but they involve many unknowns. See, for example, Kurt Gottfried and Bruce G. Blair et al., *Crisis Stability and Nuclear War* (New York: Oxford University Press, 1988), 265–268. There is also the logical paradox that Cold War U.S. and Soviet nuclear "options" all involved so many war-

heads and so much collateral damage that they transcended the very meaning of "war" as an instrument of policy, per Clausewitz. The threat of war remained politically useful but was based on a paradoxically credible willingness to perform the incredible. Fortunately, the self-referential worlds of national security bureaucrats and military planners were under some policy discipline by the desires of politicians and citizens for survival.

27. Experts recognize that actual defenses might have interaction effects among the various layers, depending on the targeting strategies of the defender, the countermeasures of the attacker, and the technologies involved. For pertinent background, see Wilkening, *Ballistic-Missile Defence*, esp. 34–37.

28. The canonical case for U.S. analysis may have been unfaithful to the actual decision-making proclivities of military planners during the Cold War. Launch on warning or other versions of prompt launch may have been the preferred Soviet option compared to retaliation after ride out, and the U.S. option for prompt launch of the ICBM force may have been higher on the list of preferred options than most policy makers acknowledged. See Bruce G. Blair, *The Logic of Accidental Nuclear War* (Washington, D.C.: Brookings Institution, 1993), 168–218. According to Blair, "A strategy of deterrence based on second-strike retaliation had become so vital a pillar of policy consensus and so much a part of the lore of strategic policy that it enjoyed virtual immunity from scrutiny, obscuring the importance of launch on warning" (176).

29. For discussion of pertinent scenarios in history and future possibilities, see Karl P. Mueller, Jasen J. Castillo, Forrest E. Morgan, Negeen Pegahi, and Brian Rosen, *Striking First: Preemptive and Preventive Attack in U.S. National Security Policy* (Santa Monica, Calif.: RAND, 2006), and George H. Quester, *Nuclear First Strike: Consequences of a Broken Taboo* (Baltimore: Johns Hopkins University Press, 2006).

Chapter 4. Missile Defenses in Context: Manageable Threat, Possible Opportunity

1. For example, see Oleg Shchedrov, "Putin Still Opposed to U.S. Missile Shield," Reuters, May 23, 2007, in Johnson's Russia List 2007, No. 118, May 24, 2007, http://www.cdi.org/russia/johnson/; and Associated Press, "Russia Says It Will Target European Sites."

2. Sheryl Gay Stolberg, "Putin Surprises Bush with Plan on Missile Shield," *New York Times*, June 8, 2007, http://www.nytimes.com/2007/06/08/world/europe/08prexy.html.

3. Rutenberg, "Putin Expands on His Missile Defense Plan."

4. Ibid.

5. "Putin Waiting for U.S. Response."

6. "RF ABM Proposals May Change Configuration of Global Relations."

7. Ibid.

8. Walter Pincus, "Senate Panel Faults Missile Defense Plan: Location in Eastern Europe Is Criticized," *Washington Post*, July 5, 2007, in Johnson's Russia List 2007, No. 148, July 5, 2007, http://www.cdi.org/russia/johnson/.

9. Ibid.

10. Ibid.

11. Ibid.

12. Ibid.

13. Ibid.

14. This terse summary ignores many nuances in U.S. and Soviet military thinking during the Cold War. For pertinent history with regard to U.S. missile defenses, see Donald R. Baucom, *The Origins of SDI, 1944–1983* (Lawrence: University Press of Kansas, 1992), and Frances FitzGerald, *Way Out There in the Blue: Reagan, Star Wars and the End of the Cold War* (New York: Simon and Schuster, 2000). A pessimistic assessment of the Reagan missile defense program, and of U.S. arms control policy during the Reagan-Gorbachev years, appears in Richard Rhodes, *Arsenals of Folly: The Making of the Nuclear Arms Race* (New York: Knopf, 2007), chaps. 10–13. For the Soviet and post-Soviet Russian experience, see Mathers, *Russian Nuclear Shield*.

15. For diverse perspectives on deterrence in the Cold War compared to later, see Payne, *Deterrence in the Second Nuclear Age*; Gray, *Second Nuclear Age*; Cimbala, *Nuclear Weapons and Strategy*; and Smith, *Deterring America*.

16. On the general topic of nuclear proliferation and its contemporary aspects, see Henry Sokolski, ed., *Taming the Next Set of Strategic Weapons Threats* (Carlisle, Pa.: U.S. Army War College, Nonproliferation Policy Education Center and Strategic Studies Institute, June 2006), and Henry Sokolski, ed., *Prevailing in a Well-Armed World: Devising Competitive Strategies against Weapons Proliferation* (Carlisle, Pa.: U.S. Army War College, Nonproliferation Policy Education Center and Strategic Studies Institute, March 2000). On the relationship between nuclear proliferation and terrorism, see Allison, *Nuclear Terrorism*, esp. chaps. 7–8 on risk reduction measures.

17. See Jim Yardley and David E. Sanger, "In Shift, Accord on North Korea Seems to Be Set," *New York Times*, February 13, 2007, http://www.nytimes.com/2007/02/13/world/asia/13korea.html; and Bill Powell, "North Korea Has Agreed to Shut Down Its Nuclear Program: Is He Really Ready to Disarm?" *Time*, February 26, 2007, 32–33.

18. On political issues related to North Korean security, see Young Whan Kihl and Hong Nack Kim, eds., *North Korea: The Politics of Regime Survival* (Armonk, N.Y.: M.E. Sharpe, 2006). On North Korea's motives for having nuclear weapons and their relationship to other military capabilities, see Andrew Scobell and John M. Sanford, *North Korea's Military Threat: Pyongyang's Conventional Forces, Weapons of Mass Destruction, and Ballistic Missiles* (Carlisle, Pa.: U.S. Army War College, Strategic Studies Institute, April 2007).

19. For U.S. intelligence community thinking on Iran, see Director of National Intelligence John Negroponte, "DNI Annual Threat Assessment 2006," cited in Anthony H. Cordesman, *Iran's Nuclear and Missile Programs: A Strategic Assessment*, rev. (Washington, D.C.: Center for Strategic and International Studies, August 31, 2006), 23. For political assessments of Iran's nuclear intentions and possible U.S. responses, see Henry Sokolski and Patrick Clawson, eds., *Getting Ready for a Nuclear-Ready Iran* (Carlisle, Pa.: Strategic Studies Institute, October 2005).

20. Herspring, *Kremlin and the High Command*, 155–193.

21. On Russian plans for strategic nuclear force modernization for the 2015–20 time period, see Isakova, *Russian Defense Reform*, 34–38.

22. See Pavel K. Baev, "The Trajectory of the Russian Military: Downsizing, Degeneration, and Defeat," chap. 1 in *The Russian Military: Power and Policy*, ed. Steven E. Miller and Dmitri Trenin (Cambridge, Mass.: MIT Press, 2004), 43–72.

23. See Stephen J. Blank, "Potemkin's Treadmill: Russia's Military Modernization," in *Strategic Asia 2005–06: Military Modernization in an Era of Uncertainty*, ed. Ashley J. Tellis and Michael Wills (Washington, D.C.: National Bureau of Asian Research, 2005), 175–205.

24. For additional information on methodology, see Cimbala and Scouras, *New Nuclear Century*.

25. For example, our simple model assumes only additive gains for the defense by deploying additional layers, but some analysis suggests that additional defensive layers would have multiplicative instead of additive effects. This is especially the case if BMD development and deployment proceed from "tail to head" (ground-based to space-based or other boost-phase intercept) instead of the other way around. For expert assessment on this and other BMD performance issues, see Wilkening, *Ballistic-Missile Defence*, esp. 34–41, and Weigand, *Heads, Not Tails*.

26. For counterarguments to the effect that the era of mutual deterrence may have ended and an era of U.S. nuclear "primacy" places Russia's deterrent at risk, see Lieber and Press, "Rise of U.S. Nuclear Primacy."

27. Sergei Ivanov, Russia's first deputy prime minister and immediate past defense minister, has alluded to this possibility. Referring to the INF Treaty signed by President Ronald Reagan and President Mikhail Gorbachev in 1987 as "a relic, a rudiment of the Cold War," Ivanov noted that dozens of nations have developed intermediate-range ballistic missiles since the pact was signed, and some of those states are located near Russia's borders. See Vladimir Isachenkov, "Russian Leader Assails U.S. Defenses," Associated Press, May 23, 2007, in Johnson's Russia List 2007, No. 118, May 24, 2007, http://www.cdi.org/russia/johnson/.

28. The role of nonstrategic nuclear forces in Russian military doctrine and strategy has been important, and a matter of some contention, from the debates over the draft military doctrine published by the Ministry of Defense in October 2000.

Nonstrategic nuclear weapons have since been discussed in a variety of contexts by Russian defense officials and commentators, including (1) their role in negating or deterring possible attacks by opponents capable of attacking Russia with strategic conventional weapons based on information superiority (so-called Sixth Generation Warfare), (2) their use for the purpose of avoiding military defeat in a conventional war while deescalating the conflict to Russian advantage, and (3) their role in helping to preserve combat stability, or continuity of mission performance during enemy attacks, as a factor of equal or greater importance to the survivability of nuclear forces. For historical perspective including the early Putin years, see Jacob W. Kipp, *Russia's Nonstrategic Nuclear Weapons* (Ft. Leavenworth, Kans.: Foreign Military Studies Office, May–June 2001), available at http://leav-www.army.mil/ fmso/documents/russias_nukes/russias_nukes.htm.

29. Vladimir Sivolob and Mikhail Sosnovskiy, "A Reality of Deterrence: Algorithms for Nuclear Use Should Become a Component Part of Military Doctrine," *Nezavisimoye Voyennoye Obozreniye*, October 22, 1999, 4, cited in Kipp, *Russia's Nonstrategic Nuclear Weapons.*

30. Kipp, *Russia's Nonstrategic Nuclear Weapons.*

31. Herspring, *Kremlin and the High Command*, 129–135 and 157–162.

32. On this point see Herspring, *Kremlin and the High Command.*

Chapter 5. Nuclear Disarmament: Can the United States and Russia Lead the Way?

1. For informed scholarly analysis with contrasting viewpoints, see Colin Gray, "To Confuse Ourselves: Nuclear Fallacies," 4–30; Lawrence Freedman, "Eliminators, Marginalists, and the Politics of Disarmament," 56–69; and Michael McGwire, "The Elimination of Nuclear Weapons," 144–166, all in John Baylis and Robert O'Neill, eds., *Alternative Nuclear Futures: The Role of Nuclear Weapons in the Post–Cold War World* (Oxford: Oxford University Press, 2000).

2. For a recent example see the discussion in Ivo Daalder and John Holum, "A Nuclear-free World," *Boston Globe*, October 5, 2007, http://www.brookings.edu/ scholars/idaalder.htm.

3. "Treaty between the United States of America and the Russian Federation."

4. Cirincione, *Bomb Scare*, 93, summarizes pertinent figures on progress in destroying and securing former Soviet weapons.

5. See Brian D. Taylor, *Russia's Power Ministries: Coercion and Commerce* (Syracuse, N.Y.: Maxwell School of Citizenship and Public Affairs, Syracuse University, October 2007), for detailed analysis.

6. Thom Shanker and Mark Landler, "Putin Says U.S. Is Undermining Global Stability," *New York Times*, February 11, 2007, http://www.nytimes.com/2007/02/11/ world/europe/11munich.html.

7. Robert Burns and Matthew Lee, "Putin Warns against U.S. Missile Defense," Associated Press, October 12, 2007, in Johnson's Russia List 2007, No. 214, October 12, 2007, http://www.cdi.org/russia/johnson/.

8. For example, see Shchedrov, "Putin Still Opposed to U.S. Missile Shield," and Associated Press, "Russia Says It Will Target European Sites."

9. Nikolayev, "Hypersonics Will Punch Holes."

10. Stolberg, "Putin Surprises Bush with Plan."

11. Rutenberg, "Putin Expands on His Missile Defense Plan"; "Putin Waiting for U.S. Response."

12. There is also some apparent interest on the part of Russian defense and arms control experts in a version of minimum deterrence. See Weitz, *Russian-American Security Cooperation*, passim.

13. For pertinent scenarios and discussion, see Quester, *Nuclear First Strike*, 24–30 and passim.

14. Forces are the author's estimates and are notional and not necessarily predictive of actual future deployments. See also, for Russian forces, Podvig, *Russian Nuclear Arsenal*, and Isakova, *Russian Defense Reform*, 34–38.

15. See, for example, Blair, *Logic of Accidental Nuclear War*, 175–187 and passim.

16. Carl von Clausewitz, *On War*, edited and translated by Michael Howard and Peter Paret (Princeton, N.J.: Princeton University Press, 1976), bk. 1, chap. 3, 104–108. See also Hew Strachan, *Clausewitz's On War: A Biography* (New York: Atlantic Monthly Press, 2007), 143 and passim; Colin S. Gray, *Another Bloody Century: Future Warfare* (London: Weidenfeld and Nicholson, 2005), 31–35; and Stephen J. Cimbala, *Clausewitz and Escalation: Classical Perspectives on Nuclear Strategy* (London: Frank Cass, 1991).

17. The author gratefully acknowledges Dr. James Scouras for use of his AWSM@ nuclear exchange model. He is not responsible for its application here, nor for any arguments or conclusions in this study.

18. Cirincione, *Bomb Scare*, 125–126 and 139–157. See also Allison, *Nuclear Terrorism*, 140–175.

Chapter 6. Nuclear Proliferation in Asia: Risks and Opportunities

1. Allison, *Nuclear Terrorism*, 61–63.

2. Lawrence Korb with Peter Ogden, *The Road to Nuclear Security* (Washington, D.C.: Center for American Progress, December 2004), 5.

3. See Mueller et al., *Striking First*, for an assessment of past and present U.S. experience. Unnecessary confusion in the American policy debate about preemption and preventive war strategies is noted in Colin S. Gray, *The Implications of Preemptive and Preventive War Doctrines: A Reconsideration* (Carlisle, Pa.: Strategic Studies Institute, U.S. Army War College, July 2007).

4. Cirincione, *Bomb Scare*, 43 and passim. According to Cirincione, the following states have abandoned nuclear weapons programs, nuclear weapons, or both since the NPT entered into force: Argentina, Australia, Belarus, Brazil, Canada, Iraq, Kazakhstan, Libya, Rumania, South Africa, South Korea, Spain, Switzerland, Taiwan, Ukraine, and Yugoslavia (43).

5. Bracken, *Fire in the East*, esp. 95–124.

6. Michael O'Hanlon, *Technological Change and the Future of Warfare* (Washington, D.C.: Brookings Institution, 2000), 7–31.

7. A hopeful expert assessment appears in David Albright and Jacqueline Shire, "Slowly, but Surely, Pyongyang Is Moving," *Washington Post*, January 24, 2008, A19, http://www.washingtonpost.com. See also Sang-Hun, "North Korea Says"; Powell, "North Korea Has Agreed," 32–33; and Glenn Kessler, "Conservatives Assail North Korean Accord," *Washington Post*, February 15, 2007, A01.

8. Quester, *Nuclear First Strike*, 49.

9. Pertinent sources include Susan L. Craig, *Chinese Perceptions of Traditional and Nontraditional Security Threats* (Carlisle, Pa.: U.S. Army War College, Strategic Studies Institute, March 2007), esp. 36–37; Carolyn W. Pumphrey, ed., *The Rise of China in Asia: Security Implications* (Carlisle, Pa.: U.S. Army War College, Strategic Studies Institute, January 2002); Mark A. Stokes, *China's Strategic Modernization: Implications for the United States* (Carlisle, Pa.: U.S. Army War College, Strategic Studies Institute, September 1999); Kihl and Kim, *North Korea*; Scobell and Sanford, *North Korea's Military Threat*, esp. 71–100; D. R. SarDesai and Raju G. C. Thomas, eds., *Nuclear India in the Twenty-First Century* (New York: Palgrave-Macmillan, 2002), esp. chap. 5; Richard L. Garwin, "When Could Iran Deliver a Nuclear Weapon?" *Bulletin of the Atomic Scientists,* January 18, 2008, BulletinOnline, http://www.thebulletin.org/columns/richard-garwin/20080118.html; U.S. National Intelligence Council, National Intelligence Estimate, *Iran: Nuclear Intentions and Capabilities* (Washington, D.C.: National Intelligence Council, November 2007); Sokolski and Clawson, *Getting Ready for a Nuclear-Ready Iran*, esp. chaps. 7–8; Sokolski, *Taming the Next Set of Strategic Weapons Threats*, esp. chaps. 1–3; and Sokolski, *Prevailing in a Well-Armed World*. For force projections and scenarios for the Middle East, see Anthony H. Cordesman, *Warfighting and Proliferation in the Middle East* (Washington, D.C.: Center for Strategic and International Studies, revised April 17, 2007). Projections for Russia are author's estimates; see also Podvig, *Russian Nuclear Arsenal*.

10. I am grateful to James Scouras for the use of his AWSM@ model in this analysis. He is not responsible for any arguments and conclusions in this study.

11. This point is made in the larger context of an argument for further Russian and American nuclear arms reductions, and for strengthening the nuclear nonproliferation regime, by Panofsky, "Nuclear Insecurity."

12. Clausewitz, *On War*, bk. 1, chap. 3, 104.

13. See Cirincione, *Bomb Scare*, for pertinent discussion.

Chapter 7. Ending a Nuclear War: Should We Even Try and Would Missile Defenses Help?

The epigraph is from Gen. Matthew B. Ridgway, U.S. Army (Ret.), *The Korean War* (New York: Doubleday, 1967), 245. General Ridgway was supreme commander of UN Forces in Korea and U.S. Far Eastern Forces and later supreme allied commander, NATO, and U.S. Army chief of staff. Ridgway's argument in this book was that the United States should avoid getting into self-escalating wars by defining clear political objectives that are attainable with available resources, consistent with international realities, and congruent with our U.S. constitutional understandings of civil-military relations. Unfortunately, each administration in Washington, D.C., has to relearn these lessons, sometimes at high cost.

1. See, for example, Stephen J. Cimbala, ed., *Strategic War Termination* (New York: Praeger, 1986); Paul K. Davis, "A New Analytic Technique for the Study of Deterrence, Escalation Control and War Termination," in *Artificial Intelligence and National Security*, ed. Stephen J. Cimbala (Lexington, Mass.: Lexington Books, 1986), 35–60; and George H. Quester, "War Termination and Nuclear Targeting Strategy," chap. 14 in *Strategic Nuclear Targeting*, ed. Desmond Ball and Jeffrey Richelson (Ithaca, N.Y.: Cornell University Press, 1986), 285–305. For a perspective on this issue at the end of the Cold War, see the essays in Stephen J. Cimbala and Sidney R. Waldman, eds., *Controlling and Ending Conflict: Issues before and after the Cold War* (Westport, Conn.: Greenwood Press, 1992).

2. However, the specific circumstances of a nuclear first use might vary considerably, so some uncertainty exists about how states affected by, or observing, the event might react. See Quester, *Nuclear First Strike*, esp. 24–73.

3. For pertinent critiques of deterrence theory as applied to post–Cold War issues, see Gray, *Second Nuclear Age*, esp. 88–93; and Payne, *Deterrence in the Second Nuclear Age*, passim. See also Morgan, *Deterrence Now*, 238–284.

4. On the issue of rationality and deterrence, see Morgan, *Deterrence Now*, 42–79.

5. Paul Bracken, "War Termination," chap. 6 in *Managing Nuclear Operations*, ed. Ashton B. Carter, John D. Steinbruner, and Charles A. Zraket (Washington, D.C.: Brookings Institution, 1987), 197–214.

6. Ibid., 201.

7. Paul Bracken, "Delegation of Nuclear Command Authority," chap. 10 in *Managing Nuclear Operations*, ed. Ashton B. Carter, John D. Steinbruner, and Charles A. Zraket (Washington, D.C.: Brookings Institution, 1987), 352–372, esp. 355ff., offers similar if slightly different distinctions between "provincial" and "political" control. Provincial control includes strategic and tactical control of the armed forces; political control deals with grand strategy, which is essentially policy.

8. Various aspects of this issue are discussed in Paul Bracken, *The Command and Control of Nuclear Forces* (New Haven, Conn.: Yale University Press, 1983).

9. Perspectives on this and related problems appear in Albert Wohlstetter and Richard Brody, "Continuing Control as a Requirement for Deterring," chap. 5 in Carter, Steinbruner, and Zraket, eds, *Managing Nuclear Operations*, 142–196. See also Bracken, "Delegation of Nuclear Command Authority," 359. As Bracken observes, delegation of nuclear command authority by political leaders to others will not happen except in the most dire circumstances—which are exactly those in which a nuclear war will most likely take place (356).

10. This perspective is developed in Peter Douglas Feaver, *Guarding the Guardians: Civilian Control of Nuclear Weapons in the United States* (Ithaca, N.Y.: Cornell University Press, 1992), 12–28. See also, in the same volume, his comments on civilian control after the decision to use nuclear weapons, 55–66.

11. See Andrew and Leslie Cockburn, *One Point Safe* (New York: Doubleday, 1997), for pertinent cases and arguments based on Russian post–Cold War experience in the 1990s.

12. Ibid., 240–244.

13. This argument is well presented with pertinent scenarios in Quester, *Nuclear First Strike*, esp. 24–52.

Conclusion: Missile Defense and U.S.-Russian Nuclear Strategy

1. Jared Diamond, *Collapse: How Societies Choose to Fail or Succeed* (New York: Viking Press, 2005), 419–440.

2. James Brooke and David E. Sanger, "North Koreans Say They Hold Nuclear Arms," *New York Times*, February 11, 2005, A1, A8.

3. See Yardley and Sanger, "In Shift," and Powell, "North Korea Has Agreed," 32–33.

4. Bracken, *Fire in the East*, esp. chap. 4, 5.

5. Matthew G. McKinzie, Thomas B. Cochran, Robert S. Norris, and William Arkin, *The U.S. Nuclear War Plan: A Time for Change* (Washington, D.C.: Natural Resources Defense Council, June 2001), chap. 5.

6. U.S. Department of State, *Moscow Treaty on Strategic Arms Reductions: Fact Sheet* (Washington, D.C.: White House, Office of the Press Secretary, May 29, 2002).

7. Roger W. Barnett, *Asymmetrical Warfare: Today's Challenges to U.S. Military Power* (Washington, D.C.: Brassey's, 2003), esp. 95–110.

8. North Korea test fired a short-range ballistic missile into the Sea of Japan on May 1, 2005, within several days after Vice Adm. Lowell Jacoby, director of the U.S. Defense Intelligence Agency, testified to the U.S. Senate that North Korea was now capable of arming a missile with a nuclear weapon. See "N. Korea Missile Test Raises New Fears," Associated Press, May 2, 2005, http://cnn.netscape.cnn.com/ns/news/story.jsp?idq=/ff/sto/.

9. U.S. Department of Defense, "Findings of the Nuclear Posture Review," briefing, January 9, 2002, Washington, D.C.. See also "Nuclear Posture Review," excerpts, http://www.globalsecurity.org/wmd/library/policy/dod/npr.htm.

10. Missile Defense Agency, *A Historical Beginning*, BMDS booklet, 2nd ed. (Washington, D.C.: Department of Defense, 2005). See also U.S. Government Accountability Office, Report to Congressional Committees, *Status of Ballistic Missile Defense Program in 2004*, GAO-05-243 (Washington, D.C.: Government Accountability Office, March 2005).

11. For possibilities, see Weitz, *Russian-American Security Cooperation*, 12–19.

12. Joseph Cirincione, "U.S. Missile Defense vs. Democracy," *Globalist*, October 24, 2007, in Johnson's Russia List 2007, No. 222, October 25, 2007, http://www.cdi.org/russia/johnson/. Cirincione prefers that the United States deploy no missile defenses in Europe but regards cooperation with Russia as better than unilateralism. Vladimir Putin showed apparent readiness to assist other states engaged with Iran on nuclear proliferation during his visit to Tehran in October 2007. See also Rose Gottemoeller, "The Nuclear Gambit with Iran," *Moscow Times*, October 24, 2007, in Carnegie Endowment for International Peace, *Proliferation News*, October 25, 2007, www.CarnegieEndowment.org/NPP/.

13. For pertinent background and expert assessment, see Herspring, *Kremlin and the High Command*, 168–176 and passim.

Bibliography

Albright, David, and Jacqueline Shire. "Slowly, but Surely, Pyongyang Is Moving." *Washington Post*, January 24, 2008, A19.

Allison, Graham T. *Nuclear Terrorism: The Ultimate Preventable Catastrophe*. New York: Time Books–Henry Holt, 2004.

Arbatov, Alexei. "Is a New Cold War Imminent?" *Russia in Global Affairs*, July–September 2007. In Johnson's Russia List 2007, No. 175, August 16, 2007. http://www.cdi.org/russia/johnson/.

Arquilla, John, and David Ronfeldt, eds. *Athena's Camp: Preparing for Conflict in the Information Age*. Santa Monica, Calif.: RAND, 1997.

Associated Press. "Experts See Decline in Russian Military." November 13, 2007. In Johnson's Russia List 2007, No. 236, November 14, 2007. http://www.cdi.org/russia/johnson/.

———. "N. Korea Missile Test Raises New Fears." May 2, 2005. http://cnn.netscape.cnn.com/ns/news/story.jsp?idq=/ff/sto/.

———. "Russia Says It Will Target European Sites of U.S. Missile Shield Proceeds." *International Herald Tribune Europe*, June 3, 2007. http://www.iht.com/articles/ap/2007/06/04/europe/EU-GEN-Russia-Putin-US.php/.

Baev, Pavel K. "The Trajectory of the Russian Military: Downsizing, Degeneration, and Defeat." In *The Russian Military: Power and Policy*, ed. Steven E. Miller and Dmitri Trenin, 43–72. Cambridge, Mass.: MIT Press, 2004.

Ball, Desmond, and Jeffrey Richelson, eds. *Strategic Nuclear Targeting*. Ithaca, N.Y.: Cornell University Press, 1986.

Barnett, Roger W. *Asymmetrical Warfare: Today's Challenges to U.S. Military Power*. Washington, D.C.: Brassey's, 2003.

Baucom, Donald R. *The Origins of SDI, 1944–1983*. Lawrence: University Press of Kansas, 1992.

Baylis, John, and Robert O'Neill, eds. *Alternative Nuclear Futures: The Role of Nuclear Weapons in the Post–Cold War World*. Oxford: Oxford University Press, 2000.

Belida, Alex. "U.S. Untroubled by Russia's Plans to Develop Missile Defense Shield." *Voice of America*, January 15, 2003. In Johnson's Russia List, No. 7020, January 16, 2003. http://www.cdi.org/russia/johnson/.

Biddle, Stephen. *Military Power: Explaining Victory and Defeat in Battle*. Princeton, N.J.: Princeton University Press, 2004.

Blair, Bruce. "The Impact of National Missile Defense on Russia and Nuclear Security." *Defense Monitor* 8 (December 1, 2000). http://www.cdi.org/dm/2000/issue8/nmdrussia.html.

Blair, Bruce G. *The Logic of Accidental Nuclear War*. Washington, D.C.: Brookings Institution, 1993.

Blank, Stephen J. *After Two Wars: Reflections on the American Strategic Revolution in Central Asia*. Carlisle Barracks, Pa.: U.S. Army War College, Strategic Studies Institute, July 2005.

———. "Potemkin's Treadmill: Russia's Military Modernization." In *Strategic Asia 2005–06: Military Modernization in an Era of Uncertainty*, ed. Ashley J. Tellis and Michael Wills, 175–205. Washington, D.C.: National Bureau of Asian Research, 2005.

Boot, Max. *War Made New: Technology, Warfare, and the Course of History, 1500 to Today*. New York: Gotham Books, 2006.

Bracken, Paul. *Fire in the East: The Rise of Asian Military Power and the Second Nuclear Age*. New York: Harper Perennial, 1999.

Brooke, James, and David E. Sanger. "North Koreans Say They Hold Nuclear Arms." *New York Times*, February 11, 2005, A1, A8.

Burns, Robert, and Matthew Lee. "Putin Warns against U.S. Missile Defense." Associated Press, October 12, 2007. In Johnson's Russia List 2007, No. 214, October 12, 2007. http://www.cdi.org/russia/johnson/.

Carter, Ashton B., John D. Steinbruner, and Charles A. Zraket, eds. *Managing Nuclear Operations*. Washington, D.C.: Brookings Institution, 1987.

Center for Defense Information. "Likely Nuclear Arsenals under the Strategic Offensive Reductions Treaty." (Moscow Treaty.) January 21, 2003.

———. "Nuclear Issues: Russian Nuclear Arsenal, May 2, 2005." http://www.cdi.org/friendlyversion/printversion.cfm?do/.

Cimbala, Stephen J. *Nuclear Weapons and Strategy: U.S. Nuclear Policy for the Twenty-first Century*. London: Routledge, 2005.

Cimbala, Stephen J., and James Scouras. *A New Nuclear Century*. Westport, Conn.: Praeger, 2002.

Cimbala, Stephen J., and Sidney R. Waldman, eds. *Controlling and Ending Conflict: Issues before and after the Cold War*. Westport, Conn.: Greenwood Press, 1992.

Cirincione, Joseph. *Bomb Scare: The History and Future of Nuclear Weapons.* New York: Columbia University Press, 2007.

———. "U.S. Missile Defense vs. Democracy." *Globalist,* October 24, 2007. In Johnson's Russia List 2007, No. 222, October 25, 2007. http://www.cdi.org/russia/johnson/.

Clausewitz, Carl von. *On War.* Edited and translated by Michael Howard and Peter Paret. Princeton, N.J.: Princeton University Press, 1976.

Cockburn, Andrew, and Leslie Cockburn. *One Point Safe.* New York: Doubleday, 1997.

Congressional Research Service. *Missile Defense: The Current Debate.* Washington, D.C.: Congressional Research Service, July 19, 2005.

Cooper, Jeffrey. "Dominant Battlespace Awareness and Future Warfare." In *Dominant Battlespace Knowledge: The Winning Edge,* ed. Stuart E. Johnson and Martin C. Libicki. Washington, D.C.: National Defense University Press, 1995.

Cordesman, Anthony H. *Iran's Nuclear and Missile Programs: A Strategic Assessment.* Washington, D.C.: Center for Strategic and International Studies, August 31, 2006.

———. *Warfighting and Proliferation in the Middle East.* Washington, D.C.: Center for Strategic and International Studies, April 17, 2007.

Craig, Susan L. *Chinese Perceptions of Traditional and Nontraditional Security Threats.* Carlisle, Pa.: U.S. Army War College, Strategic Studies Institute, March 2007.

Daalder, Ivo, and John Holum. "A Nuclear-free World." *Boston Globe,* October 5, 2007. http://www.brookings.edu/scholars/idaalder.htm/.

David, Leonard. "U.S. Defense Report: China Working on Anti-Satellite Systems." http://www.space.com/news/050727_China_military.

Davis, Paul K. "Behavioral Factors in Terminating Superpower War." In *Controlling and Ending Conflict: Issues before and after the Cold War,* ed. Stephen J. Cimbala and Sidney R. Waldman. Westport, Conn.: Greenwood Press, 1987.

———. "A New Analytic Technique for the Study of Deterrence, Escalation Control and War Termination." In *Artificial Intelligence and National Security,* ed. Stephen J. Cimbala, 35–60. Lexington, Mass.: Lexington Books, 1986.

Diamond, Jared. *Collapse: How Societies Choose to Fail or Succeed.* New York: Viking Press, 2005.

Feaver, Peter Douglas. *Guarding the Guardians: Civilian Control of Nuclear Weapons in the United States.* Ithaca, N.Y.: Cornell University Press, 1992.

Federation of American Scientists. "Nuclear Forces Guide." Regularly updated. http://www.fas.org/nuke/guide/.

FitzGerald, Frances. *Way Out There in the Blue: Reagan, Star Wars and the End of the Cold War*. New York: Simon and Schuster, 2000.

Freedman, Lawrence. "Eliminators, Marginalists, and the Politics of Disarmament." In *Alternative Nuclear Futures: The Role of Nuclear Weapons in the Post–Cold War World*, ed. John Baylis and Robert O'Neill, 56–69. Oxford: Oxford University Press, 2000.

Gareev, Col. Gen. Makhmut Akhmetovich. *M. V. Frunze: Military Theorist*. Washington, D.C.: Pergamon-Brassey's, 1988.

Garwin, Richard L. "Ballistic Missile Defense Deployment to Poland and the Czech Republic." Paper presented at the Erice International Seminar, 38th Session. Yorktown Heights, N.Y., August 21, 2007. Available at http://www.fas.org/rlg/081507BMDPe.pdf.

———. "When Could Iran Deliver a Nuclear Weapon?" *Bulletin of the Atomic Scientists*, January 18, 2008. BulletinOnline, http://www.thebulletin.org/columns/richard-garwin/20080118.html.

Gottemoeller, Rose. "The Nuclear Gambit with Iran." *Moscow Times*, October 24, 2007. In Carnegie Endowment for International Peace, *Proliferation News*, October 25, 2007. http://www.CarnegieEndowment.org/NPP/.

Gray, Colin S. *Another Bloody Century: Future Warfare*. London: Weidenfeld and Nicolson, 2005.

———. *The Second Nuclear Age*. Boulder, Colo.: Lynne Rienner, 1999.

———. *Strategy for Chaos: Revolutions in Military Affairs and the Evidence of History*. London: Frank Cass, 2002.

Gronlund, Lisbeth, David Wright, George Lewis, and Philip Coyle. *Technical Realities: An Analysis of the 2004 Deployment of a U.S. National Missile Defense System*. Cambridge, Mass.: Union of Concerned Scientists, May 2004.

Herspring, Dale R. *The Kremlin and the High Command*. Lawrence: University Press of Kansas, 2006.

Hildreth, Steven A. *Missile Defense: The Current Debate*. CRS Report for Congress. Washington, D.C.: Congressional Research Service, July 19, 2005.

Hitchens, Theresa. "Update on U.S. Military Space Policy and Strategy." July 8, 2005. Center for Defense Information, http://www.cdi.org/program/document.cfm.

Isakova, Irina. *Russian Defense Reform: Current Trends*. Carlisle, Pa.: U.S. Army War College, Strategic Studies Institute, November 2006.

Jervis, Robert. *The Meaning of the Nuclear Revolution*. Ithaca, N.Y.: Cornell University Press, 1989.

Kihl, Young Whan, and Hong Nack Kim, eds. *North Korea: The Politics of Regime Survival*. Armonk, N.Y.: M. E. Sharpe, 2006.

Kipp, Jacob W. *Russia's Nonstrategic Nuclear Weapons*. Ft. Leavenworth, Kans.: Foreign Military Studies Office, May–June 2001. http://leav-www.army. mil/fmso/documents/russias_nukes/russias_nukes.htm.

Knight, Amy. "Is Kremlin Infighting Destabilizing Russia? A Bitter Power Struggle among Putin's Security Chieftains May Explain Renewed Hostility against the West." *Toronto Globe and Mail*, October 16, 2007. In Johnson's Russia List 2007, No. 216, October 16, 2007. http://www.cdi. org/russia/johnson/.

Knox, MacGregor, and Williamson Murray, eds. *The Dynamics of Military Revolution, 1300–2050*. Cambridge: Cambridge University Press, 2001.

Korb, Lawrence, with Peter Ogden. *The Road to Nuclear Security*. Washington, D.C.: Center for American Progress, December 2004.

———. "Visualize Iraq: In Space." *Seattle Times*, July 21, 2005. Available at Center for Defense Information, Space Security, http://www.cdi.org/ program/document.cfm/.

Kramer, Andrew E., and Thom Shanker. "Russia Suspends Arms Agreement over U.S. Shield." *New York Times*, July 15, 2007. http://www.nytimes. com/2007/07/15/world/europe/15russia.html/.

Lieber, Keir A., and Daryl G. Press. "The Rise of U.S. Nuclear Primacy." *Foreign Affairs*, March/April 2006. http://www.foreignaffairs.org/ 20060301faessay85204/.

Linzer, Dafna. "Bush Officials Defend India Nuclear Deal." *Washington Post*, July 20, 2005. http://www.washingtonpost.com.

Mathers, Jennifer G. *The Russian Nuclear Shield from Stalin to Yeltsin*. New York: St. Martin's Press, 2000.

McGwire, Michael. "The Elimination of Nuclear Weapons." In *Alternative Nuclear Futures: The Role of Nuclear Weapons in the Post–Cold War World*, ed. John Baylis and Robert O'Neill, 144–166. Oxford: Oxford University Press, 2000.

McKinzie, Matthew G., Thomas B. Cochran, Robert S. Norris, and William Arkin. *The U.S. Nuclear War Plan: A Time for Change*. Washington, D.C.: Natural Resources Defense Council, June 2001.

Miller, Steven E., and Dmitri Trenin, eds. *The Russian Military: Power and Policy*. Cambridge, Mass.: MIT Press, 2004.

Missile Defense Agency. *A Historical Beginning*. BMDS booklet, 2nd ed. Washington, D.C.: Department of Defense, 2005.

Morgan, Patrick M. *Deterrence Now*. Cambridge: Cambridge University Press, 2003.

Mueller, Karl P., Jasen J. Castillo, Forrest E. Morgan, Negeen Pegahi, and Brian Rosen. *Striking First: Preemptive and Preventive Attack in U.S. National Security Policy*. Santa Monica, Calif.: RAND, 2006.

Nelson, Robert W. "Lowering the Threshold: Nuclear Bunker Busters and Mininukes." In *Tactical Nuclear Weapons: Emergent Threats in an Evolving Security Environment*, ed. Brian Alexander and Alistair Millar. Washington, D.C.: Brassey's, 2003.

Nikolayev, Mikhail. "Hypersonics Will Punch Holes in American Missile Defense. Problem Is, the New Weapon Will Not Be Fielded Soon." *Nezavisimoye Voyennoye Obozreniye*, March 21, 2007. In Johnson's Russia List, No. 69, March 22, 2007. http://www.cdi.org/russia/johnson/.

Norris, Robert S., and Hans M. Kristensen. "Russian Nuclear Forces, 2005." *Bulletin of the Atomic Scientists* 61, no. 2 (March/April 2005): 70–72. http://www.thebulletin.org/article_nn.php?art_ofn=ma05n/.

———. "U.S. Nuclear Forces, 2005." *Bulletin of the Atomic Scientists* 61, no. 1 (January/February 2005): 73–75. http://www.thebulletin.org/article_nn.php?art_ofn=jf05norris/.

Office of the Secretary of Defense. Assistant Secretary of Defense and Director, Defense Research and Engineering. *Space Technology Guide, FY 2000-01*. Washington, D.C.: GPO, 2001. http://www.fas.org/spp/military/stg.htm.

O'Hanlon, Michael. *Technological Change and the Future of Warfare*. Washington, D.C.: Brookings Institution, 2000.

Panofsky, Wolfgang K. H. "Nuclear Insecurity." *Foreign Affairs*, September–October 2007. In Johnson's Russia List 2007, No. 180, August 23 2007. http://www.cdi.org/russia/johnson/.

Payne, Keith B. *Deterrence in the Second Nuclear Age*. Lexington: University Press of Kentucky, 1996.

Perrow, Charles. *Normal Accidents: Living with High-Risk Technologies*. New York: Basic Books, 1984.

Pincus, Walter. "Senate Panel Faults Missile Defense Plan: Location in Eastern Europe Is Criticized." *Washington Post*, July 5, 2007. In Johnson's Russia List 2007, No. 148, July 5, 2007. http://www.cdi.org/russia/johnson/.

Podvig, Pavel. *The Russian Nuclear Arsenal*. Stanford, Calif.: Stanford University, Center for International Security and Cooperation, and International Relations and Security Network, 2006.

———, ed. *Russian Strategic Nuclear Forces*. Cambridge, Mass.: MIT Press, 2001.

Polmar, Norman. "Improved Russian Missile Tested." June 4, 2007, Military.com, http://www.military.com/forums/0,15240,138051,00.html.

Pry, Peter Vincent. *War Scare: Russia and America on the Nuclear Brink*. Westport, Conn.: Praeger, 1999.

Pumphrey, Carolyn W., ed. *The Rise of China in Asia: Security Implications.* Carlisle Barracks, Pa.: U.S. Army War College, Strategic Studies Institute, 2002.

Quester, George H. *Nuclear First Strike: Consequences of a Broken Taboo.* Baltimore: Johns Hopkins University Press, 2006.

———. "War Termination and Nuclear Targeting Strategy." In *Strategic Nuclear Targeting,* ed. Desmond Ball and Jeffrey Richelson. Ithaca, N.Y.: Cornell University Press, 1986.

Rhodes, Richard. *Arsenals of Folly: The Making of the Nuclear Arms Race.* New York: Knopf, 2007.

Ridgway, Gen. Matthew B., U.S. Army (Ret.). *The Korean War.* New York: Doubleday, 1967.

Roberts, Kristin. "U.S. Offers to Keep Shield on Stand-by: Officials." Reuters, October 23, 2007. In Johnson's Russia List, October 23, 2007. http://www.cdi.org/russia/johnson/.

"Russia Plans ICBM to Counter U.S. Missile Shield." *Spiegel On Line International,* August 6, 2007. http://www.spiegel.de/international/world/0,1518,498338,00.html.

Rutenberg, Jim. "Putin Expands on His Missile Defense Plan." *New York Times,* July 3, 2007. http://www.nytimes.com/2007/07/03/us/03putin.html.

Sagan, Scott D., and Kenneth N. Waltz. *The Spread of Nuclear Weapons: A Debate.* New York: W. W. Norton, 1995.

Samson, Victoria. *An "F" for Missile Defense: How Seven Government Reports in Two Months Illustrate the Need for Missile Defense to Change Its Ways.* Washington, D.C.: Center for Defense Information, 2006.

Sanders, Patricia. *Missile Defense Program Overview for the European Union, Committee on Foreign Affairs, Subcommittee on Security and Defense.* Washington, D.C.: Department of Defense, June 28, 2007.

Sang-Hun, Choe. "North Korean Reactor Is Shut, U.N. Confirms." *New York Times,* July 16, 2007. http://www.nytimes.com/2007/07/16/world/asia/16cnd-korea.html?ref=world/.

SarDesai, D. R., and Raju G. C. Thomas. *Nuclear India in the Twenty-First Century.* New York: Palgrave-Macmillan, 2002.

Schelling, Thomas C. *Arms and Influence.* New Haven, Conn.: Yale University Press, 1966.

Scobell, Andrew, and John M. Sanford. *North Korea's Military Threat: Pyongyang's Conventional Forces, Weapons of Mass Destruction, and Ballistic Missiles.* Carlisle, Pa.: U.S. Army War College, Strategic Studies Institute, April 2007.

Sessler, Andrew M., John M. Cornwall, Bob Dietz, Steve Fetter, Sherman Frankel, Richard L. Garwin, Kurt Gottfried, Lisbeth Gronlund, George N. Lewis,

Theodore A. Postol, and David C. Wright. *Countermeasures: A Technical Evaluation of the Operational Effectiveness of the Planned U.S. National Missile Defense System*. Cambridge, Mass.: Union of Concerned Scientists, April 2000.

Shanker, Thom, and Mark Landler. "Putin Says U.S. Is Undermining Global Stability." *New York Times*, February 11, 2007. http://www.nytimes.com/ 2007/02/11/world/europe/11munich.html.

Sharp, Jane M. O. "Missile Madness." *World Today*, December 2007. In Johnson's Russia List 2007, No. 245, November 28, 2007. http://www.cdi. org/russia/johnson/.

Shchedrov, Oleg. "Putin Still Opposed to U.S. Missile Shield." Reuters, May 23, 2007. In Johnson's Russia List 2007, No. 118, May 24, 2007. http://www.cdi. org/russia/johnson/.

Smith, Derek D. *Deterring America: Rogue States and the Proliferation of Weapons of Mass Destruction*. Cambridge: Cambridge University Press, 2006.

Sokolski, Henry, ed. *Prevailing in a Well-Armed World: Devising Competitive Strategies against Weapons Proliferation*. Carlisle, Pa.: U.S. Army War College, Nonproliferation Policy Education Center and Strategic Studies Institute, March 2000.

———. *Taming the Next Set of Strategic Weapons Threats*. Carlisle, Pa.: U.S. Army War College, Nonproliferation Policy Education Center and Strategic Studies Institute, June 2006.

Sokolski, Henry, and Patrick Clawson. *Getting Ready for a Nuclear-Ready Iran*. Carlisle, Pa.: Strategic Studies Institute, U.S. Army War College, October 2005.

Sokov, Nikolai. *Russian Strategic Modernization: The Past and Future*. Lanham, Md.: Rowman and Littlefield, 2000.

Solovyev, Vadim. "Report on Russian Expansion of Offer to Create Joint Missile ABM System." *Nezavisimoye Voyennoye Obozreniye*, July 15, 2007. In Johnson's Russia List 2007, No. 155, July 16, 2007. http://www.cdi. org/russia/johnson/.

Stokes, Mark A. *China's Strategic Modernization: Implications for the United States*. Carlisle, Pa.: U.S. Army War College, Strategic Studies Institute, September 1999.

Stolberg, Sheryl Gay. "Putin Surprises Bush with Plan on Missile Shield." *New York Times*, June 8, 2007. http://www.nytimes.com/2007/06/08/world/ europe/08prexy.html.

Strachan, Hew. *Clausewitz's On War: A Biography*. New York: Atlantic Monthly Press, 2007.

Taylor, Brian D. *Russia's Power Ministries: Coercion and Commerce*. Syracuse, N.Y.: Maxwell School of Citizenship and Public Affairs, Syracuse University, October 2007.

Toffler, Alvin, and Heidi Toffler. *War and Anti-War: Making Sense of Today's Global Chaos*. New York: Warner Books, 1993.

"Treaty between the United States of America and the Russian Federation on Strategic Offensive Reductions." May 24, 2002. *Arms Control Today*, June 2002. http://www.armscontrol.org/documents/sort.asp/.

Trenin, Dmitri. "NATO and Russia: Sobering Thoughts and Practical Suggestions." *NATO Review*, Summer 2007. http://www.nato.int/docu/review/2007/issue2/english/art1.html.

———. *Russia's Nuclear Policy in the 21st Century Environment*. Paris: IFRI Security Studies Department, 2005.

Tyson, Ann Scott. "U.S. Missile Defense Being Expanded, General Says." *Washington Post*, July 22, 2005, A10. http://www.washingtonpost.com.

Tzu, Sun. *The Art of War*. Edited and translated by Samuel B. Griffith. London: Oxford University Press, 1971.

U.S. Department of Defense. "Findings of the Nuclear Posture Review." Briefing, January 9, 2002, Washington, D.C. http://www.defenselink.mil/dodcmsshare/briefingslide/120/020109-D-6570C-001.pdf. See also Nuclear Posture Review, Excerpts. http://www.globalsecurity.org/wmd/library/policy/dod/npr.htm.

———. Missile Defense Agency. *The Ballistic Missile Defense System: Fact Sheet*. Washington, D.C.: Department of Defense, September 2005.

U.S. Department of State. *Moscow Treaty on Strategic Arms Reductions: Fact Sheet*. White House: Office of the Press Secretary, May 29, 2002.

U.S. Government Accountability Office. *Defense Acquisitions: Status of Ballistic Missile Defense Program in 2004*. Washington, D.C.: Government Accountability Office, March 2005.

———. *Status of Ballistic Missile Defense Program in 2004*. Report to Congressional Committees. GAO-05-243. Washington, D.C.: Government Accountability Office, March 2005.

U.S. National Intelligence Council. *Iran: Nuclear Intentions and Capabilities*. National Intelligence Estimate. Washington, D.C.: National Intelligence Council, November 2007.

Weitz, Richard. *Russian-American Security Cooperation after St. Petersburg: Challenges and Opportunities*. Carlisle, Pa.: U.S. Army War College, Strategic Studies Institute, April 2007.

Wiegand, Col. Robert C., U.S. Air Force. *Heads Not Tails: How Best to Engage Theater Ballistic Missiles?* Occasional Paper No. 53. Maxwell AFB, Ala.: Center for Strategy and Technology, Air University, February 2006.

Wilkening, Dean A. *Ballistic Missile Defence and Strategic Stability*. Adelphi Paper 334. London: Oxford University Press and International Institute for Strategic Studies, 2000.

Wisconsin Project on Nuclear Arms Control. "Iran Watch Roundtables."
    Regularly updated. http://www.iranwatch.org/ourpubs/roundtables/
    rt-iranianbomb-090105.htm.

Index

About the Author

Stephen J. Cimbala is Distinguished Professor of Political Science at Penn State Brandywine. He is the author of numerous works in the fields of U.S. national security policy, nuclear arms control, conflict termination, and related topics. Dr. Cimbala is an award-winning Penn State teacher and has consulted for various U.S. government agencies and defense contractors. He has also been quoted frequently in the media on security related topics. His recent publications include *U.S. National Security: Policymakers, Processes and Politics,* coauthored with Sam C. Sarkesian and John Allen Williams (Boulder, Colo.: Lynne Rienner, 2008); and *Russia and Postmodern Deterrence,* coauthored with Peter Jacob Rainow (Washington, D.C.: Potomac Books, 2007). He is married to Elizabeth Harder; they have two sons, Christopher and David.

The Naval Institute Press is the book-publishing arm of the U.S. Naval Institute, a private, nonprofit, membership society for sea service professionals and others who share an interest in naval and maritime affairs. Established in 1873 at the U.S. Naval Academy in Annapolis, Maryland, where its offices remain today, the Naval Institute has members worldwide.

Members of the Naval Institute support the education programs of the society and receive the influential monthly magazine *Proceedings* or the colorful bimonthly magazine *Naval History* and discounts on fine nautical prints and on ship and aircraft photos. They also have access to the transcripts of the Institute's Oral History Program and get discounted admission to any of the Institute-sponsored seminars offered around the country.

The Naval Institute's book-publishing program, begun in 1898 with basic guides to naval practices, has broadened its scope to include books of more general interest. Now the Naval Institute Press publishes about seventy titles each year, ranging from how-to books on boating and navigation to battle histories, biographies, ship and aircraft guides, and novels. Institute members receive significant discounts on the Press's more than eight hundred books in print.

Full-time students are eligible for special half-price membership rates. Life memberships are also available.

For a free catalog describing Naval Institute Press books currently available, and for further information about joining the U.S. Naval Institute, please write to:

Member Services
U.S. Naval Institute
291 Wood Road
Annapolis, MD 21402-5034
Telephone: (800) 233-8764
Fax: (410) 571-1703
Web address: www.usni.org